Ellis Island

a people's history

Ellis Island

a people's history

Małgorzata Szejnert

Translated from the Polish by Sean Gasper Bye

SCRIBE

Melbourne • London

Scribe Publications
2 John St, Clerkenwell, London, WC1N 2ES, United Kingdom
18–20 Edward St, Brunswick, Victoria 3056, Australia
3754 Pleasant Ave, Suite 100, Minneapolis, Minnesota 55409 USA

Originally published in Polish by Znak as *Wyspa klucz* in 2009
First published in English by Scribe in 2020

This publication has been supported by the
©POLAND Translation Program.

This project is supported in part by an award from the
National Endowment for the Arts.

Every effort has been made to acknowledge and contact the copyright holders
for permission to reproduce material contained in this book. Any copyright
holders who have been inadvertently omitted from the acknowledgements
and credits should contact the publisher so that omissions may be rectified in
subsequent editions.

Typeset in Adobe Garamond Pro by the publishers
Printed and bound in the UK by CPI Group (UK) Ltd, Croydon CR0 4YY

Scribe Publications is committed to the sustainable use of natural resources and
the use of paper products made responsibly from those resources.

9781911617976 (UK edition)
9781925849035 (Australian edition)
9781950354054 (US edition)
9781925938210 (ebook)

Catalogue records for this book are available from the National Library of
Australia and the British Library.

scribepublications.co.uk
scribepublications.com.au
scribepublications.com

For Marysia Drzewiecka and her home on Jamaica Hill

Contents

Part I
Rising Tide

Lenni Lenape

The little island of the Lenni Lenape Indians is called Kioshk. It lies flat on the waters of the bay, tiny as a leaf. It is overgrown with salty marsh reeds, gray ivy, and coarse low-lying grasses. Europeans have already reached America, but here, quiet and emptiness prevail; the only sounds are of water, wind, and the calling of birds.

In the Lenni Lenape language, *Kioshk* means Seagull Island; a woman is *xkwe*, a snake — *xkuk*, a horse — *nehënaonkès*, a duck — *kakw*, the sun and the moon — *kišux* (as though day and night were the same), and *Lenni Lenape* means

the True People. As time goes on, they are increasingly known as the Delaware. The new name comes from the river, or actually from Thomas, Lord Delaware — scion of an old English family and governor of Virginia. So the True People lose not only their ancient hunting grounds, but also their ancient name. They accept the foreigners' name, but they still tie their hair in a tight topknot, with a long, sharp feather stuck in it.

The Lenape lead a modest life on Seagull Island — a few canoes, huts, and campfires. They fish and gather shellfish, which are so plentiful that in time Seagull Island is renamed

Oyster Island. The oysters here are large, and fat enough to choke on. The Indians cut the oysters up with the creatures' own shells, which are razor-sharp. When burying their dead — both humans and dogs — the Lenape seal the bodies up tight with these shells; they are indestructible.

Yet the True People no longer feel safe here, and in 1630 they sell the island to the Dutch West India Company. In exchange, they take *certain cargoes or parcels of goods*[1] (a few years earlier, other Native Americans had sold nearby Manhattan in a similar fashion) and move deep into the mainland, leaving their ancestors on the island in their oyster-shell shrouds.

They will return nearly 360 years later, and will once again be called the Lenni Lenape.

Abandoned Oyster Island will pass from hand to hand. And although the shoals surrounding it grow more famous, and the island itself, with its oval shape, looks like an oyster (with a bite taken out of one side), its name changes once again, to Gibbet Island.

Pirates are hanged here, and one of these hanged men is so famous that for a time the island takes on yet another name, in his memory: Anderson.

In 1774, Samuel Ellis acquires it. He is a wealthy citizen of a huge country, though his purchase amounts to hardly anything. The Roman Coliseum takes up more than seven acres. The market square in Kraków — some 4,000 miles from here — is nearly ten acres. Seagull, Oyster, or Gibbet Island measures a little over three acres.

Samuel Ellis's Transactions

The fish merchant Samuel Ellis lives among the 25,000 inhabitants of Manhattan, at 1 Greenwich Street — a muddy road that is constantly flooded by the Hudson.

Perhaps he gazes on his new acquisition from his window when the bay is calm. Even in the present, as I write this (it is autumn and the trees in Battery Park are bare), the island is visible from here. Here meaning the place where Samuel's house might have stood. Greenwich Street still bears the same name, but now, rather than house no. 1, at the point where the street begins, a concrete cube towers skyward, and cars continually plunge into an opening at its base. This is the entrance to the underwater Brooklyn–Battery Tunnel, which took over a million pounds of dynamite to carve out.

That being said, back then, no. 1 might have stood closer to the riverside: it could have been, for instance, at the spot where in 1926 the Dutch erected an ostentatious gift to the citizens of New York — a giant flagpole. A bas-relief on the pedestal commemorates the contributions its donors made to the New World: a merchant in a ruff, a hat, and buckled shoes hands an Indian a string of beads; they both look very pleased.

Or perhaps Samuel Ellis would stand a few yards further along Greenwich Street — maybe here, where a silver and gold ball was installed a few years ago, after being dug out from under the ruins of the World Trade Center. This shining sphere had stood in front of the Twin Towers as a monument to civilization and an aspiration for global unity; it was a masterpiece of artistry and technical skill, but now it looks like a crushed apple with its skin partly stripped off. Wherever it is Samuel Ellis might have lived, and wherever he might have looked out on his new acquisition, he had no concept of what he had bought.

The Key — that's what the great architect Frank Lloyd Wright, or rather his intellectual heirs from the Taliesin Fellowship, wish to call the island. On it they intend to build *Metropolis*, a tangle of glass domes and cylinders, metal wires, and hanging terraces so dense it does not require a large space. But we are not there yet; for now, Samuel Ellis is living in his house on Greenwich Street, the 18th century is three-quarters through, and Wright's people won't announce their idea until the second half of the 20th century. In any case, they won't receive support for the drawings, or the name, although everyone can see how well-suited it is. A key can unlock the world or lock it. Exactly like Ellis Island.

Samuel Ellis has so little idea what he has purchased that barely four years after the transaction he will announce in the local newspaper his intention to give up this *pleasant situated island*, while incidentally advertising the other goods he has to spare — timber fit for constructing docks, a few barrels of excellent herring as well as some of inferior quality (though still fit for shipping), a few thousand red herring from his own smokehouse (guaranteed to withstand a journey to any corner of the globe), and a quantity of twine for netting (cheap, but first-rate). *Also, a large Pleasure Sleigh, almost new.*[2]

We don't know what he managed to dispose of. We do know that no one wanted the island, though Samuel Ellis isn't disappointed. On the far bank of the Hudson, he has hundreds of acres, orchards, cattle, horses, stables, and granaries. Increasingly, he is abandoning the water for the land. He feels more at home in the orchards and among his cattle than in Manhattan — which is full of Yankee Patriots, while he favors the Tories and the King of Great Britain.

Any interest he retains in the little island is thanks to the fact that it has acquired his name. Having it there in Upper New York Bay must be flattering. He wishes to pass on the family name and bequeaths the island to the future child of one of his four daughters, on condition the child be a boy and named Samuel Ellis. His grandson dies in infancy, however, setting off a fierce battle for his inheritance, which is not worth getting into.

Over the years to come, the island will serve military purposes, and a corps of engineers will install artillery batteries. Barracks are built for British prisoners of war, and then pirates will once again dangle from its gallows. These executions aim to advance not only moral order, but science as well. The bodies go, or rather are shipped by boat, to the College of Surgeons in Manhattan, where on a metal table in 1831, students dissect the bodies of George Gibbs and Thomas Wansley.

The "Gibbet" name does not return, though. The island now — and forevermore — will bear Ellis's name: Ellis Island.

Liberty

By the end of the 19th century, what's happening in the bay is beyond anything any ordinary person could have imagined.

Beside Ellis Island — which is currently a munitions store for the United States Navy — some sort of tower is rising above the water with a giant cocoon protruding above it. You might be forgiven for thinking it conceals an elephant, raised on its hind legs and stretching its trunk into the air. But no elephant in the world is so large. At Bedloe's Island (today's Liberty Island), beneath the tower and the cocoon, a moored ship is loaded up with mighty, glistening shapes. They are rippled or smooth, and identifiable as segments of arms, shoulders, and drapery.

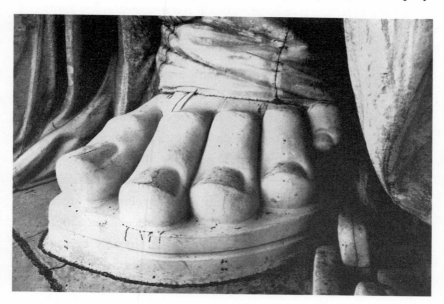

There is also a foot, oddly flattened, certainly at least as large as Samuel Ellis's sleigh.

One day, a mysterious head appears, as large as a house and looming over the water. Its eyes are directed slightly upward, gazing into undefined space. It has a straight Roman nose, a somewhat narrow upper lip and a thick lower one, and full young cheeks, although its expression is hard to define. There is no sign of pain or worry, as in the masks of antique theater, but neither does it show joy or hope. Instead, there is a detached calm, even coolness. The head is dark, but that is a question of the oxidization process — at the moment, it is in its bronze-colored phase; later it will turn red and finally, with time, it will attain a verdigris hue.

Once freed from its cocoon, the elephant trunk turns out to be an arm raising a torch.

In 1886, workers use cranes to lift up the head, place it on a brown neck, and encircle it with a crown of sharp rays. And four years later, neighboring Ellis Island — now the property of two states, New York and New Jersey — begins to grow. It does so at breakneck speed. Dockworkers dump tens of thousands of cubic feet of silt, mixed with clay, sand, and gravel, on to its shores.

Soon the surface of the island exceeds 11 acres; it is more than three times as large as Seagull, Oyster, or Gibbet Island. It would no longer fit on the market square in Kraków.

Józef Jagielski to his Wife, Franciszka

The construction of the Statue of Liberty and the tripling in size of Ellis Island are intimately linked.

They reverberate in the labor of the censors who monitor correspondence from America to the cities, towns, and villages of Russian-ruled Poland. This labor is also growing dramatically.

In 1891, as the island grows like a mushroom after rain, sacks full of letters are leaving America in the holds of steamships, and sometimes even sailing ships. They are written by semi-literate people or dictated to scribes who themselves are not much better educated.

In nearly all the letters, the word *szyfkarta* — ship's ticket — appears again and again.

> My dear wife, Christ be praised, I send word to you
> my dear wife that I am healthy wich I wish you and the
> children alsoe, good helth and fortune from the Good
> Lord and I send word that I rote a letter to you, 11 weeks
> have past and I have no reply from you and I do not
> know what that means, if the letter did not reach you or
> you have not replyed to me, and send word if you have
> received the monney I sent you 15 rubles, so rite back
> rite away if you got it or not. And send word if you got it
> and do not wish to reply, if you are angry, if you do not
> want me, because I can get angry too and what can I tell
> you, because in America a man can get lots of wifes for
> not much money. I was meant to send you a ship ticket
> but I will not until you send me a letter back and I will
> send you the ship ticket and you will come to me along
> with the children and all the best to you my dear wife and
> beloved children …

This is what Józef Jagielski writes from Pittsburgh, Pennsylvania to Franciszka Jagielska, in Dulsk, Golub-Dobrzyń county, on the border between the Russian and German partitions of Poland. Alongside the Russian postmark on this letter from husband to wife, as on thousands of other envelopes from America, the censor has written *zaderzhat'* — withhold.

The tsarist government does not wish its Polish subjects to receive ship's tickets from relatives who have managed to leave the country. Workers are emigrating at a disturbing rate and any means of reining this in is worthwhile.[3]

Józef Jagielski sailed to America to get the lie of the land and prepare for his family to join him (he most likely departed a year or two before sending the letter the censors retained and filed). He disembarked at the southern tip of Manhattan, known as the Battery, at Castle Garden immigration station, clearly visible from Ellis Island.

Castle Garden, round as a doughnut, has been, in turn: a fort defending New York, a large arena to entertain the city's citizens (fireworks, hot-air balloon rides, exhibitions of marble busts and paintings), a concert hall, a venue for public gatherings, a bathing resort, a launching point for boat races, and an indoor market. In 1885, it became an immigration station for the state of New York, meaning it welcomed

the majority of immigrants entering the United States.

When Józef Jagielski arrives, Castle Garden station's best days are behind it. It has managed to process eight million immigrants and can no longer keep up with the surge of new ones. Huge numbers are sailing to America who want for bread, safety, and freedom in their home countries. German, Scandinavian, Irish, French, Dutch, and Alsatian men and women are arriving; joining them are Poles, southern Italians, Greeks, Czechs, Russians, and Jews of various origins — mainly Russian and Austro-Hungarian, since Poland has been erased from the map. They no longer come on sailing ships but on steamships, packed like sardines on to the lower decks, while the shipowners profit handsomely from these impoverished people.

Józef Jagielski probably has neighbors from Poland on the ship with him. His letter to his wife Franciszka ends up in the same box as several dozen other letters from America withheld by the censor in 1891, addressed to wives, brothers, and brothers-in-law living near Golub-Dobrzyń in the province of Płock. One of his neighbors from Poland might be, for instance, Wojciech/Albert Melerski (currently resident in New York's Woodlawn Cemetery), who sends a ship's ticket to his brother-in-law Graboski, advising: *get yourself together rite away and come as quick as possible becuse if you worry about it to much you will have to wate a long time for work* ... Or Władysław Borkowski from Pittsburgh, who promises his wife Marianna a ship's ticket but asks: *please send word of my belloved orphans and if the youngest girl is walking and talking good.* Or Piotr Borowski from Brooklyn, New York, who promises his brother Antoni: *as for the free ticket you will get it on March 15.* Or Jan Cybulski (address not determined), who tells his wife Józefina that he hopes to send her a ship's ticket in four days and admonishes her: *you do not need any packs I mean do not bring any bundels with you exept clothes to travel in, if you have any bedclothes then sell them.* Or Jan Jesionkowski from New Jersey, who will not send his brother-in-law Karol Fenzka a ship's ticket, but says he should sell his farm and come *because hear you and your wife and children will eat things you wood not see there on Chrismas and Easter.* Or Walenty Lewandowski in Collinsville, Connecticut, who writes to his dear wife Filcia not to be afraid to join her husband *because heere it will be better then if I was an organist and do not be afraid crossing the see, because who ever is most afraid has the most complicated journey.* Or Stanisław Wasilewski, also from Collinsville, who gently chides Teofila — "Filcia" — Lewandowska that her husband (probably the aforementioned Walenty) is waiting for a letter and is *full of longing.* Or Anna and Jan Tifs from Adams, Massachusetts, who send a "ship tiket" to their sister Maria Edelman and admonish her: *do not bring a ider-down with you because you will have a lot of troubel at the border, bring a winter shawl ...*[4]

The censor's box also contains many letters sent to America from this place on the banks of the Drwęca River.

Let's hope the neighbors stick together as they enter America, because processing at Castle Garden is hell for the new arrivals. It is also a tough slog for the immigration service, which is subject to growing criticism from the press, the administration, and politicians. Joseph Pulitzer is an immigrant from Hungary who himself came to America via Castle Garden in 1864. Now, 23 years later, at the age of 40, he is the editor of the *New York World*, in whose pages he attacks the station for disorganization, degrading treatment of immigrants, and violating the law. This is the same Pulitzer who in 1904 will found the most famous journalism prize in the world.

America needs a modern, comfortable station where a new spirit will prevail. It should be cut off from the streets — where conmen, thieves, and human traffickers immediately descend on the immigrants — and under the control of the federal government.

Commissioner Weber's Faith

The first choice is Bedloe's Island, where the Statue of Liberty now stands. But an uproar breaks out not only in New York, where Pulitzer protests (they'll turn the Statue of Liberty into the Tower of Babel!), but in Paris as well, where the statue's creator, sculptor Frédéric-Auguste Bartholdi, is appalled, calling the idea monstrous and blasphemous.

Pulitzer's newspaper has considered Ellis Island before. The idea was met with reservations, however, for the island is small and lies in shallow waters. The chief official charged with investigating the situation on-site is very unhappy with it:

> We were on a little revenue cutter and asked the officer
> to take us to Ellis Island. He said he could not get the
> boat there, because the water was not deep enough. I told
> him then to take us as near to it as he could; and he went
> within 30 rods of it, I should think, or perhaps less. The
> difficulty of reaching it and the observations we had at
> that distance from us, where it seemed to be almost on a
> level with the water, presented so few attractions for an
> immigrant depot that we steamed away from it under the
> impression that even if we could get rid of the powder
> magazine which is there now, and could secure the island,
> it was not a desirable place ...[5]

But Castle Garden is closed in 1890. Immigration traffic is directed to a nearby building with a decorative stone façade, known as the Barge Office, since long ago barges running to and from the nearby islands docked there. The building is cramped and processing passengers is even more challenging than at Castle Garden. But everyone knows the discomfort will be short-lived, since work has commenced on Ellis Island and is gathering pace every day.

On the island, the munitions are removed, buildings are erected, and canals are dredged to accommodate ferry traffic. Whatever is dug out is used to cover and expand the island. That same year, Republican president Benjamin Harrison invites a businessman from Buffalo — John Baptiste Weber, a loyal Republican — to Washington to offer him the newly created and nationally vital position of Commissioner of Immigration at the Port of New York, shortly to be headquartered on Ellis Island.[6]

Any candidate for this position, who will serve a four-year term and always be appointed directly by the president of the United States, must have a perfect résumé and a strong character. Colonel John B. Weber, a Civil War veteran, meets these conditions. Yet there is one potential surprise. The colonel comes from a good family of Alsatian farmers, loyal Frenchmen and women (his mother came to America in 1830 on a sailing ship which took six weeks). He is definitely a Catholic, but when asked about his faith, declares it to be *American*. Though admittedly, this response comes under particular circumstances.

Since the station on Ellis Island is still under construction, Commissioner Weber is not needed there yet. The United States government therefore sends him to Russia in an attempt to determine why all the Jews of that country wish to come to America.

Weber's mission is exceptionally important for American immigration policy. The country has absorbed the first wave of immigration — mainly English, Irish, and German — but has fears about the second, which it considers less desirable, having its origin in Southern and Eastern Europe. Most concerning is the rising tide of poor Jews from Russia and the Polish territories under Russian rule. Opponents suggest these Jewish arrivals are so thoroughly degraded, backward, and physically and morally weak that they are unfit to join into American life and may become *public charges*. For more or less a quarter-century, this will be the most-used expression on Ellis Island, until giving way to the phrase *Red Scare*.

John Weber's journey east in many respects resembles the journey taken by the French aristocrat the Marquis de Custine into the Russian Empire over half a century before. The two men share a sense of foreignness and wonder.

> Custine: I was about to enter the Empire of fear; and fear prevailed just as much as sadness, so I was frightened and sad ...[7]

> Weber: Government in Russia and the United States represent the antipodes, the two extremes of human freedom. We here have liberty of speech; there you cannot have a public gathering without permission of the authorities; here freedom of the press, there a governmental censorship ... The use of the hectograph is not permitted unless previous license for its use has been obtained. Enthusiasm is by order; flags and bunting are displayed on state occasions according to instructions from the police ...[8]

> Custine: This population of automatons seems like one-half of a chess game — for one man directs all the pieces, and his invisible opponent is humanity. Here, one does not move, one does not breathe except by imperial permission or command; therefore all is dark and constrained, a great silence hangs over life and paralyzes it.

Colonel Weber is 44. In this era someone of his age is already on the older side, but the Russian mission must invigorate him, for he works with extraordinary energy, contacting victims and witnesses of pogroms; shackled prisoners in provincial jails; women working in a stocking factory earning forty *kopeks* (twenty cents) a day and who can only afford *black-bread watered with tears*; bankers with an income of 4,000 to 7,000 rubles a year, who nonetheless are pariahs; students who have struggled their way through the quota system; an orphanage; soldiers and mutilated veterans (*I thank God I was a UNION and not a RUSSIAN soldier*); and a hospital where he investigates and confirms what he

can hardly believe: that Pasteur's life-saving rabies vaccine is forbidden to Jews, because they are Jews. He uses bribes to clear his path and is unafraid to conceal his identity. He goes to Moscow, Minsk, Warsaw, Grodno (Hrodna), and Vilna (Vilnius). In Kovno (Kaunas), he asks people why they want to go to America. They respond: *because in that direction there lies hope.*

All suffer, mainly from humiliation — even the bankers. The laws regulating settlement are growing harsher. Jews have the right to reside only within the limits of the so-called Pale of Settlement, including provinces in today's Lithuania, Belarus, Ukraine, and Poland. For many years this order has excluded economically independent and educated Jews, though access to colleges and universities is drastically limited by quotas. Recently, however, even these emancipated Jews, long settled in the so-called *interior*, have been ordered to remove themselves to the Pale.

> Among those ordered out while I was there were
> cashiers, clerks, correspondence chiefs, and bookkeepers

of banks; heads of business departments; manufacturers — pioneers in important industries built up by Jews, who in Russia are the leaders in what we call progress and enterprise ...

Colonel Weber is so shocked by the violations of human rights he witnesses that in his report he grows emotional:

Time and distance pales the horror and sometimes I wonder if I was not a victim of hallucinations extending over a few weeks of my life spent in Russia. I wish they could be forgotten but at present they hang over me like a nightmare. The emaciated forms, the wan faces, the deep sunken cheeks, the pitiful expression of those great staring eyes reminding one of a hunted animal, are ever present and will never leave me. Sleeping or waking I see these people literally with outstretched hands, appealing, oh, so pitifully, for help, and we are helpless.

Helpless? This is just rhetoric — the United States has a great task ahead of it. John B. Weber continues:

It is inhumane of us to push these people back into the pit from which they have crawled. When we do this we should extinguish the torch [in] the outstretched hand of the Goddess of Liberty in New York's beautiful Bay ...

In Grodno, approaching the end of his journey, Colonel Weber is summoned from his hotel to the police station. He is so offended that he hires the best carriage in the city — an idea that jars with his modest soldierly nature and experience. The colonel knows appearances don't mean much. His comrades from the war with the South included two brothers, Dave and Billy. The former was exceptionally stylish and elegant, the latter the opposite: he had a puffy face, his hair was in disarray, his buttons were drab; he would get tangled up in his pant legs and only polish the front of his boots. Yet during the famous Battle of Hanover Court House in Virginia, it was Billy who turned out to be the hero. Yet Weber's pragmatism tells him that in Russia, a country of appearances, it is important to keep them up. He therefore rides down to the police station in imperial style. (Custine: *they take ostentation for elegance, luxury for courtesy* ...)

The police chief (in his account, Weber uses the Russian word *pristav*) is new and eager. Weber fears he has suspicions or information about the American's mission that could displease the tsar's government. The *pristav*'s assistant examines the commissioner's passport carefully, checking his name and place of birth. Then, unexpectedly, he asks his religion.

Without a moment's hesitation, the colonel answers: *American.*

His declaration catches the clerk by surprise, but the *pristav* whispers to him in Russian — *never mind his religion, these Americans have none.* The reason he is accommodating is that, at an opportune moment, Weber's interpreter slipped him a ten-ruble bribe. Commissioner Weber includes this in the expense report for his expedition, which he presents to the Department of the Treasury in Washington.

The report of his journey is distributed to eminent persons in Europe, including the cabinet ministers of Russia. The Russian censor returns it to the registered sender, marked "Forbidden."

At least Commissioner Weber receives a return message, unlike Józef Jagielski and his neighbors, whose letters disappear without a trace. Weber, who now has experience of tsarist censorship, does not know what is permitted in correspondence from Polish emigrants. If he knew, he would probably note it in his papers — and perhaps make an intervention.

Annie Moore's Ten Dollars

It is 1 January 1892. John Baptiste Weber has risen early, before sunrise, an easy feat for a former soldier. Today is the day Ellis Island goes into service. It is a historic date for the island, and in years to come it will be known as a historic date for America, and an important one for the world.

On a day like today, the colonel would never admit what he wrote later in his memoirs — that when he accepted President Harrison's nomination as commissioner, he knew nothing about the immigration service.

It was the same when he was elected sheriff of Erie County, New York — he knew nothing of the law, but was sure he would manage (he had been 14 when he joined the 65th Militia Regiment, and went on to command the African-Americans of the 89th United States Colored Infantry during the Civil War). His only fear was that he might be required to witness executions. He quickly looked into the legislation and found a rule stating the sheriff could send a substitute observer.

When he became assistant postmaster of Buffalo, all he knew was that you had to put a stamp on an envelope.

A person can learn anything with enough persistence and confidence. What tries his patience most are road junctions: regardless of all his other duties, for 12 years Colonel Weber has worked on intersections, a task he considers exceptionally important. America is becoming a country where roads and railroad tracks are growing denser and more interlinked, creating a network that is unsafe for people and problematic for businesses. While living in Buffalo, the colonel constantly found himself falling into these snares. He calculated that to get from his house on the outskirts to his office downtown he had to cross 55 different roads. So now he works tenaciously to make America understand the necessity of dividing traffic and constructing safe crossings, tunnels, and overpasses.

It's hard to say how much the colonel's passion is the result of personal tragedy. He does not speak of his private life. At the age of 21, while on leave during the third year of the Civil War, he married Miss

Elizabeth J. Farthing of Buffalo. Elizabeth died falling from a carriage when the horse reared, probably after being startled on the road.[9]

Today, Colonel Weber is making the rounds of Ellis Island on foot, with no risk of collision. He is performing an inspection.

The island's entire staff have taken position at their stations. At the southern tip of Manhattan, three ships are waiting impatiently — the *Victoria*, the *Nevada* and the *City of Paris*, full of immigrants who have no idea they are taking part in an important occasion. The heads of the shipping lines and the captains of each ship are perfectly aware, however, and every one of them hopes that a passenger from their list will be given first priority, which will bring publicity and, hence, money.

Commissioner Weber has likely known since the morning, or maybe even since yesterday evening, who the first will be.

Annie Moore is still a girl and today is her birthday. Fifteen years ago, on 1 January, she was born in Cork, Ireland. She arrived yesterday evening on the SS *Nevada* along with her brothers, 11-year-old Anthony and seven-year-old Philip, whom she's been looking after for the entire journey. They are poor, with only one item of luggage between them. Unable to afford a cabin, they have been packed into steerage (the name comes from the neighboring steering tackle), the lowest level for passengers, also known as the *Zwischendeck*, or between-decks. Steerage, to judge from the already-rich literature on the subject, would be better called Purgatory.

Still, Annie is a hardworking girl and has maintained her upbeat spirit and even her elegance. She wears a fitted jacket and her blonde head is topped with a round hat, which she holds with one hand to stop the winter wind on the Bay from blowing it away. This we know from monuments, of which Annie Moore has two nowadays — one at Ellis Island, where she arrived, and the other in Ireland, whence she departed.

Annie's parents are already awaiting her and her brothers — they came to New York beforehand and reside on Monroe Street in Manhattan.

The steamer *Nevada* is unloaded first. The steerage passengers (107 according to some sources, 148 according to others) are led off the ship by the immigration officers, who place them on a transfer boat decorated with banners. Merrily, with music playing and amid the ringing of ships' bells and joyful whistles, the boat takes them from Manhattan to Ellis Island. In modern times, that trip takes a little over ten minutes, and it was probably about the same length back then.

Annie Moore and her little brothers come down the gangplank and are the first to set foot at the station.

There is no risk in their arrival, because an eminent official of the Treasury Department in Washington, Charles M. Hendley, has already conducted an initial investigation and made certain the United States will accept all three.

The reason for choosing Annie, with Colonel Weber's certain knowledge and approval, is simple. One need only examine the passenger register of the ship on which the Moore siblings arrived — it's available online. The 107 steerage passengers include eight from Ireland, ten from England, two from Germany, 14 from Sweden, two from France, and two from Italy. The majority, 77, have come from Russia — but nearly all bear Jewish names: Isak, David, Sclome (Shlome), Faige, Juda, Sara, Elias, Hersch, and so on.

The inaugural passenger ought to have been chosen from the largest national group. However, Jewish immigrants are not viewed as suitable godparents for a new immigration station, whose opening cannot risk offending America. To honor a Jewish immigrant would be to show kindness to the very least-desired group. Instead, the first guest at Ellis Island should prompt warmhearted, welcoming feelings for the new arrivals. Annie Moore is meant to be a heroine out of a fairytale — a neat little Cinderella who will turn into a princess in America.

Commissioner Weber welcomes the young lady and offers her a gift to wish her a good start to her new life: a gold $10 Liberty coin. It's fitting, since the Statue of Liberty is visible from the island in all its splendor, though only from the back or the side, since it must welcome ships coming from the ocean.

Annie curtsies and assures the colonel she will never part with this treasured memento.

Peter Mac Looks at the Luggage

The first immigrants to enter the huge building — with its countless windows, steep roof, and peaked towers, more resembling a seaside casino than an inspection station for the poor — feel the same thing under their feet that they have felt the last few weeks onboard their ships: solid wood. The timber came from North Carolina and Georgia; the floor is pine, seasoned, and the walls are made of green lumber — pine and spruce — so arrivals from villages and towns are greeted by the familiar scent of the forest and home. The Sheridan & Byrne company was supposed to mount stainless metal siding on the exterior walls, but it's not known if they did so. In light of the events that will soon follow, it seems doubtful.

The building is 400 feet long and 150 feet wide. It is equipped with central steam heating, electricity, and modern bathrooms. *Harper's Weekly* writes it can receive 10,000 immigrants a day. This later turns

out to be an exaggeration. A day of 5,000 at Ellis Island feel like the wrath of God. But even so, the island is probably the largest caravanserai in the world.

Ever since he was named commissioner, Colonel Weber has been meticulously assembling the island's staff. He began with a visit to Castle Garden. He arrived unannounced and mixed in with the crowd. He witnessed terrified people being shoved every which way by charlatans and con artists. He observed the immigration workers and spoke with a man who commanded his respect. Soon he had three lists. A good one, for honest workers; a neutral one, for workers whose moral qualifications he lacked enough information to assess; and a bad one, for workers who shouldn't be trusted with tasks on Ellis Island.

For help in the first months of his job, Commissioner Weber brings in Charles Semsey and James O'Beirne, who share wartime connections with Weber. Major Semsey, a clerk at Castle Garden, served in the 45th New York Infantry Division and, like, Weber, fought in Virginia. He is 13 years older than the colonel. His real first name is Kálmán.

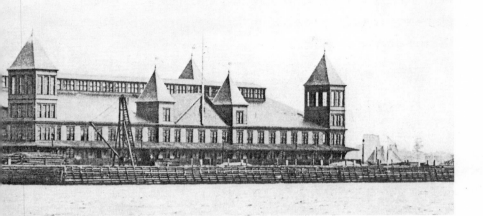

He comes from an aristocratic Hungarian family and was born in Bártfa in the mountains of Hungary (today's Bardejov in northeastern Slovakia), and his relatives include Andor von Semsey, a mineralogist and discoverer of a beautiful crystal called semseyite, samples of which in the 21st century fetch high prices at specialist auctions.

O'Beirne, born in Ireland and two years younger than Weber, also fought in Virginia. He advanced to the rank of general. He takes pride in having stood guard at President Lincoln's deathbed and then helping track down his assassin, the actor John Wilkes Booth. After the Civil War, as a correspondent of the *New York Herald* (a mighty newspaper that sent Stanley to Africa in 1871 to find Livingstone), he reported on battles with Native Americans. O'Beirne is a daredevil and individualist, qualities that before long he'll find hard to reconcile with the discipline of an immigration station.

Colonel Weber occupies an office in the corner of the second floor of the pine structure, which also houses a telegraph office, a currency exchange bureau, an information stand, a lunch buffet, and a railroad ticket office, while his deputy O'Beirne moves into a similar room at the opposite end.

One of the workers on the Castle Garden "good" list is Peter McDonald, who has been handling luggage for 20 years. He can tell at a glance what country a bag is from. He knows more about their origins than his own.

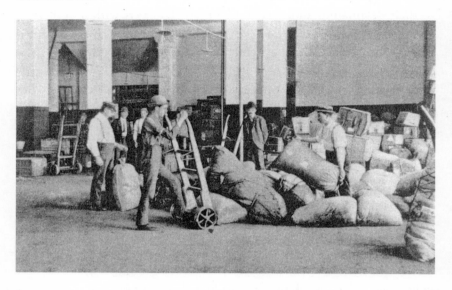

When the new luggage room is opened, with space for 12,000 passengers' worth of bundles, suitcases, and trunks, Peter Mac, as he's known here, is 43. He knows his date of birth — 1849 — but he doesn't know where he was born — in Ireland, New York, or Fall River, Massachusetts. Nor does he know if the people who raised him were his own parents or friends of theirs who took him on when his mother died.

Luggage handler Peter Mac in his round work cap, white shirt, and pants with suspenders (the job is so good Peter has started to show a paunch) conducts the movements of possessions transported from every corner of the globe. Some of his observations are obvious, but now and then he gets a surprise. For instance, he's used to every nation roping up its bundles differently — and he knows which loops and knots were tied in his beloved Ireland (where his wife is from), which in Sweden, which in Italy, and which in Switzerland.

Danes, Swedes, and Norwegians have the most tightly packed luggage. Peter thinks they bring the most out of any nationality — mattresses, featherbeds, bed frames, drawers, kitchen chairs — but try and explain to them they'll pay a fortune to have it all delivered to their destination and they'd die rather than part with it. The suitcases of the English and French are in better condition than others' and certainly are the most modern. Greeks and Arabs have bundles large as mountains, gathering up five or six hundred pounds' worth of various objects, squeezing them all together, and wrapping them up in carpets and scarves. Sometimes it takes six men to lift an object like that.

As Peter stands guard over the suitcases and bundles, he maintains that, improbably, he's never lost a thing. But he can't get over how the Poles behave. They're actually registered on their travel documents as Russian, Austrian, or German, but after so many years working at Castle Garden, Peter Mac can distinguish the sounds of different languages. Polish speakers don't like putting their bags in storage and instead haul them everywhere they go. They attach the greatest importance to eiderdowns, often carrying them on their heads or shoulders, using one hand to prop them up while the other drags a trunk with children clinging on.[10]

Another man carefully observing this deluge of people and possessions is Dr Victor Safford, who's being offered the position of physician on Ellis Island. He's come in for an interview, but he still has some time, so he watches. He's got a very sharp eye, and what he sees at Ellis Island so fascinates him he's prepared to accept a large pay cut to get to know this remarkable place better. He's looking forward to the professional challenge and has to admit he likes the immigration service medical uniform, which resembles that of a Navy officer.

Like Peter Mac, he's also struck by the immigrants' reluctance to part with their possessions and, as befits a surgeon, he notes the hazardous results. No problem if a wicker basket bashes into someone, because the wicker will give way and not break anyone's ribs. But collisions with boxes and chests clearly packed with metal objects are more severe. You also have to watch out for large bundles on the shoulders of strong Slavic girls. A bale like this,

> may feel superficially soft and fluffy, but besides a feather
> bed or two it is likely to contain a pair of andirons, iron
> pots or kettles, or various other Eastern European Lares
> and Penates of a substantial, practical character.[11]

If the girl turns around suddenly, anyone unlucky enough to be standing nearby will feel the momentum of her cargo as it swings around. Yet in Dr Safford's opinion, nastiest of all are the tidy little boxes of the English, not only hard but also metal-cornered, so they cause injury.

Victor Safford has literary talent and imagination, seeing iron hidden in featherbeds and predicting the strength of a blow from bundles supposedly stuffed with down. Meanwhile, when the clerk Augustus Sherman observes the immigrants, he is most focused on what he sees on the surface. He's only 27, but with his gray suit, tie, starched collar, and signet ring, he looks more like an old bachelor. He closely follows this improbable human hodgepodge of gestures, facial features, glances, attitudes, hairstyles, sidelocks, beards, hats, yarmulkes, turbans, headscarves, aprons, tunics, shoes, felt boots, and woven bast slippers. For the moment, Augustus, the well-educated son of a wealthy trader from Pennsylvania, is an ordinary staff clerk on Ellis Island.

Can he sense what the future holds? First he will become a senior clerk, then chief clerk, then confidential secretary to the island's commissioner — yet it's his photographs that will make him truly famous.

One of the youngest employees is Byron Hamlin Uhl, a native of Monticello, Indiana. He's 19, but extremely promising — no-nonsense, hard-working, and meticulous. He's been hired as a stenographer and is skilled in the shorthand method of Sir Isaac Pitman — no longer a new system, but still the most popular one, adopted by at least 500 of the world's most important languages since it innovatively eliminates unnecessary vowels.

A reporter for the *New York World* is thrilled. He raves that the immigrants' comfort and safety are finally at the level one would wish for, and adds: *Everything worked like a charm.*[12]

Buttonhook, Tiffany

The buttonhook — a small instrument, barely a few inches long, sometimes straight, sometimes elegantly ornate, but practical, above all — enjoys spectacular success from the end of the 19th century at least until the First World War. One of its successes, entirely unique to Ellis Island, we will see shortly. But the main reason for the buttonhook's success has to do with women's drive for emancipation.

" MOTHER, WHEN YOU'VE
FINISHED WITH FATHER, I
SHOULD LIKE TO BORROW
HIM FOR A MINUTE ! "

A woman wants to be mobile, nimble, and energetic. She intends to cross her legs and show off her ankle in a shapely little boot, move through crowds on the street, and travel. She wants to gesticulate, perhaps at rallies and meetings where she demands her voting rights. Her mind turns to sports. Such a woman needs more than clothes held together with capricious ribbons; they have to be properly buttoned up.

The zipper does not yet exist. It has actually been patented by Whitcomb Judson, but it looks more like a roller chain and fails to make a mark at the 1893 Chicago World's Fair.

So boots and dresses are equipped with rows of tiny buttons. A dozen on each foot and another twenty on a corset is a lot of work, yet a progressive, mobile woman dresses herself, without help from servants.

Satirical magazines, particularly British ones, print many epigrams and cartoons about roping husbands and lovers into buttoning, and lending these helpers to other lady friends. Yet the best helper, always available, is the buttonhook.

The homeland of the buttonhook is Victorian England. They are manufactured in workshops in Birmingham, London, Sheffield, and Chester. The most famous are the factories of Adie & Lovekin, Levi & Salaman, Goldsmiths & Silversmith Co., and Crisford & Norris, which sign their wares. American buttonhook manufacturers on the other hand do not brand their items, though one that does is the already famous Tiffany & Co. This being Tiffany, you can imagine what their buttonhooks look like, or rather their handles: rainbow enameled, opalescent, sculpted into flower sepals or butterfly wings. More daring ladies can buy a buttonhook from Tiffany's in the shape of naked Eros, stretching out luxuriantly. Buttonhooks like these are attached to a chain like jewelry and worn on the corset or at the belt.

An ordinary buttonhook has a metal or bone handle with a hook extending from it, thick and smooth enough not to injure. There are victims, though. Four-year-old Canadian Alfred Courtemanche fell on the floor while holding one, driving it through his nose and into his brain.

The passengers inspected at Ellis Island haven't heard that story — they couldn't have, since it doesn't happen until 1921[13] — but they find the buttonhooks the medical service is equipped with to be fearsome.

Ellis Island needs a large number of buttonhooks because the tools have to be constantly disinfected, meaning that, even without government penny-pinching, they must be plain and made with rust-free metal; they are surely bought from a cheap factory.

They might, for instance, come from the factory of Abraham Shavinovitz of Kadzidło, Poland. Abraham emigrated to America through Ellis Island. He has a beard, a mustache, and sidelocks, and his eyes — gentle but alert — peer out from under a round cloth cap. A photograph of him survives, along with the information that he set himself up as a craftsman on Manhattan's Lower East Side. He makes buttonhooks. Did he bring these skills from his village? Doubtful, but not impossible. Kadzidło, about a hundred miles north of Warsaw, teemed with small Jewish workshops: cobblers, tailors, tanners, and their products — shoes, frock coats, sheepskin jackets, all of which of course had little buttons, little holes, little loops — so a buttonhook after all might appear at the end of the production chain.[14]

Yet the Ellis Island service has no interest in what an immigrant did before setting off for America unless his family is accompanying him, which would suggest more stability in his new country. If Ellis Island kept information saying Shavinovitz produced suitable hooks on the Lower East Side, he was probably a supplier for the island. Maybe he even brought his wares personally. Since he was processed at Ellis Island, he knows they can't get along without buttonhooks.

General O'Beirne's Ten Dollars

John Baptiste Weber often benefits from the help of the stenographer Byron Uhl, who likes working on the island so much he'll stay here to the end of his days. The colonel, on the other hand, has no trouble imagining leaving his current job behind. His voyage to Russia has once again awakened the desire to get to know strange lands and cultures. As he gazes out his office window over the bay, teeming with steamships, he imagines a journey to far away, to Japan, for instance. He got the idea 16 years ago at the Centennial Exhibition in Philadelphia. He saw famous inventions from the newest minds, from Bell's telephone and Heinz's ketchup to the steel cables of the Brooklyn Bridge and Corliss's Centennial Engine. When President Ulysses S. Grant of the United States and Emperor Dom Pedro of Brazil climbed up to release the steam and set the pistons in motion inside their cyclopean cylinders, a tremble ran through the 12.5-acre floor (1.5 acres larger than the surface of Ellis Island on opening day). The packed crowd of guests (free entry for 120,000 people) trembled along with it.

Yet it was somewhere different, unexpected, that really shook John Baptiste Weber, then 34 years old. Strolling through the vast spaces of the Philadelphia exhibition, amid American states' pavilions resembling hunting lodges, he happened across a square building with a plain roof, labeled *Japan*. Inside, he saw painted fabrics as light as fog, and a grasshopper with fragile wings and limbs that looked real even though it was carved from hard green stone and was at least five times larger

than life, its curved back forming a small serving tray. This elegant piece was so powerful it could hold its own against the cables of the Brooklyn Bridge or Corliss's Engine.

Yet Colonel Weber defers his Japanese dreams. He devotes all his energy to implementing an organizational and moral regime at the immigration station. Principles must be developed and enforced relentlessly. But the fly in the ointment is General O'Beirne. He apparently takes a dim view of reporting to a lower-ranking veteran and,

the moment Colonel Weber sets off on a business trip to Washington, O'Beirne issues a directive that sets Ellis Island reeling. He orders officials to arrest any immigrants unable to present $10 to the inspector for the cost of onward rail travel through the United States, since only a small share of foreigners will remain in the environs of New York. The majority will continue to Chicago, Detroit, or Pittsburgh, and many are headed for distant states: Kansas, Nebraska, the Dakotas, or even California, which lure them with ads the size of barn doors, though they might better be called heaven's gates. One such billboard shows a chariot with a maiden in loose robes — breasts bare, holding

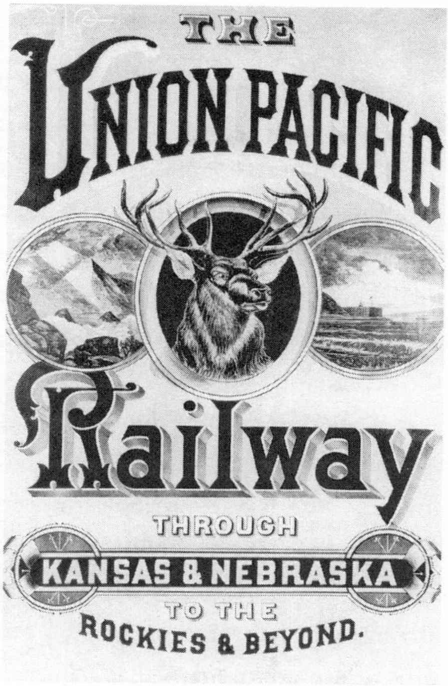

out a garland — and a youth, also half-naked, tugging at the reins of four racing steeds. The dynamic caption suggests the location of this scene is *Dakota, Land of Golden Grain*. This image isn't quite truthful, however, since Dakota attracts immigrants in part because of its expanded rail system, meaning horse-drawn vehicles play a reduced role. What's more, the artists forgot to mention the Puritan morality the immigrants will have to deal with out there.

California, on the other hand, beckons with goods pouring out of a golden horn of plenty (bananas, oranges, pineapples ...) and land for the taking:

> Room for Millions of Immigrants
> 43,795,000 Acres of Government Lands Untaken
> Railroad & Private Land for a Million Farmers
> A Climate for Health & Wealth Without Cyclones or Blizzards[15]

So O'Beirne's order is justified to a degree (though travel costs are generally covered beforehand by the immigrants, or their friends and loved ones). But $10 is a fortune at this time. Ship records from this period show passengers traveling in steerage have either five dollars or no money at all. Naturally we can presume they're concealing their true wealth, just in case. But even if they are concealing it, then, according to common knowledge, it's in a tiny place — the heel of a shoe.

Ambitious O'Beirne's decision causes the immigration service at Ellis Island to refuse 300 immigrants entry into the US, provoking lamentations from them and their families waiting at the wharf, crowding and chaos on the island, as well as confusion and quiet rebellion from the island's clerks. Luckily, Weber returns quickly, reverses the order — which has no basis in existing immigration policy — and releases all the detainees.

Weber disciplines the whole staff just as he disciplined O'Beirne. At their very first meeting he states clearly that the principles in force on the island are both simple and inflexible. The staff are to care for the immigrants, direct their movements, and make it easier for them to go through processing. Ill-will in this regard or taking advantage of foreigners will be punished with immediate termination of employment. What's more, there are no second chances for anyone who violates these principles. It's too hard to catch someone red-handed to risk giving them another opportunity. Appeals will therefore not be considered.

The colonel feels like lord of the island and has been granted such authority by the president. He quotes the words Benjamin Harrison spoke after Weber was sworn in:

> We have taken over a serious task, and you shall have full latitude in carrying it to a successful conclusion.[16]

This task finds its expression in the reams of immigration laws. The most recent Act, issued in 1891, is liberal when it comes to money. It maintains the tax rate in force for the last ten years — 50¢ per immigrant — and dedicates the revenue thus collected to health inspections for new arrivals, among other things. But at the same time the Act makes it clear whom the United States does not desire: idiots, insane persons, paupers or persons likely to become a public charge, polyg-amists, persons suffering from a loathsome or dangerous contagious disease, and persons who have been convicted of a felony or other infamous crime or misdemeanor involving moral turpitude.

Another group still not permitted entry are the Chinese, under a special law from 1882,[17] and contract workers, excluded by the Immigration Act of 1885.

Enforcing these regulations requires an iron fist and a hard heart, qualities the colonel demonstrates by giving guilty employees no opportunity to reform. Sure enough, he has already fired a Polish interpreter who was directing immigrants to a dishonest employment agency (proposing $50 in wages a month, while the union office was guaranteeing more than twice as much), while collecting a commission of 50¢ per person. No pleas or arguments can help, not even that this interpreter is well-educated, a Republican protégé, and ultimately a Polish count.

The colonel goes softer on the immigrants. He even takes the liberty of publishing the following reflection, to the irritation of his superiors in the capital:

> It is charged that foreigners furnish a larger percentage
> of paupers and criminals than the native element.
> This is probably true, but it is hardly because they
> are foreigners, but because they are the poorer half
> of society, and consequently less able to cope with
> misfortune or to withstand temptation. It is not so
> creditable to a rich man to refrain from stealing a loaf of
> bread as it is to a hungry one.[18]

Cholera

In the second half of the 19th century, the great shipping companies attain power comparable to that of the masters of coal and steel. This stems to a large degree from their new cargo — immigrants to the United States.

When the station on Ellis Island is beginning operations, some of the most powerful companies running ships between the United States and Europe are Cunard, Norddeutscher Lloyd, and Hamburg–American. It only takes a glance at the arrangement of passenger berths on their vessels to realize they've bet their money on steerage. Their brochures refer to this deck as "third class". *Steerage* or *Zwischendeck* doesn't sound as nice.

Cunard is just renovating the *Etruria*, which has 800 steerage berths onboard, while the new, powerful, elegant *Campania* has 1,000. Norddeutscher Lloyd has 600 third-class berths on the *Berlin*; 700 on the *Hanover* (its successor of the same name can fit 1,850 people in steerage); 1,907 on the *Weimar*; 1,000 on the *Kaiser Wilhelm II*. This last ship was built in 1889 at the Vulcan shipyard in Stettin (today's Szczecin, Poland). Hamburg–American has, according to various sources, either 1,100 or 800 third-class bunks on the *Rugia*, 1,400 on the *Scandia* (both ships also from Vulcan), 1,200 on the *Moravia*, and 700 on the *Normannia*.

The number of bunks on the worst deck grows each time a ship is renovated, mainly to the detriment of second class. First class is naturally the smallest.

It's no surprise the passenger lines decide to hold a celebratory luncheon to welcome the new immigration commissioner for New York. His main hosts will be Messrs Vernon H. Brown of Cunard, Gustave H. Schwab of Norddeutscher Lloyd, and Emil L. Boas of Hamburg–American. These companies have 3,200 agencies in the United States. Mr Boas is not only an efficient manager but also a bibliophile. He knows that Commissioner Weber — so by-the-book on the island — has a weakness for cultural marvels, so gives him an expert talk on the latest acquisitions of his maritime library, which takes up increasing amounts of space in the Boases' residence on West 74th Street, between two marvelous parks — Riverside and Central.

The colonel can't get out of attending the luncheon, though he has no enthusiasm for meeting these men. Big business' game always involves politics, but he's decided that as commissioner of Ellis Island he needs to be as much a Republican as a Democrat. He's noticed the big businessmen gleefully piling blame for their problems on the previous administration to score points with the new one, and he has no desire to get drawn into that. And besides, every day on the island he sees passengers who've been through a journey in steerage. As he shakes hands with Messrs Brown, Schwab, and Boas, he wonders what they'd look like after such a two-week endurance course.

So the lunch goes awkwardly.

> I told them, in substance, that I was there to administer the immigration laws which they understood better than I ...[19]

A few months later, on 30 August 1892, the *Moravia*, a small sail-and-steam ship with one smokestack and two masts, sails into New York Bay. She has, as we already know, 1,200 bunks in steerage and an additional 100 in first class. There is evidently no second class, because none is mentioned in the passenger registry. The ship collected her passengers in Hamburg 13 days earlier. The deputy chief doctor at the port of New York, Dr Tallmadge, goes onboard to inspect and the captain tells him that the American consul in Hamburg issued the ship a health certification. Yet Dr Tallmadge demands a precise report from the ship's doctor, David Israel, because for a few days New York has had disturbing news of cholera, apparently introduced to Germany by Jewish immigrants from Russia *en route* to America, and it's not certain if this is an instance of the most severe variety — Asiatic cholera. The captain of the *Moravia* has no choice, then, but to confess that over the 13-day journey they threw overboard the corpses of 12 children and two adult cholera victims. (Thirteen of these victims are described as having Polish nationality. Their names: Schustiewitz, Rutzawisky, Czarayska, Rogasekepsky, Rutizinsky.) Further investigation reveals that Hamburg has in fact witnessed an epidemic the city authorities are not reporting. Supposedly the sick are quarantined north of the city center, on the banks of the Elbe, and the river has borne microbes into the city.

Panic breaks out in New York, and only increases when, a few days after the *Moravia* (already known as a death ship), even more ships from Hamburg arrive at port: the *Normannia*, the *Rugia*, and the *Scandia*. They too threw bodies overboard; the *Scandia* committed 32 victims to the waves. Politicians and the press note that the disease affected steerage passengers and members of the crew. The passengers in cabins (with one exception on the *Scandia*) remained healthy. This event nearly coincides with a letter from a reader in the *New York Times*:

> We do not want and we ought to refuse to land all or any
> of these unclean Italians or Russian Hebrews. We have
> enough dirt, misery, crime, sickness, and death of our
> own without permitting any more to be thrust upon us.[20]

The chief doctor of the Port of New York, Dr William T. Jenkins, a handsome 40-year-old Mississippian with an elegant handlebar mustache linked to his sideburns (the image of this man, who is to save New York City, immediately appears in the press), decides the dangerous ships may not approach the shore. Anyone leaving the ships will be shot, and anyone trying to board without authorization — which some daring New York reporters have already tried — risks the same. Passengers in cabins may no longer approach steerage or vice-versa. The sick are taken to hospitals on Hoffman and Swinburn Islands, but an initial quarantine must take place before the ships dock.

It's easy to imagine how the healthy passengers feel, trapped on crowded ships where the disease still lurks. Yet Dr Jenkins is convinced he is acting rightly. He fears losing control of the situation if the quarantine takes place on land. So the written protests sent to Manhattan by the *Normannia*'s first-class passengers — a New Jersey senator, an editor from New York, a popular priest, a well-known theater businessman, and above all the music-hall star Lottie Collins, whose hit *"Ta-ra-ra Boom-de-ay"* is being hummed on the carbolic-acid-drenched streets — are all fruitless.

Only once the danger has passed, when the ships and their whole stock of travelers have undergone intensive disinfection, does a ferry bring the survivors to Ellis Island for normal processing.

This stops the infection from reaching the island, which Commissioner Weber should thank God for, since his station is unprepared to battle an epidemic. If it had a well-equipped hospital, modern laboratories, and could provide the at-risk and sick with specialist care, further deaths on the condemned ships would surely cease. Let us remember that, by this time, the developed world is already benefiting from the discoveries of Louis Pasteur and Robert Koch.

The fear of cholera lasts longer than the epidemic itself. At departure ports, many steamship companies refuse to let emigrants onboard. The lower decks sit empty. Traffic to Ellis Island is reduced, and so is the money to serve the immigrants, since revenue from the fee per head falls. Colonel Weber ought to reduce the staff, though he'd rather eliminate his own position to reduce costs. The administration does not accept his proposal, however.

Now that the crisis is over, the commissioner can devote more attention to organizing the manifests.

Franciszka Jagielska, Manifests

The manifests that interest Commissioner John Baptiste Weber are passenger lists. However, for a manifest to be truly a manifest, not just a list of names, it must include a large amount of useful information for the immigration service and — to the commissioner's mind — for the newcomers' protection, since this prevents them from vanishing without a trace in a foreign land. Ships' captains have kept passenger lists since time immemorial, but they and the steamship companies handle them with varying reliability. The task at hand is to expand and standardize the information on the lists, and demand they be filled out honestly and legibly.

Requiring the manifests is one matter, archiving them is another. For the time being, they're a nightmare for the island's clerks, accumulating in stacks on desks.

The manifests begin with the ornately calligraphed title *List of Passengers: District of the City of New York, Port of New York* and an oath formula. For instance:

> I [illegible name written here], Master [this word crossed
> out and "1st Officer" written in] of the SS München, do
> solemnly, sincerely and truly swear that the following
> List or Manifest, subscribed by me, and now delivered by
> me to the [illegible] of the Port of New York is a full and
> perfect list of all the Passengers taken on board said vessel
> at Bremen, from which port or ports the said vessel has
> now arrived, and that on said List is truly designated the
> age, sex, calling, ability to read and/or write, country of
> citizenship, native country, last residence, whether citizens
> of the United States or not, the location of compartment
> or space occupied, the intended destination or location,
> State or Territory, the number of pieces of baggage, and

the date and cause of death of any such passengers who
may have died on the voyage; also the port of embarkation
and a statement as far as it can be ascertained with
reference to the intention of each immigrant passenger
as to a protracted sojourn in this Country, as required
by "The Passenger Act 1882" and Regulations of the
Secretary of the Treasury; So help me God.

There follows the signature of the first officer of the SS *München*,
the clerk who collected the oath, and the date — 16 August 1892.[21]

Today, over a century since that date, ships' manifests are one of
America's greatest treasures.

In the year Ellis Island goes into service, all the immigration
stations in the United States combined process around 580,000 immigrants. Of those, the island's share is almost 446,000, which speaks
emphatically to its importance.

Surely the brothers, wives, and brothers-in-law whose families
promised them ship's tickets a year ago would make their way to the
island too? On the other hand, we shouldn't expect them to arrive before
the new Ellis station is open, because, as we know, letters with tickets
and promises of tickets were withheld by the tsar's censorship, and re-
establishing contact and making family decisions must have taken many
long months, if it were possible at all. How could they manage, after
all, since follow-up letters were confiscated as well? The telegraph now
exists, but isn't available to the impoverished people of Płock Guberniya.

Did Franciszka Jagielska come to join her husband Józef, who
threatened that *in America a man can get lots of wifes for not much
money?* Today we can seek the answer online. American websites can
match user-entered names and presumed dates of birth with data from
the ships' manifests. They search passenger registers and make them
available onscreen in scanned originals or legible printouts. It could
never have occurred to Commissioner Weber when he demanded these

documents from the steamship companies that at the start of the 21st century tens of millions of people would want to view these manifests to learn about their unknown families.

The internet tells us Franciszka Jagielska does not sail to Ellis Island either that year or the next. Neither does Graboski, who was sent a ship's ticket by his brother-in-law Melerski; nor Marianna Borkowska and her children, sent for by her husband Władysław; nor Antoni Borowski, invited by his brother Piotr; nor Józefina Cybulska, who was to rejoin her husband Jan; nor Karol Fenzka, who was to pay his own way and join his brother-in-law Jan Jesionkowski; nor Maria Edelman, who was to receive a *ship tiket* from Anna and Jan Tifs; nor Teofila-Filcia Lewandowska, whose husband Walenty is still *full of longing*.

But another reason we can't find them could very well be because the manifests stored at Ellis Island went up in smoke.

On 14 April 1897, just past noon, a violent fire breaks out on the island. The green lumber ignites with a bang and an aroma. Over three hours, the large station building turns into a charcoal slag heap. Everyone is successfully evacuated.

Colonel Weber Returns to Buffalo

Colonel Weber read about the fire in the paper. It's been four years since he was commissioner of Ellis Island. In 1893, the Democrat Grover Cleveland became President of the United States and, as per procedure, recalled the Republican Weber from this strategic governmental post.

On Ellis Island, the station is being reconstructed, or rather rebuilt from scratch, this time out of brick, stone, concrete, and steel. Its architects, William Alciphron Boring and Edward Lippincott Tilton, studied at the École des Beaux Arts in France and are influenced by the turn-of-the-century fashion for monumental French Renaissance revival. Their design appeals, or else they wouldn't have won the bid and the gigantic fee of $26,000. The new main building resembles not a seaside casino like the old one, but instead a gaudy train station. Lending it dignity are four towers with glistening domes, griffins, and eagles on the red-and-white façade, and American flags in cartouches. The carved women's heads beneath the keystones have the straight noses and indifferent

47

gaze of the Statue of Liberty. The large windows with countless panes are enclosed in stone arches probably large enough to fit a tugboat. The main hall where the crowds of arrivals will undergo inspection is 200 feet long, 100 feet wide, and 56 feet high.

The island is growing again — now it is over 15.5 acres. The new land area is coming into being, as before, out of silt, clay, sand, and gravel, but now with the fire-consumed remains of the first station buildings and rock rubble from New York's subway tunnels mixed in. Binding all this together is hot ash from the heat-and-power station on Ellis Island.

It is actually no longer one island, but two. A new island extends in a strip alongside the old one. A stretch of water is left between the two as a convenient ferry channel. A few hospitals will be built on Island 2 (numbering spaces is very helpful; it was tested out on the streets of New York), almost certainly a partial result of the Hamburg cholera scare.

Colonel Weber has returned to Buffalo, where he's now absorbed in designing the Pan-American Exposition in that city. He is its commissioner general. The event will attract eight million guests, including the 25th President of the United States, the Republican William McKinley. On 6 September 1901, as the president is shaking hands with those gathered in the Temple of Music, he is fatally shot by an anarchist.

The assassination takes place a short distance from the Electricity Building — whose lights, visible for 20 miles, thrill even Edison; a stone's throw from a pavilion of devices with godlike powers — incubators for newborns; and beside the Japanese gardens and Japanese village, John Weber's favorite place to relax.

This is the colonel's curse. He was the exhibition's host, but couldn't protect its most important guest from death. Weber defended immigrants, but the president was shot by the descendent of a Polish immigrant: Leon Czolgosz.[22] Weber worked for the economic success of his city, but the cost of the exposition dwarfed the money earned. Two months after the attack, the Temple of Music is razed to the ground.

William Williams, Plymouth Rock

Plymouth Rock, an inconspicuous boulder weighing 20,000 pounds, lies today, wave-lapped, under a lightly built white portico that stands on the banks of a bay of the Atlantic Ocean. This is where the *Mayflower* galleon landed in 1620. Although during the first winter half the *Mayflower's* Pilgrims died of hunger, cold, and disease, the memory of this tragedy isn't held against the rock, which today is a holy relic of the United States — America's cornerstone.

For 120 years since the English Pilgrims, exhausted from their journey of over two months, set foot on the rock, it has lain there peacefully, sometimes in the water, sometimes out, covered with algae and seagulls. When the decision was made to build a wharf, the 94-year-old Presbyterian Thomas Faunce remembered family stories about the landing and decided to bid the rock farewell. The inhabitants of Plymouth bore the old man to the water's edge on a chair, and it would appear his farewell touched their hearts, because some time later they relocated the rock to the meeting house. Yet it didn't wish to abandon the shore and split into two pieces. The lower one was left *in situ*, the upper one taken into town.

Years later, it was decided to correct this barbaric act committed in good faith. A quadrangular Victorian building was placed over the lower stone on the shore, neither tombstone nor triumphal arch. The upper part of the rock was brought from town and placed upon the lower.

In 1920, this somewhat bulky marker is replaced by a marble portico with Doric columns, funded by the Colonial Dames of America and designed by the famous architects Charles McKim, William Mead, and Stanford White. The stone rests safely beneath it, protected by metal bars. It's calculated a third of the memorial stone's mass was lost when it was moved. Despite patriotic appeals, no one in possession of these remains has brought them back to Pilgrim Memorial State Park.

Plymouth Rock symbolizes good ancestry. The descendants of the Mayflower Pilgrims belong to the American aristocracy, even if their ancestor was just a poor craftsman who showed too much humility in the face of nature's cruelty and God's wrath and succumbed to both in that first winter.

Ellis Island is not Plymouth Rock. It is formed of clay, silt, and ash. The island is a Cinderella compared to Plymouth Rock and everything that hunk of granite entails, and the pompous edifice erected on it in 1900 doesn't change that. So it might come as a surprise that the new commissioner at Ellis Island will be William Williams, whose ancestor and namesake Colonel William Williams signed the United States' Declaration of Independence in Philadelphia in 1776 as a delegate from Connecticut (alongside 55 other remarkable signatories). The Williamses sailed to America in 1630, ten years after the *Mayflower*, so we can say with confidence their family history rests firmly on Plymouth Rock.

In 1902, Commissioner Williams accepts President Theodore Roosevelt's nomination. We see them both in a photograph. They stride around the island, or rather the president does, in a wind-blown coat and broad-brimmed hat, smiling, his arm extended in greeting, while the diminutive commissioner with his dark jacket, bare head, and short-cropped hair has stopped and is looking ahead in an expectant pose, as though wanting to see to just one more thing.

He is 40, a Republican, though, as the *New York Times* emphasizes, he has never been active in politics. Nor has he had the opportunity to meet the president previously, though they share a connection from an important episode in Williams' life — both men fought in the Spanish-American War of 1898. Williams graduated from Yale and Harvard. To accept his new post, he abandons a successful law practice; not at once, but after careful consideration. The office is located at 35 Wall Street, an address so good it requires no comment.

Ten years ago, under the Benjamin Harrison administration, William Williams made a name for himself in a dispute over seals. The animals have breeding grounds next to the Pribilof Islands, in the American part of the Bering Sea. The United States forbade killing the animals on the islands and in adjacent waters, but nonetheless the British ventured into the area, exploiting loopholes in the regulations. A couple of British ships were caught and a long dispute broke out. An arbitration tribunal was ultimately convened. Young William Williams provided legal support to the United States, in whose judgment hunting seals on land was legitimate, but the method of mass murder by hunting at sea was illegitimate, piratical, and *contra bonos mores* — contrary to good morals. (In such hunts females are killed, because they are difficult to distinguish from males in the water, and many of the killed seals sink.)

The United States therefore proposed legislation banning such practices. Yet because such an appeal went beyond the limits of the current administrative system, the American lawyers said in addition that the tribunal should defend moral law as laid out in the fundamental principles of right.

Although the United States lost the dispute, and was forced to pay nearly half a million dollars in compensation, William Williams remained convinced that the future would vindicate the American position.[23]

Taking the boat out to Ellis Island every day does not take away from time William Williams spends with his family because he hasn't started one. He's a bachelor and likes it that way. For three years he's lived in central Manhattan at the University Club, founded by Yale men. They are America's know-it-alls, eggheads, but ones with plenty of money. The splendid club building was designed by its members McKim, Mead, and White, the same architects who raised the marble portico over Plymouth Rock.

McSweeney's Stables

In taking on the role of Ellis Island commissioner, Williams faces a Herculean task. The law of the jungle prevails at the freshly opened facility; it's more a stable than a station. The fire has left its organization, not yet fully consolidated, in ruins, because of the need to abandon the island while the wreckage was cleared, the ground expanded, and the new buildings erected. The station was temporarily relocated to the Barge Office building in Manhattan, which had been used for immigration control in the past, between the closure of Castle Garden and the opening of Ellis Island. This transfer to the city once again left immigrants at the mercy of con artists. Now conditions familiar from the old Castle Garden prevail in the new buildings at Ellis Island, as the insightful Dr Victor Safford puts it.

William Williams sees bones scattered on the floor of the dining room, unwashed bowls being refilled several times with soup, immigrants eating with their hands because they haven't been given knives or forks, sometimes not even spoons. They're put to work, pushed around, and insulted. The detention quarters — known without inhibition as *pens*, where a share of the arrivals await questioning and possible deportation — stink of filth. The men running food stands, wearing official caps with American eagles, demand dishonest prices and pressure people into purchases for which they haven't the slightest need.[24]

The rot beneath the surface is even worse. President Roosevelt must have been aware of this, because he's dismissed the station's current leadership — the blundering Thomas Fitchie, along with his deputy, the devil on his shoulder Edward McSweeney — and sent in William Williams, a superb lawyer and at the same time an idealist who respects both humans and animals.

What could be rottener than filth, rough behavior, and rip-off prices?

Once the poor immigrants from steerage have successfully cleared all the checks, they are forced to hand over five dollars for the right to leave the station, which should be theirs for free. Given the enormous number of passengers, some of the staff are making a killing. If an immigrant has more money — which can sometimes be determined from the manifest — they undergo a harsher investigation, which they can buy their way out of. People are released who should be detained and detained when they have every right to be in the United States. The determining factors are money and the chaos that corruption produces. Labor contracts offer a particular opportunity for abuse; the unions, who oppose an imported workforce, are at war with big business, which needs one. In the push and pull of these great powers, significant bribes can be reaped for supporting one side or the other. An immigrant's fate in all this is of no significance.[25]

Little by little, a series of investigations brings these conditions to light. Fitchie and McSweeney's dismissals are followed by the firing of senior clerks who ignored corruption on the island and may have benefited from it.

But what were the unquestionably honest officials doing? It's hard to imagine the stenographer Byron H. Uhl not noticing anything. We can only assume he had too much respect for hierarchy to act against the commissioner and his deputy, especially since he so loved his job at Ellis Island. What about Augustus F. Sherman, who was promoted to senior clerk at this corrupt time? He limited his own field of vision to the small aperture of a lens in a box camera on tall legs. His testimony, preserved on black-and-white light-sensitive sheets, is invaluable, although it unmasks no criminality at Ellis.

Dr Victor Safford, of course, noticed what was happening on the island, and recorded his thoughts:

> [W]e should remember that wherever one finds ships he
> will find at least an attenuated form of piracy and that
> wherever one sees travelers he can find extortion and
> robbery.[26]

Races, Victor Safford

As Dr Safford watches the travelers, he feels compelled to instill some kind of order in this chaos, yet it's not administrative order he has in mind, but a natural one. The throng of people is a jumble of all the races. But which races?

This troubles Victor Safford as a scientific problem, but if it could be solved, it would be tremendously helpful to the immigration service. They struggle to codify the identity of arrivals from conquered lands, who sometimes don't know themselves who they really are. And then there's the question of the Jews. Dr Safford, for his part, can tell perfectly who he's dealing with. For instance, this man with the haughty gaze and the fork and spoon protruding from the top of his boots is a

Slovak; this one, slightly taller, more aloof, gentler in his movements, is a Pole; this man, taller than the Pole with a pale, seemingly bleached appearance, is a Lithuanian; this dark-haired, well-built, muscular, mustachioed man in a short-cut coat is a Hungarian; these slim but stooped men with bony faces are Croatians; these ones who look similar but are heavier-set are from Krajina; while these massive, swarthy, suntanned men come from Dalmatia. Meanwhile this man, whose skull is so vaulted that his hat sits high on the tips of his ears — a skull that would absolutely prefer a turban — is a Jew. The man waiting for him has a silky van Dyck beard and is dressed like a wealthy man of Wall Street, but he is also a Jew.

Victor Safford doesn't really know how he can recognize all these different types; he's a doctor, after all, not a clairvoyant. He suspects it happens subconsciously *by reason of certain distinctive peculiarities which each displayed as a living being in active motion.* He adds: *Muscular enervation and coördination reflect the soul itself.*[27]

These deliberations of Safford's may seem excessively vague, but the doctor really is developing a list of races, or rather perfecting one, since the notion of race has been applied to immigrants since 1899, not out of ideological considerations, but due to the practical needs of the administration. This is easily visible in the case of Italians. These are arriving *en masse* from the unified Kingdom of Italy and all are Catholics, yet they must be divided into two races — Northern and Southern Italians. Immigration officials consider these two separate nations, differing from one another in language, temperament, appearance, and dress; the ones from the south don't know how to read and write or use a sink, and they wear rags. Northerners come from Piedmont, Lombardy, Veneto, Emilia, and territories adjacent to France, Austria, and Switzerland. Southerners are from Sicily and Sardinia. Genoese are also counted as southerners. And what about the middle? It isn't on the list.

Other races include African (*black*), Pacific Islanders (*including*

Hawaiian), Portuguese (*including Brazilian*), Welsh, Scottish, Polish, Ruthenian (*including Ukrainian*), Romanian, Russian, Spanish (*including Catalan*), Armenian, West Indian (*including Cuban*), Dutch and Flemish, and another several dozen. At the end of this long list is the category *Other Peoples*, and packed into it are those groups not arriving in large numbers for the moment — including Arabians (*Muslims*), Albanians (*unless accidentally counted as Greeks or Turks*), Georgians, Gypsies (*Roma*), Persians, and so on.[28] As a result of this detailed inventory, the *Other Peoples* subgroup has practically the same character as the whole list of races and we should not read any implications into its name.

Other Peoples might, however, be a fitting description of those characters Augustus Sherman sometimes comes across at the island and enthusiastically photographs; some catch his eye because of a deformity or impairment.

Here is a man with a handsome hairstyle and straight posture, but four arms and four legs. The extra limbs extend from his belly — in the picture, he displays them with dignity. We can assume August Sherman was interested not so much in this immigrant's particular disability as in his pride in it, which has ensured him bread and even a cabin: he sailed second class on the SS *Adriatica*. His name is Perumall Sammy. The list of races does not place him among *Other Peoples* but in the separate group *East Indians*.

William Williams, Ellis Rock

Commissioner Williams signs his name to the cleaning regulations for Ellis Island.

Each laborer is equipped with a bucket, a hard brush, a rough sponge, rough towels or rags, and three brooms of various kinds.

Everyone is to work with the energy required by private corporations and individual employers in the city of New York. Anyone who neglects this will be dropped from the payroll.

First they wash the bathrooms. Then the men's dormitories.

Remove the blankets. Lay aside those requiring washing. Beat and neatly fold the others. Change all blankets on Mondays and Fridays (this sentence is added to the document by hand).

Brush beds with turpentine and kerosene. Wipe off walls.

Hang beds uniformly.

Wash the floors.

Now everyone goes over to the women's dormitories. They do the same as in the men's.

Then they disperse to their own sections. Disinfect the floors with carbolic acid. Disinfect the bathrooms. Wash the women's exclusion room, the special inquiry room, the steamship agents' room.

Between 7.15 and 9.15 am, fill all the ice-coolers.

Constantly empty all wastepaper baskets and refuse cans. After the first round, do another. At night as well. Burn all refuse.

On Tuesdays, Thursdays, and Saturdays remove insects from beds, radiators, and crevices. Do so with a special machine.

Wash the windows every ten days.

The day cleaners (66 people, nine of them women) leave Manhattan on the ferry at 6.20 am and remain on Ellis Island until 5.30 pm. Lunch break from 12.00 to 12.45 pm. The night staff numbers 15 people, five of them women.

We don't know if the commissioner has delegated drawing up these rules to one of his employees, Byron Uhl for instance, or compiled them himself. The latter can't be ruled out. He is meticulous.

Working at the island in 1909 alongside the cleaners are 64 inspectors, 96 clerks, 64 guards, 32 interpreters, and 24 matrons. The list does not include doctors — perhaps they are counted as clerks, or perhaps are considered separate as belonging to the Public Health Service.[29]

The island's administration is divided into divisions — from the first, executive, to the seventeenth, miscellaneous, their names and characters bearing witness to the fact that absolutely everything has received attention.[30]

Maud Mosher, Matron

Maud Mosher becomes a matron at Ellis Island at the age of 32. She writes in her diary that for her the invitation to the island was *a thunderbolt out of a clear sky*. She's afraid not of the function itself, which she knows well, but the place where she is to carry it out.

The spirit of adventure prompted me to accept the position.

She comes from Illinois. She's known a variety of jobs, for instance, as a traveling saleswoman — to put it bluntly, a peddler — but her most important task thus far has been caring for Native Americans in Wichita, Kansas. She tended to them as a government social worker and was ultimately promoted to the rank of matron. Her work was noticed. That is why she was invited to Ellis Island. She is to defend young immigrant women from human traffickers. *White slave traffic* is reaching a troubling scale and is difficult to combat, since the traffickers use sophisticated methods to smuggle and control their merchandise.

Maud Mosher arrives at the island in 1903. She answers questions from one watchman after the other and looks around, the way Dr Safford did while awaiting his job interview a few years earlier.

> I had been in the government service before for seven
> years as a teacher among the Indians so although I was
> really from the "wild and woolly west" I knew a few
> things about the government service, although in this
> new and strange place they did seem to be very few and
> far between.
>
> That first day at the Island was an interesting one
> but very disheartening also. I first took the oath of office,
> swearing to uphold and defend the constitution of the
> United States against all enemies and to do my duty to
> the best of my ability. I was now a Matron on probation
> only. If I served my probationary period successfully, I
> would be sworn in to the permanent service.

That day, the chief matron takes Maud for a walk around the island to show her the processing procedures. She explains to her trainee that today she has time for her because Ellis Island is examining relatively few immigrants, some 3,000.

To me, writes Maud Mosher,

> it looked as though all the poor people of Europe had
> come in on that day. Out in Kansas no one was so very
> wealthy but no one was so very poor ... In all my life I
> had never seen people so desperately poor except some
> of the reservation Indians and we always thought they
> were so poor because they were an uncivilized people
> — but these were people from the civilized countries of
> Europe, so of course, they must be civilized. That is what

Americans think ...

As I stood and watched the immigrants coming in, it
looked as though they would never cease, every minute was
an hour ... The Doctors were examining their eyes and
scalps ... 2 Matrons, very grave and dignified, stood there
looking and occasionally taking some woman or woman
and man out of the ranks. Officers stood at different places
giving strange commands in foreign tongues. Little children
were crying, tugging at the mother's skirts, the tears making
streaks down their tired dirty faces ... So many look weak
and starved, so many were filthy and dirty ... so low and
degraded looking, and so poor, so dreadfully poor! And I
— I had to stay, I had to stay.[31]

Matrons on Ellis Island have two tasks, Maud finds. The first,
clearly, is to help female immigrants as they are processed on the
island, and care for those unlucky ones who are detained for investigation or deportation. The second task, a discreet one, is observation,
because there is much suspicious activity. They must keep an eye on
the immigrant men, and also the women, perhaps them above all. The
dangerous conjecture of *a public charge* is followed by a new one: *moral
turpitude*. The matrons are to help women, but they must do so according to laws defending their country against loose morals.

But is Maud Mosher suspicious enough? Or is she too caught up in
the drama of this place?

She has just laid eyes on the Kissing Gate:

There are so many joyful meetings at this place that the
officers call it the Kissing Gate. The manner in which the
people of different nationalities greet each other after a
separation of years is one of the interesting studies at the
island. The Italian kisses his children but scarcely speaks

to his wife, never embraces or kisses her in public. The
Hungarian and Slavish people put their arms around one
another and weep. The Jew of all countries kisses his
wife and children as though he owned all the kisses in the
world and intended to use them all up quick.

The joyful Kissing Gate is located next to the Stairs of Separation,
leading down from the largest hall of the new building, where the
arrivals' initial inspections take place. The stairs are broad and solid,
like everything in the island's new buildings. They're divided into
three pathways by heavy barriers. The left leads to the ferry to New
York. The right, to the railroad ticket office: with a ticket from here
you may board a train at the enormous station on the New Jersey coast,
visible with the naked eye from the station and reachable by ferry, and
travel into America. Those who come down along the right or left wall
of the staircase are free to go and can kiss their loved ones crowded at
the foot of the stairs in all the ways in the world. Those who are sent
on the middle route, between the barriers, are in deepest despair. Bereft
and terrified. The middle line of stairs cuts them off from their families,
their traveling companions, their hope for a new life. Now they are
prisoners of the United States, though unsentenced.

After her first day on Ellis Island, Maud can't regain her composure:

I was so disheartened, so overwhelmed, so frightened that
I could not sleep that night. The endless procession kept
still moving on, the Doctors were examining eyes, eyes,
eyes and the babies were crying, crying and I could do
nothing; the people were so poor and low and degraded
and I — just an atom thrown on the tide. I wanted to run
away right back to Kansas and go on teaching shorthand
forever and ever. I felt as though I never could take up
the work at the Island but I had to stay.

Maud Mosher is one of the first "boarding matrons." She boards the ships before the immigrants are taken by ferry to Ellis and has the right to question passengers in cabins. Her main task is to search for prostitutes or girls brought to the United States as slaves.

The aptly named Margaret Dye Ellis, an activist of the Women's Christian Temperance Union, has designed appropriate costumes for the young boarding matrons: long skirts with bloomers underneath. New York's reporters can't get enough of watching the girls climbing swaying ladders on to the ships, but Commissioner Williams predicts a fiasco. And rightly so: the boarding matrons' investigative efforts yield no information, the indignant women passengers lodge complaints, and the male staff of Ellis Island watch all this unfold with derisive superiority. Maud Mosher complains in her journal that the inspectors block her way on to ships, send her back to shore, and humiliate her in an unpleasant tone, saying: *There is nothing down there for you.*

After three months of this practice, the boarding matrons stop working as a unit. They assist the male inspectors.

Still, no one on the island has any doubt — human trafficking is dramatically expanding.

The Smell of the Ships, Victor Safford

Doctor Victor Safford has not only a sharp eye, but also a very sensitive nose. When he came to Ellis Island for the first time, back before the fire, he could tell from a distance that the Georgia pine the new station was built with was still green, judging by its smell.

To Safford's mind, nothing in the world smells sweeter and purer than a vessel fresh from the shipyard. It bears the scent of pine, oak, and young spruce, combined with the aroma of Stockholm tar, oakum, and new rigging, enriched with a note of fresh shellac. This enchanting aroma is so strong not even the steel plating of the hull or the steam engine and boilers can suppress it. Anyone who hasn't smelled a ship in a long time would delight to breathe in even the air trailing from the ventilators of a new steamer.

All new ships have a similar smell. Over time, their bouquets begin to differ. It's their cargo that's responsible for the change. The aroma of sugar and molasses, pleasant at first, becomes tiresome; green coffee can even cause yellow fever or beriberi; while old whaling ships that haven't hunted a sperm whale in half a century still reek of them from a long way away.

Yet nothing so marks a ship as the trade in African slaves. Even after one voyage, this cargo leaves a stench of rotting flesh that will never leave the hull.

Some phenomena defy explanation. Why does an American warship smell differently from a Spanish one? Because the Spanish eat so much garlic? Unlikely, since American vessels smell different from British ones, though their cuisine is similar.

It appears the doctor considers a ship's aroma to be its speech, which humans aren't always able to understand.

Victor Safford has boarded many ships to perform medical inspections, but his particular sensory perception of a sea vessel's aura probably originates elsewhere. How does he know the odor left by the poverty, wounds, and despair of the enslaved, since — as he admits — he's never had to deal with a ship that transported them? Someone must have told him the story.

When the doctor accepts his job at Ellis Island, Moses Atwood Safford — a lawyer and sailor from Maine, and a Baptist — is still alive. In 1861, as the United States was furiously expanding its navy and training crews for war with the Confederates, he enlisted as a non-commissioned officer on the USS *Constellation*, a slim three-mast frigate. He was 28. He served three years on the ship, where neither drills, nor storms, nor skirmishes kept him from writing his diary, which happily survived and is — according to maritime historians — unparalleled as a testimony of life at sea in that era. Before the *Constellation* joined the battle with the South, it tracked down slave traders and freed 700 black victims from three ships on the coasts of Africa. Moses Atwood Safford would therefore have heard on his frigate about the qualities of slave ships and it must have been he who passed this knowledge on to Victor Safford.

The two men were surely related. Both came from the same town of Kittery, Maine. Both bore the same last name, and Victor Safford's middle name was Moses. The doctor not only knew the aforementioned diary but — bibliographical sources show — edited it himself in 1933 (14 years before his death) and placed the manuscript in the archive collections of the USS *Constellation* in Baltimore, Maryland. The *Constellation* is the only ship from the Civil War era to have survived until today. It stands at Pier 1 in Baltimore and operates as a museum.

The sailor and doctor must have been close, because they repose under a single stone in the Baptist cemetery in Kittery, a photograph of which can be found on the internet. At the top is carved the name Safford; below, first names and dates, including: *Moses A. 1833–1914* and *Dr Victor M. 1867–1947*.

The fact that they were not just close relatives, but father and son, is conclusively proved by information in the International Genealogical Index, available online.

Now let us return to the early 20th century. Father and son are alive. Victor Safford is working on Ellis Island and analyzing olfactory impressions, not from hearsay, but firsthand.

We are already aware that, as he watches the latest contingent of immigrants haul their luggage across the island, Dr Safford knows how to determine their race — according to their posture, the energy of their movements, and their appearance. Now he assures us that, based on their scent, he can guess which shipping line they took to America, even though their ship has stayed at the Port of New York while they themselves are transferred by the ferry that runs between the port and Ellis Island. As passengers of the White Star Line pour out of the ferry, they smell different from passengers of Norddeutscher Lloyd, who in turn smell different from Cunard passengers. Arrivals on the Hamburg–American line have a particular smell, and those from Holland–America yet another. Victor Safford maintains this is unrelated to the passengers' origin, since all these companies transport a similar mix of nationalities. It isn't the people who differ by scent, but rather the decks they've departed.[32]

The doctor does not explain this peculiar fact. Nonetheless, we can be sure his nose is mainly catching the air of between-decks, because Ellis Island processes primarily steerage passengers; those who can afford cabins usually come ashore back at the port, having already been processed on their ships.

One wonders if Dr Safford has told Matron Maud Mosher, who is meant to fight white slave traffic, about his discoveries. One fears this meticulously concealed trade will leave no despair-scented trace to give it away. The slaves have either accepted their fate freely, or are as yet unaware.

Franciszka Jagielska Thirty-Three Ways

From the moment Ellis Island reopens (on 17 December 1900), the size of the crowds passing through keeps growing. In 1901 — nearly 389,000 immigrants; in 1902 — over 490,000; in 1903 — over 630,000.[33]

They do not include Franciszka Jagielska, or Graboski, or Marianna Borkowska and her children, or Antoni Borowski, or Józefina Cybulska, or Karol Fenzka, or Maria Edelman, or Teofila-Filcia Lewandowska. We don't know if Filcia slipped out of the documents, if she stayed on the banks of the Drwęca, or if her husband Walenty is still *full of longing*.

Or maybe we don't know how to find them, because the names they bore in Płock Guberniya might appear completely differently on the manifests. To search for Franciszka Jagielska as carefully as possible, we would have to type the following versions into the search engine (the program provides a list of them): jagielska, jagielski, jagielsky, jagietska, gagielska, jagialska, jagialsky, jagielzki, jakielski, jakielsky, jaqielski, jagierska, jagelska, jagielka, jagiolsky, jogielski, jakiolski, and many more, 33 variants altogether, multiplied by the approximate dates of birth we consider likely.

It's no wonder these names were altered and simplified, first on the ships, and then on the island. Some of the most famous names include Andrjuljawierjus, Grzyszczyszyn, and Koutsoghianopoulos, which survive in oral histories. They're treated like relics under special care.

William Williams, the Club in Manhattan

Commissioner William Williams' apartment at the University Club in Manhattan consists of a small hallway, a living room with a bathroom attached, and a bedroom; it's no larger than 650 square feet. A remarkably modest apartment. American citizens equal to Williams in status and background have beautiful residences on Washington Square, as described by the famous author Henry James, who at this very moment intends to visit the commissioner on the island.

The apartment is warm; the central heating works flawlessly. William Williams (or rather his valet) doesn't light the fire in the living room. The logs lying in the firebox and tied with string have gone gray with age.

Through the tall bedroom window is a small balcony. It looks out on Fifth Avenue, with a view of the bright, recently built St Patrick's Cathedral.

It was no sure thing William Williams would get this spot. The club's distinguished council wanted no permanent residents in the rooms. Yet, after some discussion, they decided the club would set aside four apartments, one for *the honorable William Williams, Yale 1884*, and the second and third for alumni of the same school, classes of 1860 and 1895. The fourth room was held in reserve.[34]

When William Williams moves into his rooms, the club numbers around 1,700 members. To get an idea of their social significance and

wealth, we must leave the commissioner's small living room and walk through the building's main entrance, beneath an enormous portal featuring a head of Minerva. There are hardly any skyscrapers in Manhattan as yet. It is an era of the palaces of the new bourgeoisie (the most exquisite ones belonging to the Vanderbilts), and this pseudo-Renaissance club building, faced with pink Maine granite, also masquerades as a palace. The architects borrowed a little from Sienna (Palazzo Spannocchi), a little from Bologna (Palazzo Albergati), a little from Rome (Palazzo Spada), and a little from Florence (Palazzo Strozzi). But even more palatial than the exterior are the great hall and the three-story dining room, with crystal chandeliers, a gallery for musicians, a large fireplace in the western alcove, and rows of cabinets where you can stand face-to-face with George Washington as painted by Gilbert Stuart or a noblewoman by Sir Joshua Reynolds. All this, however, pales in comparison to the library, which is patterned after the Vatican. Under a richly painted ceiling of high, vaulted arches stand packed shelves, dark tables, and old globes. Members may view a 1511 printing of Ptolemy's *Geography* and original drawings by Piranesi.

What a shame the library's collection is no longer overseen by Lyman Hotchkiss Bagg (a Yale graduate), famous author of *Ten Thousand Miles on a Bicycle* — 900 pages, 76 pages of index, nearly 23,000 footnotes, 3,000 subscribers. He has recently resigned from his position. Or maybe it isn't a pity, since at any rate William Williams would have no time to talk with this eccentric. Instead the commissioner seeks solitude, he spends his time in the library's side rooms reserved for focused work, at one of the tables with the silver inkwells. There he can write his rules and directives. He returns to his own accommodation late at night and maybe its modesty even soothes him after the lavishness of the club's common spaces.

Every day at around 8.00 am the commissioner boards an official boat to the island. First he has to get a few miles down Manhattan, but the New York City subway is still under construction. Trolleys and the first electric trains on elevated tracks above the streets are indeed running, but we must presume William Williams uses a carriage or a car with a driver. Automobiles are increasingly popular: in 1899, the newspapers report the first deadly car accident on West 74th Street near Central Park.

Augustus Sherman, Photographer

Senior Clerk Augustus Sherman's hobby has caught Commissioner Williams' eye, and, for some time, Sherman has been treated as Ellis Island's official photographer.

Yet he photographs what he wants. He doesn't seem to be given ongoing assignments, covering visits or celebrations. He couldn't have fulfilled them anyway — his pictures require thought and time. The commissioner admires some of Sherman's images so much he requests prints and keeps them in his desk drawer.

Augustus Sherman has a completely different working method to the photographer Lewis W. Hine, who took portraits of immigrants at Ellis Island in 1905 and remembers it this way:

> We are elbowing our way thro [sic] the mob at Ellis trying to stop the urge of bewildered beings oozing through the corridors, up the stairs and all over the place, eager to get it all over and be on their way. Here is a small group that seems to have possibilities so we stop 'em and explain in pantomime that it would be lovely if they would only stick around just a moment. The rest of the human tide swirls around, often not too considerate of either the camera or us. We get the focus, on the ground glass of course, then, hoping they will stay put, get the flash lamp ready ... By that time most of the group was either silly or stony or weeping with hysteria because the bystanders had been busy pelting them with advice and comments, and the climax came when you raised the flash pan aloft over them and they waited, rigidly, for the blast.
> It took all the resources of a hypnotist, a supersalesman and a ball pitcher to prepare them to play the game and then outguess them so most were not either wincing or shutting their eyes when the time came to shoot.[35]

Augustus Sherman doesn't push his way through the throng. He photographs people for whom the gates to America have been closed for now or for ever, and are waiting in the detention rooms. But because he spares no effort or time, he can make them feel at home, persuade them to pose in costumes seemingly out of the most fabulous opera scenes, or only in their underwear if they have such a marvelous torso as the Polish wrestler Zbyszko Cyganiewicz. Sherman wrote *Zybszko* in black ink on the print and so the misspelling has remained in photo books.[36]

Sherman's status as a senior clerk means he knows in advance what people or groups warrant particular attention, and — even if there's no reason to detain them — he finds ways to get them in front of his lens and arrange them appropriately.

By height, for instance.

That's how eight very well-behaved, intelligent, and handsome children are lined up, wearing little jackets with shiny buttons and white collars, with large berets — flat and stiff as hot-water bottles for relieving morning hangovers — on their heads. This little group, who arrived on the steamship *Coronia*, would be fun to look at if we didn't know they were orphans whose mothers had perished in Russia in the 1905 pogrom. They've sailed to the United States under the care of a Jewish humanitarian organization.

Similarly lined up are ten Germans — Russian citizens — who arrived on the *Pretoria*. The father, Jakob Mittelstadt, clutching his cap, the mother in an apron, their first-born daughter also in an apron, then seven boys, from a teenager to almost an infant, in plain coats and heavy boots.

Or a group of 13 from the Netherlands: the proud parents — father with a grey beard, mother in a hat — and 11 siblings, the eldest could be the father of the youngest at the end of the line, who's only just begun standing on his own; each has a white paper pinned to his or her chest with the name of their destination.

Most of Sherman's models wear such labels. The wave may surge and people can get lost in it.

The Third Island, the Radiator, Oysters

In 1904, just over 606,000 immigrants disembark at the island, a little less than the previous year, but 1905 is a record — over 788,000, and there is every indication that even that record will be broken.

Ellis Island is expanding again. Alongside Island 2 they are beginning to sketch out Island 3, fashioned from already familiar materials, plus some new ones — leftover stone from the buildings erected on Islands 1 and 2, as well as sand, earth, and rock from the excavations under those buildings. The third island has therefore partly sprung from its older sisters.

A geologist wanting to test these binding agents would find remnants of shells, hard as slate. This is waste from the ancient homesteads of the Lenape Indians, a trace of the long-ago riches of New York's waters. In the 17th century these waters apparently provided half the world's supply of oysters. Over the next two centuries, the local mollusks voyaged to the tables of London, Paris, and other cities of Europe, while in America they made a nutritious repast for all the states. They're sold for pennies at street stalls, in outdoor markets, and in basement taverns. The trade pauses in the warmer months — from the start of May to the end of August — but on 1 September, the long-awaited start of oyster season is joyfully celebrated and red balloons fly over the tavern entrances. Yet this custom is dying out. The waters of the bay are increasingly polluted, the oysters are becoming stunted, and little by little the New York Department of Health is banning exploitation of the beds, in light of serious suspicions that it isn't only immigrants spreading typhus and other diseases — the culprits could also be these mollusks, harvested from waters contaminated by a civilization that is the New World's pride and joy.

Even Ellis Island no longer resembles an oyster with a bite out of one side. From above, it looks like a comb with three teeth, or a

radiator. The strips of land are separated by strips of water, their banks are connected with footbridges. The island is now over 20.25 acres in area, making it over six times its original size, more than twice as large as Kraków's market square.

The third island, 4.75 acres, will be the base for addressing some pressing needs. There, a contagious diseases hospital is to be erected.

Buttonhook, Trachoma

Trachoma (from the Greek *trăchýs* — rough, coarse) has long been familiar in the Polish lands. The disease's folk name is *jaglica* — from *jagło*, millet — while doctors call it Egyptian ophthalmia.

Tomasz Kuczkowski, *Court Advisor to the Russian State, Medical Doctor, Knight of the Orders of St Vladimir Fourth Degree and St Anne Second Class with Diamonds*, composes a scientific book on trachoma, published in 1822.[37]

In the introduction, he pays tribute to the civic spirit of the Renaissance poet Jan Kochanowski (quoting his words, *Let us serve noble glory* ...) and the paternal spirit of Grand Duke Constantine toward the valorous defenders of the motherland. He goes on to inform us that, from 1819 to 1821, the main Polish hospital treated 2,095 eye patients, of whom 1,926 recovered, 58 went completely blind, 56 partially blind, and the remainder are still in treatment.

The British statistics are even more alarming.

> In 1810, the government was burdened with 2,317
> completely blind soldiers. At the current time, according
> to a calculation by Dr William Adams, the number of all
> those blinded by infectious disease in the whole British

army has reached 4,500, on whom the public treasury
must spend 92,600 pounds sterling.

Twenty-eight years after this book, another publication comes
out on the Egyptian disease, a work by the Medical Council of the
Kingdom of Poland. The Council explains this affliction's exotic name.
The ophthalmia *began to manifest itself in Europe among the soldiers
of various nations after Napoleon's campaign in Egypt, i.e. after 1799.*
Following that, it appeared in Malta, Great Britain, Elba, Sicily, various
parts of Italy, the Prussian Army, the Belgian Army — where it raged
viciously in 1818 and 1819 — and in Warsaw — where it affected 8,000
active army soldiers in 1834, before spreading to Russia.

The Council lays out the precise stages of the disease. First sand
forms under the eyelids, then

the membrane connecting the eyelids becomes apparently
velvety, whey-like fluid begins to secrete from the glands
at the edges of the eyelids, which begin to excrete mucus
in the form of fibers resembling egg-white.

The second stage of the disease is aversion to light, the upper eyelid
swells like half an egg, and its surface goes grey. The velvety membrane
becomes grainy, and the fluid — *pus-like, yellowish, greenish, dotted, like
cottage cheese.* Added to this is *pain as though from a burning coal.*

The third stage: the connecting membrane becomes covered in
wart-like grains, frequently as large as peas. The eye waters or swells.

Next comes an ominous sentence: *This disease spreads by contagion.*[38]

Trachoma infection may come from sacred sources, such as the
waters of St Vitus in Stary Żywiec, where the faithful rinse their eyes in
the belief they will be cured.

America is terrified of this disease. Immigrants with trachoma are
to be mercilessly deported.

Many years later, Dr Grover A. Kempf, who conducted medical inspections on the island, recalled:

> I entered the work at Ellis Island ... The doctors would
> examine the eyes for trachoma ... To turn the eyelid
> I used the good old buttoner — button shoes were
> common in those days, and there was a little loop [used]
> to button shoes, [we] used [it] to turn the eyelid — it was
> the most efficient way of turning the eyes ever devised.[39]

One hundred and three years after the opening of the station, the

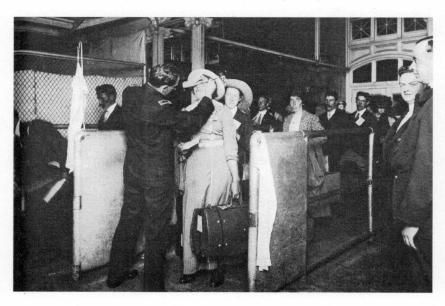

author and filmmaker Robert Bober presents his readers with a photograph of his great-grandfather Wolf Leib Frankel from Przemyśl, who was deported from Ellis due to trachoma. The dignified old man in a prayer shawl has his glazed, lashless eyes fixed on a book. His head rests on one large, old hand. A grey, fan-like beard reaches down to his chest.

The picture was taken after Wolf Frankel's arrival in America or a few months after his deportation. When Dr Kempf or another inspecting doctor peeled back his eyelid, using a hook possibly produced by Savinovitz from Kadzidło, Wolf Leib was clean-shaven. He intended to enter American life as a younger and more modern man. But after being turned back, he decided to return to his old skin. He didn't want to live in Przemyśl without a beard. He stopped over in Vienna and waited for it to grow back.[40] Did he save his eyes too? His great-grandson doesn't say.

Nor do we know what happened to the eyes of a 30-year-old immigrant from Russia who arrived at Ellis Island under the name Leie Kwarczinsky. She came to join her husband, who'd found work as a blacksmith in the New York subway. He worked 12 hours a day for $15 a week. Leie brought three children with her: three, seven, and nine years old. At Ellis Island she was found to have trachoma. She was assured she could stay if she was cured, but after four months of painful treatments at the island hospital she was still sick. Her husband, additionally burdened with supporting the children, couldn't afford to continue treatment. The evening of Christmas Eve 1908, she was deported to Russia on the German ship *Scharnhorst*.[41]

Six years later, the British sank the SMS *Scharnhorst* near the Falklands, but that's another story.

An Immigrant Like an Automobile, Victor Safford

Maud Mosher surveys the line of immigrants, and her eyes fill with tears. Dr Victor Safford maintains a detached distance, perhaps defensively. He calmly picks off the fleas he's caught from an Italian ship (they've left red spots on his neck) as he considers this problem: what is the difference between assessing an automobile one wishes to purchase, and assessing a person who is to be allowed into the United States?

It is a no more difficult task to detect poorly built,
defective or broken down human beings than to recognize
a cheap or defective automobile. It requires of course
some training and experience to do either, but in any case
difficulty usually arises not so much in recognizing that
something is wrong as in determining and demonstrating
just what is wrong. With immigrants the metaphor may
be carried still further. Ordinarily when a person goes
to a doctor he is helped to locate the cause of trouble by
the patient himself, who relates his subjective symptoms.
The alien who comes before the immigration medical
officer is usually interested only in leading the medical
officer to believe that nothing is wrong, and one might
as well waste time waiting for an automobile to tell of its
internal feelings as to hope to get diagnostic help from the
subjective symptoms of a diseased immigrant ...
[T]he wise man who really wants to find out all he can
about an automobile, or an immigrant, will want to see
both in action, performing as well as at rest, and to watch
both at a distance as well as to scrutinize them close at
hand. Defects, derangements, and symptoms of disease
which would not be disclosed by a so-called "careful
physical examination," are often easily recognizable in
watching a person twenty-five feet away.[42]

That is precisely what takes place on the island. After entering a large
vestibule on the ground floor of the station's main building, the immigrants climb up one floor, under the watchful eye of doctors who, as
we already know, wear military-looking uniforms. People arriving
from the subjugated nations of Europe fear nothing and no one more
than men in uniforms, who embody oppression in their towns and
villages — so they do everything to stay out of sight: hiding behind

someone taller, disappearing into their coats, or covering themselves with their bundles. These naïve methods have been quickly discovered, catalogued, and laid out in instructions, and the doctors know exactly whom to pull out of the crowd for further investigation.

A medical inspector giving the immigrants a quick visual once-over must pay attention to six elements: the skin of the head, the face, the neck, the arms, the gait, and their general condition — physical and mental.

If any of the above is invisible to the naked eye, the doctor will stop the immigrant to make sure there is nothing suspicious going on.

A high collar. This must be unbuttoned to check if there is a goiter or an ulcer lurking underneath.

A hat. Often used to cover ringworm or mycosis.

A thick head of curls. As above.

A cap pulled low over the eyes. This could conceal conjunctivitis or trachoma.

A hand hidden under a coat, a scarf, or a bag. The limb may turn out to be deformed, paralyzed, missing fingers, or afflicted with tinea.

Luggage. This can be used to conceal deficient posture. The immigrant must lay their bags on the ground and walk about ten feet without them.

Children above the age of two clinging to their mothers. The mother must proceed as above.

It is calculated that on days with larger intake, when Ellis Island accepts four to five thousand people, each doctor has more or less six seconds to visually scan a single person. The medical inspectors, also known as "line inspectors," are increasingly known for their "six-second physicals."

If the six-second inspectors notice something and consider further, closer investigation to be necessary, they must give instructions using a piece of chalk. If a person is suspected of a mental defect, the inspectors draw an X on their clothes. If a mental defect is very likely, they draw a circle around the X. B is back, C — conjunctivitis, CT — trachoma, E — eyes, F — face, Ft — feet, G — goiter, H — heart, K — hernia, N — neck, P — physical and lungs, Pg — pregnancy, Sc — scalp, S — senility.

Sometimes they don't bother with camouflage, instead writing a whole word in chalk, usually on the immigrant's chest or back: *arms*, *legs*, *skin*, *nails*.

Next, another doctor will examine the people marked with chalk, standing them in a well-lit place near a large window. On the island they call them the "eye men." They will make a closer inspection of suspicious eyes, heads, and hands. Sometimes they will ask about something with the help of an interpreter. They might free an immigrant from suspicion or confirm it. In the latter case, they lead the patient into one of the medical rooms for further examination, sometimes psychological.

Until 1998, there was no known case in the history of the island of someone escaping the clutches of the chalk symbols. But that was the

year an 84-year-old Spanish woman named Espuga Manuela Carnero returned to Ellis Island. She had emigrated to America in 1920 with her mother and brother. She was six, but could remember the inspector marking her brother's jacket with chalk. Her mother pulled the jacket off him so quickly and dexterously that no one noticed a thing. Somehow, the boy wasn't pulled out of line, nor separated from his family. Espuga Manuela Carnero came to Ellis Island to tell that story and record it, because it is never too late to tell others how you must fight to the end, even when resistance seems hopeless.[43]

A Ghost in the House, Henry James

When, in 1904, the author Henry James sails from Europe, where he has spent most of his life, to America, where he was born, he is over 60 and renowned. He's published the novels *Daisy Miller*, *The Portrait of a Lady*, *Washington Square*, and *The Bostonians*. He

observes the changes in his home country. He is moved by the influx of new people. He wishes to see the gateway to America, the station on Ellis Island, and Commissioner Williams is happy to show him.

James describes William Williams as *the eminent Commissioner of this wonderful [immigration] service* and thanks him in this way in his novelistic essay *The American Scene*, published in 1907.

He is thankful to him for his hospitality and permissiveness, for Williams enabling him to see the drama of this *poignant and unforgettable* place. *Before this door,* writes James of the immigrants at Ellis,

> which opens to them there only with a hundred forms
> and ceremonies, grindings and grumblings of the key,
> they stand appealing and waiting, marshalled, herded,
> divided, subdivided, sorted, sifted, searched, fumigated
> …

Henry James is convinced a sensitive US citizen who's had the chance to see the work on Ellis Island will come away from the island a different person.

> He has eaten of the tree of knowledge, and the taste will
> be for ever in his mouth. He had thought he knew before,
> thought he had the sense of the degree in which it is
> his American fate to share the sanctity of his American
> consciousness, the intimacy of his American patriotism,

with the inconceivable alien; but the truth had never come home to him with any such force ... I like to think of him, I positively have to think of him, as going about ever afterwards with a new look, for those who can see it, in his face, the outward sign of the new chill in his heart. So is stamped, for detection, the questionably privileged person who has had an apparition, seen a ghost in his supposedly safe old house. Let not the unwary, therefore, visit Ellis Island.[44]

William Williams on the Millennium

These thoughts, which perhaps influence James to naturalize in the United Kingdom before his death (he dies nine years after the publication of *The American Scene*), trouble William Williams too. Both come from the same wealthy background, their families long resident in America; if they did not meet at Harvard Law School, it is only because James is 19 years older.

The commissioner sees to it that the arrivals are treated honestly and respectfully, because he is a man of honor, order, and discipline. He suspends a gateman who used coarse language with an immigrant for two weeks without pay. He fires a watchman who instead of gently waking a sleeping man in a dormitory, frightened him by pounding on the canvas of the bed on which he was sleeping. He sends a telegraph boy to jail for giving an immigrant a counterfeit coin, and informs all his employees in writing:

Swindling immigrants is contemptible business, and whoever does this, under whatever form, should be despised. It is the duty of all Government officials to go out of their way to protect immigrants against every kind of imposition. Let everyone at Ellis Island clearly understand that all impositions, whenever detected, will be punished as severely as the law admits.[45]

When Williams realizes the large transportation companies are cheating immigrants not only on ticket prices (selling them third class for the price of first) but also by sending them on circuitous routes with stopovers (so their accomplices, the accommodation owners, can earn more), he orders that tickets should be sold directly to their final destinations and sends his inspectors to monitor travel conditions *incognito*.

He keeps the various immigrant aid organizations honest. When a Hungarian immigrant organization writes to a Hungarian family in West Virginia to wire money for relatives, he sharply reprimands them, because these relatives are sufficiently provided for.

He evicts from the island representatives of Scandinavian House, Austro-Hungarian House, and the Polish St Joseph's House because he has to draw a line between true missionaries and the people running these flophouses. The latter, in his view, take false credit for being caregivers, when all they care for is their business. They charge excessive fees and exploit immigrants for labor.

He opposes deportations lacking sufficient legal justification. When Charles Semsey, the Civil War veteran hired on the island back in the days of John Baptiste Weber, wants to repatriate 11 Cuban children invited to a Theosophical school in California, Williams presents the case in Washington and the group is accepted by the United States.

Under Commissioner Williams' governance, the station operates efficiently, courteously, and even sensitively. Postcards are introduced with pre-printed information for immigrants to send for free from Ellis to their loved ones in the United States, sparing them the cost of an expensive telegram. The card states where their relative is staying, how

to come and meet them, and that they may contact them by telephone at the station's expense. The commissioner orders that all children over 12 who are detained at the island have their temperature taken daily.

One of Augustus Sherman's photographs shows the great lengths the station sometimes goes to in caring for its immigrants. The photo is touchingly propagandistic: it has six waving American flags, but that doesn't detract from the fact we are seeing a real playground on the roof of one of the buildings on Ellis Island. A small wagon on spoked wheels with *Uncle Sam* written on the side is besieged with tawny-haired immigrant children holding those very flags, while another child has climbed on a rocking horse, and it's not difficult to imagine the gorgeous view of the Bay, the Statue of Liberty, and Manhattan stretching out in all directions from the playground. Or that from time to time the rooftop resounds with the cheerful voice of a caregiver, who holds up soap and a brush and sings in English:

> This is the way we wash our face,
> Wash our face, wash our face.

This is the way we brush our hair,
Brush our hair, brush our hair ...

So it would seem everything works like a dream, but when the annual tide of immigrants reaches 800,000, William Williams tells a *New York Times* journalist that is 300,000 too many. *Aliens have no inherent right to land on American soil.*[46] In Williams' view, the old immigration laws are no longer up to the task. New limits are needed, because the growing wave of immigrants from the southern and eastern regions of Europe is worse than the older wave from the northern regions: they are physically weaker, sick or sickly, and mentally slack.

It was exactly these kinds of views about the new immigrants' inferiority that John Baptiste Weber protested at the end of the last century. We might wonder why the two commissioners have different opinions — is it because they come from different backgrounds, or because Weber took over the station earlier, when the wave was just building up?

Commissioner Williams would like to introduce a test to exclude illiterates. He has already introduced a requirement for immigrants to possess $10 (the same amount as General O'Beirne demanded) and intends to raise this sum to $25, though he never manages to.

He's appealed to Theodore Roosevelt to liberate him from Joseph Murray, his feckless and inefficient assistant commissioner. He hasn't kept in mind Murray is a protégé of the president and the president will not be dictated to. Williams receives a refusal and, in early 1905, he bids the island farewell.[47]

Williams leaves on a ferryboat recently christened in Delaware with a bottle of champagne; he attended the ceremony. The boat was built specially for Ellis Island and bears the island's name. It is 160 feet long and crosses back and forth across the Bay 18 hours a day. It transports not only immigrants (it can fit 1,000 on the lower deck), but also island employees. The commissioner has his own cabin with a swinging table and a soft locker seat, where he could even catch a nap if the ride were longer. In the evening on the ferry, round lanterns in round iron housings are lit. The large, smooth, oak wheel of the ship glistens as though cast from bronze, and the whole vessel is still infused with the seductive aromas of wood, pitch, shellac, and so on.

William Williams parts with the lovely boat and steps out on to land. He returns to his legal practice in Manhattan, and in his free hours he enjoys the luxuries of his club. These luxuries are multiplying. There are billiard rooms, avenues of palm trees in clay pots as large as amphoras from Greek archeological sites, and a sunny atrium with wicker armchairs, and soon there will be a swimming pool. The club caters to the physical and mental health of its members and benefactors. The library's collection is subject to censorship — it collects works dedicated to the humanities, art, travel, geographical exploration, and sports, but does not tolerate books on finance and business. The council has decided that the club is a refuge from the economic activity of the city; a meeting place for socialization and rest, more among personal friends than business associates. So William Williams may sink into a chair with some relaxing reading (for instance about traveling 10,000 miles by bicycle), and at times look up from his book at the exquisite painting by Henry Siddons Mowbray on the vaulted ceiling — a barefoot shepherdess with a skimpy bodice hugging her breasts, who is also reading a hefty book she props on a stone, titled *Philosophy*.

William Williams leaves the battle with the great wave of immigration to his successors. A year into his work at Ellis Island, he said he believed it possible to curb bad practices and ensure good service for the immigrants. But Ellis would never be paradise: he didn't believe that *the millennium can ever exist here.*[48]

Part II
Flood

The Nut-seller's Song, Robert Watchorn

The portrait of Robert Watchorn that opens his autobiography depicts a handsome, gray-haired man of aristocratic bearing, in a black jacket and pinstripe trousers, winding the slim chain of a pocket watch around his finger, lost in thought. The painting is by the sought-after portraitist Thomas Stephen Seymour, who can boast not only of his high-quality clientele but that his parents lived in the first multi-story building in Texas.

This portrait would not look out of place on the walls of the University Club in Manhattan. Yet the sitter never studied at either Harvard or at Yale.

He was born in a workers' block in the small mining community of Alfreton in England and left school at the age of 11 to earn money in the mine; he had five younger siblings.

He starts this job in April 1869 (Charles Dickens is still alive; 30 years earlier he finished *Oliver Twist*). The boy's duty is to open and close the ventilation doors in the mine corridors. They can't be open either too long or not long enough, and when he has to let through a horse-drawn mine trolley loaded with coal, he sweats with fear, because the old nag is dragging it so slowly.

He opens the first door at 6.00 am and closes the last at 6.00 pm. He hands the envelope with his pay over to his mother without ever opening it. The first time he does open it is when he turns 21. When he brings home his first wages, his mother says in tears: *Bobbie! This is like coining your body and soul painfully cheap.*

Bobbie has to work so hard because his father wastes too many hours and pence at the local pub, the Swan and Salmon. So Bobbie himself swears temperance and joins the Methodists, whom he trusts. He truly gains a moral support — on their advice he even registers for night school and goes every evening. He doesn't return home until late.

Small-time traders stand at the corners of Alfreton's lanes. These are the men who couldn't get work in the mines. One sells bags of nuts and attracts customers with song:

> To the West, to the West, to the land of the free,
> Where a mighty Missouri flows down to the sea
> Where a man is a man ...

Robert Watchorn knows the nut-seller well and sometimes asks him specially for that song.

> The song kept the picture of the Missouri River in my
> mind, giving me no rest from the thought of emigrating.
> Accordingly, a few days after my twenty-second birthday,
> I made use of all my available resources and bought
> passage from Liverpool to New York on the Cunard liner
> Bothnia, due to sail Saturday, May 14, 1880.[49]

There is no immigration station yet on Ellis Island. The Statue of Liberty has not yet been erected. Watchorn lands at Castle Garden with five pounds leant to him by his Methodist spiritual mentor and another two pounds from his vicar. He also has a knife, a fork, and a spoon, a blanket, a towel, a piece of soap, and a small amount of underwear. The good old traveling chest he lugs on his shoulder, knocked together in home-made fashion by his mother and the woman next door, is sure not to catch the attention of Peter McDonald, recently made head of the baggage staff. What might have caught Peter Mac's eye is when the chest's owner puts it down and gets into a fistfight. It turns out a lemonade salesman didn't give him his change, and now is even accusing him of stealing. The young man fights back so energetically the police investigate and determine he was in the right.

This is Robert Watchorn's first encounter with America. Despite everything, it rouses his hopes.

He takes a job at a mine in Pennsylvania. Every day he has to load six freight cars weighing two tons each; they are tall, with closed sides. To load his cargo, he first has to split the glazed lumps of anthracite into smaller chunks. His overseer is a sadist and one day they have an altercation, leading Watchorn to run away from his shift. That rebellion shapes his destiny. In the next mine he observes the cars being weighed and works out the miners are being cheated. He himself is losing 84¢ a day (nearly half his daily earnings), and there are 300 loaders working in the mine.

He calls a workers' meeting. They win out — the weighing will take place under the miners' observation. This is the start of Watchorn's union activism.

But first he returns the five pounds and two pounds to his friends, in the same banknotes they gave him, untouched. Now that he feels more confident in America, he pays for passage for the nut-seller from Alfreton — the one who sang about the Missouri. *He came and soon found suitable and remunerative employment and enjoyed fifteen additional years of happy and contented life.*

Watchorn becomes, in succession, treasury secretary of the United Mine Workers of America, an associate of the governor of Pennsylvania, an immigration clerk at Ellis Island, and commissioner of the immigration station in Montreal, where he works with the Canadians to tighten the border against illegal Chinese immigration. In 1905, President Theodore Roosevelt names him commissioner of Ellis Island, with the enormous salary of $6,500 a year. The very same president who first appointed a man from Plymouth Rock now bestows governance of the island on a man from steerage.

From the Bible, Edward Steiner

William Williams hosted Henry James at the island; Robert Watchorn hosts H.G. Wells. The fact that each commissioner hosts a writer from his own social class is surely coincidental.

Wells, like Watchorn, was a child of the English poor and had to leave school early to help his family.

When he comes to Ellis Island, he is already the famous author of *The Time Machine, The Invisible Man,* and *The War of the Worlds,* and is gathering observations for a non-fiction book titled *The Future in America.* Commissioner Watchorn leads him to the gallery above the great inspection hall and they both look down on the *crowd creeping step by step through the wire filter*[50] *of the central hall of Ellis Island into America.*

> "You don't think they'll swamp you?" I said.
>
> "Now look here," said the Commissioner, "I'm English-born — Derbyshire. I came into America when I was a lad. I had fifteen dollars. And here I am! Well, do you expect me, now I'm here, to shut the door on any other poor chaps who want a start with hope in it, in the New World?"[51]

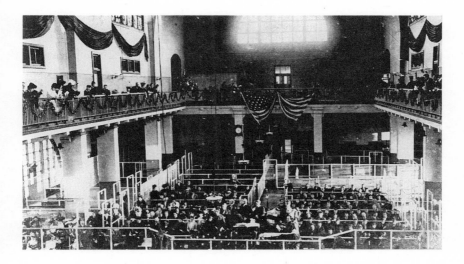

Around this time, another writer visits Watchorn: Edward Alfred Steiner. He is not as famous as Wells, but for years he has worked with immigrants as a journalist, sociologist, and clergyman. He was born in Slovakia, outside Pressburg (today's Bratislava), to a Jewish family. He emigrated to the United States, was baptized, and became a pastor. He tirelessly roams the oceanic routes, giving lectures on immigration. He observes the processing on Ellis Island:

> A Russian Jew and his son are called next. The father
> is a pitiable-looking object; his large head rests upon
> a small, emaciated body; the eyes speak of premature
> loss of power, and are listless, worn out by the study of
> the Talmud, the graveyard of Israel's history. Beside
> him stands a stalwart son, neatly attired in the uniform
> of a Russian college student. His face is Russian rather
> than Jewish, intelligent rather than shrewd, materialistic
> rather than spiritual. "Ask them why they came," the
> commissioner says rather abruptly. The answer is: "We
> had to." "What was his business in Russia?" "A tailor."
> "How much did he earn a week?" "Ten to twelve

rubles." "What did the son do?" "He went to school."
"Who supported him?" "The father." "What do they
expect to do in America?" "Work." "Have they any
relatives?" "Yes, a son and brother." "What does he do?"
"He is a tailor." "How much does he earn?" "Twelve
dollars a week." "Has he a family?" "Wife and four
children." "Ask them whether they are willing to be
separated; the father to go back and the son to remain
here?" They look at each other; no emotion as yet visible,
the question has come too suddenly. Then something in
the background of their feelings moves, and the father,
used to self-denial through his life, says quietly, without
pathos and yet tragically, "Of course." And the son says,
after casting his eyes to the ground, ashamed to look his
father in the face, "Of course." And, "The one shall be
taken and the other left," for this was their judgment day.

Is their judge Watchorn? Based on the date this takes place, yes.
But Steiner does not condemn him. The book in which he describes
their trial, he dedicates to Commissioner Robert Watchorn, *who, in the
exercise of his office has been loyal to the interests of his country, and has
dealt humanely, justly and without prejudice, with men of "Every kindred
and tongue and people and nation."* [52]

Does Steiner's account of the trial of the father and son in his book
On the Trail of the Immigrant contradict the conversation quoted by
Wells? It need not. The son might *start with hope in the New World*, the
father could potentially be a burden for the New World, where voices
cry ever more loudly that protection is needed from these burdens. In
1906, when Steiner's book is published, Ellis Island accepts 880,000
newcomers, and the next year promises more.

A Jar of Jelly Beans, Steerage

On 17 April 1907, 11,747 immigrants arrive at the port of New York. How, over a century later, can we show this to school groups visiting Ellis Island in a way that will capture their imaginations? Educators suggested filling an enormous jar with tiny jelly beans in many colors and asking them: *What do you think, was it this many?*

This is the peak day and the peak year. In this year, 1,285,349 people came to the United States (including 1,004,756 at the Port of New York). The immigration inspectors from Ellis Island process passengers from 3,818 ships.

American political cartoonists have their work cut out for them. The *New York Evening World* shows us a brief exchange between powerful Uncle Sam in his star-spangled tailcoat, with the words *United States* on the collar, and a mustachioed fellow in frilly bonnet, holding a swaddled baby with the label *This week's immigrant arrivals.* Uncle Sam is placing a large hand on the little bundle and calling out to the nurse, i.e. Commissioner Watchorn: *Don't tell me it's triplets!* And the mustachioed nurse, his round eyes popping out with fear, replies: *Triplets! It's forty-five thousand!* [53]

The large number of ships plus technological and social advances should lead to improved travel conditions, but the pressure of masses of immigrants on the shipping lines and growing demand for tickets still makes a journey in steerage an arduous trial of body and character. Steerage is becoming an issue for politicians, writers, and the press.

Our familiar pastor Edward A. Steiner buys cabin tickets for himself, but spends time with immigrants between-decks and records what he sees. In second class on the *Staatendam*, he steals water at night for the thirsty passengers in steerage. On the *Nordam* he makes sure a dying Russian boy is brought out of the abyss of the lower deck into fresh air, then not pushed back down there but put in the infirmary. He notes that on Norddeutscher Lloyd's elegant, spacious *Kaiser Wilhelm II*, 900 steerage passengers are packed in like cattle; they can neither breathe down below, where there's no air, nor come up to the deck reserved for better customers.

He notes the dishonesty of the shipping companies who charge just about twice as much for a bed in second class as for a bunk in steerage, but for that double price offer six times more space, relative privacy, and decent service.

> The steerage ought to be and could be abolished by law.
> It is true that the Italian and Polish peasant may not be
> accustomed to better things at home and might not be

happier in better surroundings nor know how to use them; but it is a bad introduction to our life to treat him like an animal when he is coming to us.[54]

Yet the Polish peasant might surprise Edward Steiner with his knowledge of steerage, conveyed back and forth by families and neighbors.

Now dear brother-in-law, take yourself about 2 roast geese, if you have them for the rode, a couple roasted ducks or chickens and about 2 loafs of hole-meal bread, because on the ship you ain't going to be able to eat what they give you, about 2 long sosages, homemade and salted good, peppered, and made with garlic and smoked good, if you like smoked cheese sosage then bring cheese ones, and if not then make cured ones but they have to be smoked first or they'll spoil on the ship and take a couple hard cheeses and if you come to the seaside at Bremen bye yourself bout 2 quarts good vodka that will be medicine for you on the ship, since then you ain't going to have no appetite for food there so have a drop from the bottle... If theres alredy a line and you see the vessel then get right out of the train car and get on the vessel over this sort of bridge, but dont forget and dont leave nothing, you got to make it on to the vessel meaning the ship fast as you can, so you can pick a good spot soon as you get inside the vessel after the first stairs down you'll see these sort of shelves there like cages on either side those are beds, pick the first bed near the stairs you come down, take the bottom compartment in that cage cuz all the stink stays up top, but on the top level, settle in quick, take the sleeping pallets off the floor if they ain't on the beds and put them on your beds, because at the ends of the vessel is where it rocks the most.[55]

In Congress, Representative Adolph J. Sabath from Illinois accuses the steamship lines of selfishness and hypocrisy. *[T]hey come in here with crocodile tears in their eyes, as is customary with all these "poor and oppressed corporations,"* when they face demands to curb their excesses and improve their customers' conditions. Americans take better care of the cattle they ship out of their ports than the steamship companies do for passengers coming in. The United States Department of Agriculture checks whether animals on ships have enough space, air, and water, while the great steamship lines pack two hundred passengers into a camped space that serves as a common dormitory, dining room, and place to spend the day. The bunk beds stand in blocks of 32, and there are no sanitary facilities, dishes, silverware, or clean water.

Representative Sabath cites an excerpt from Commissioner Watchorn's report on work at the station in 1907:

> During the year just closed 1,506 children have been
> received at this station afflicted with measles, diphtheria,
> and scarlet fever, all of which diseases are due, more or
> less, to overcrowding and insanitary conditions. Of this
> number 205 died.[56]

The immigrants landing at Ellis Island don't hold their tongues. They complain the doctors on the ships bypass steerage, that whoever manages to struggle their way through to the front of the food line will leave hungry anyway, that the holes in the ceiling drip with filth from the deck above, that the luggage — packed under bunks because there are no cupboards or shelves — slides across the deck with every rock of the ship, that the blankets are lice-ridden, that the washrooms are open only at certain times of day, and when some passengers can't hold out they relieve themselves in corners. Travelers who protest are told by the crew that anyone wanting to travel like a human being should buy themselves a cabin, because steerage is a place for cattle, not human beings.[57]

In this peak immigration year, Ellis Island station has much in common with steerage. It is designed for a maximum 500,000 immigrants a year; now it must serve over a million. At times such a mass of passengers arrives at the Port of New York that even with Ellis Island receiving the gigantic number of 5,000 immigrants per day, thousands more must wait another three or four days on their ships for clearance. Over 10 per cent of arrivals must be held at the island for further procedures, which means giving them places to sleep, feeding them, bathing them, laundering their clothes, and disinfecting them. There are too few toilets and the air is heavy because fans are unable to freshen it in the horribly crowded rooms.

The Italian interpreter Francesco Martoccia recalls:

> I was one of the four employees whose duty it was
> to distribute their detention cards. That day it took
> us all of four solid hours to distribute the cards to the
> seventeen hundred people, because, added to the general
> noise in several different languages, we were simply
> unable to work our way through the massed crowd. We
> finally solved the problem by taking our places in the

four corners of the room and distributing the cards by
shouting out at the top of our lungs the names of the
aliens. When they answered we threw the cards as near to
them as we could and let them scramble for them.[58]

Wards, Corridors

The fact that children often leave the ships diseased is the shame of the
steamship lines; the fact they die of these diseases after their arrival
on land is the shame of the American immigration service, which is
behind schedule in building the infectious diseases hospitals, despite the
lessons of the cholera epidemic.

Victor Safford estimates that fatalities among immigrants with
measles are at around 30 per cent, and this is because they are transported to city hospitals, where their treatment is delayed and, we can
also assume, conducted with less care than for those citizens whose
language and customs are comprehensible.

Commissioner Watchorn appeals to the government for money
and he has been notified that 11 hospital buildings will be constructed

on the third island under a federal program by architect James Knox Taylor. They will be built in the Italian Neo-Renaissance style like the University Club in Manhattan, but, naturally, more modestly — without molding, sculptures, or paintings. They will hold 22 wards, including: measles, scarlet fever, diphtheria, chickenpox, tuberculosis, trachoma, and venereal diseases. Alongside them will stand an electric plant, a laundry, a staff house, offices, a kitchen, a laboratory, isolation wards, an autopsy theater, and a morgue.

It appears Ellis will be an island of corridors. Nearly all the buildings are already — or will be — connected by brick passageways, straight or winding like the curtain wall of a defensive castle. All these passages are numbered, like the islands of Ellis and the streets of New York. For instance, Corridor 1 on Island 1 connects the main station building to the kitchen, laundry, and ferry dock, and is built of red brick laid in Flemish bond. Corridor 2 leads from the kitchen to the luggage office and dormitory. Corridor 8A leads from the general hospital on Island 2 to the psychopathic ward. And so on. Some of these passages seem to stretch into an infinite black abyss where it's hard to make out walls or doors. They slither tirelessly in every direction like living roots, paying no heed to the island's limited area.

Dr Salmon's Frustrations

Thomas W. Salmon, who is 31 in 1907, behaves more eccentrically than even his profession as a doctor of psychiatry can justify. He sits in front of his house on New York's Staten Island, surrounded by his children, and shoots at rats. He has holes in his shoes and stuffs them shut with newspapers. He's capable of being absent-minded enough to walk full speed through a glass door, closed of course, and has to be stitched up by a surgeon. His wife, who loves him very much in spite of everything, makes sure he never goes anywhere without a return ticket placed firmly in his pocket, because he's sure to lose his money, spend it, or give it to someone; money is something he simply doesn't understand.

History can explain this latter defect of his. His great-grandfather Nicholas, an aristocrat, lost his estate in Lorraine during the French Revolution. He escaped to Great Britain, where he settled, writing and publishing classical dictionaries. But he died young, accidentally shot at a banquet.

Thomas's father became a doctor and emigrated to America. Their household was poor. One day his mother brought Thomas to the river and urged him to leap into the water with her. Life had no meaning — she felt — especially if, like him, one side of your body is weaker and you have a club foot as well.

Thomas grew tall, slim, and handsome, but sickly. He was talented, jocular, and affable. He went to medical school in Albany, New York. He joined the United States Public Health Service and in 1904 was sent to work at Ellis Island.

There he is remembered as being discontented.

We must explain that Dr Salmon, who comes to work at Ellis Island as a psychiatrist, is in fact a general practitioner. He feels called to psychiatry and has a particular sensitivity for the fate of those who cannot decide for themselves. He saw such people while working in Greyson County, Kentucky, where the community cared for its sick and mentally ill. The poor had been given a modest farm to live on, but conditions on it were humane. The mentally ill had it worse.

> Back from the main building, apart from the little
> cottages ... [w]hen you first see the one-story brick
> building, with a high, sharp-pointed, rusty, iron fence on
> either side of it, you are reminded of a tomb. It is a tomb

... This tomb is for the living whose brains can still know
grief and despair and ... suffering bodies ... When you
open the door and enter the building [you see] fourteen
iron cages ... made of iron bars [and] sheet metal ...
Each cage contains an iron prison cot or two swinging
from the wall ... [T]hese cages ... are too far from the
windows in the brick walls for the sunlight to enter except
during [a] short period each day ... The outside door is
locked at night. There is no watchman to ... see if there
are bodily wants to be attended to ... Each morning
brings to the men and women here light and food — as it
does to the cattle in the sheds — but it does not bring to
them the slightest hope of intelligent care nor, to most of
them, even the narrow liberty of the iron-fenced yard.[59]

Ellis Island, like Greyson County, is helpless when it comes to
the mentally ill, but in the context of the rising wave of immigration,
increasing numbers of them are arriving from all over the world.
It's necessary to identify them and determine if they may remain in
America. The answer, in fact, is clear — they may not. The immigration laws are continually restricting entry to the United States for
those with mental disorders. They first ban *lunatics and idiots* (the
Immigration Act of 1882), next *all idiots and insane persons* (1891), then
*all idiots, insane persons, epileptics, and persons who have been insane
within five years previous; persons who have had two or more attacks of
insanity at any time previously* (1903), *imbeciles* and persons *mentally or
physically defective, such mental or physical defect being of a nature which
may affect the ability of such alien to earn a living* (1907). The latter Act
also eliminates mentally ill and disabled immigrants' rights to appeal
the decision of the immigration station's Boards of Special Inquiry,
which will decide their fate.[60]

Bertha M. Boody, PhD, who conducted psychological research on Ellis Island in the 1920s, put it succinctly when she wrote:

> The first thing was the kind of human material that the
> countries of the world were sending to the United States.
> The second was the kind of human material that the
> United States was accepting.[61]

With increasing frequency, the station must assess whether someone is to be deported due to their mental health. There must be provisions for detaining that someone for long enough to diagnose and prepare them for deportation, which — Dr Salmon firmly insists — must be carried out humanely.

The doctor does not doubt the deportations are necessary. The important thing is to deport those people the regulations require them to, and in order for Ellis Island to have a handle on this, it must have an appropriate diagnostic and hospital ward. This is all the more essential because recently the island's general hospital failed to prevent two patients from committing suicide.

Thomas Salmon, who helps create the psychopathic pavilion (as he calls it), does not wish it to differ in any essential way from its neighboring buildings.

> Every suggestion of the cell-like rooms which used to
> be thought necessary in hospitals for the insane should
> be avoided in the furnishing of this pavilion ... The
> duty to give these unfortunate persons the same degree
> of consideration that is shown to immigrants with other
> acute diseases is a very obvious one.[62]

And the ward is truly beautiful and modern: it has large windows, bright rooms, and even a porch. It's true the porch is closed off by a

chain-link fence, the walls are soundproof, and the rooms lock from
the outside, but that's how it has to be. Still, the rooms don't have
the steel cage-beds offered by an Austrian psychiatrist ($100 apiece),
tested out in his clinic in Vienna. Ellis Island's doctors refused his
proposal. Compared to contemporary institutions for the mentally ill
and disabled, the ward on Island 2 at Ellis is a paragon of humanitarian
medical thinking.

If its co-creator Dr Salmon is discontented, it is because now comes
the hard part: sifting out people who are an even greater mystery than
ordinary psychiatric patients, if the word *ordinary* even applies here.

How can they assess whether apparent mental illness or disability
is not the product of travel exhaustion, cultural differences rendering
some notions incomprehensible for the arrivals, difficulty making
themselves understood in a foreign language or through an interpreter,
shame, self-consciousness, or fear?

This is all so painful and nerve-wracking for Thomas Salmon that he falls out of favor with his superiors. They want him to assist in the frontline six-second medical inspections. He refuses. He's not going to keep an eye out for someone raising a collar or concealing their hand, he has a completely different job. But the island is a place of strict discipline — he will have to leave. He does, though he does not leave psychiatry.

Fiorello and Francesco

During the peak immigration period, 36 interpreters work at Ellis Island. According to a list compiled in the commissioner's office, the following languages are available: Albanian, Arabic (Syrian), Armenian, Bohemian Czech, Bosnian, Bulgarian, Croatian, Dalmatian, Danish, Dutch, Finnish, Flemish, French, German, Greek, Herzegovinian, Italian, Lithuanian, Macedonian, Magyar (Hungarian), Montenegrin, Moravian Czech, Norwegian, Persian (Farsi), Polish, Portuguese, Romanian, Russian, Ruthenian, Servian (Serbian), Slovak, Slovenian,

Spanish, Swedish, Turkish, and Yiddish.[63]

One of the best interpreters is Fiorello, an Italian by descent, short, round, energetic, and with a cheerful face. Everyone calls him "Little Flower," which slightly impugns the dignity of his service. It never occurs to anyone, and never would, that Fiorello's last name, so often passed over, will one day be known around the world as one of the busiest airports in America, where he himself will gaze down on passengers from a marble monument; the sculptor having endowed his model's round features with a lively fortitude.

Fiorello Raffaele Enrico La Guardia knows the following languages: Italian, Serbo-Croatian, German, Yiddish, a little French, and, naturally, English, because he was born in New York. He hasn't worked at the island for long. Before joining, he spends a few years as the American consul in Fiume (today's Rijeka, Croatia), on the Adriatic Sea. He's in his twenties and his office has two rooms, one of which is his bedroom.

At this time, Fiume has 30,000 inhabitants, but every month 2,500 emigrants, mainly from Austria-Hungary, set sail from its port. Cunard has just opened a regular Fiume–New York line.

The young consul reports to the United States Consulate General in Budapest, which, however, has no experience with emigration to America. So La Guardia procures and studies all the possible regulations and reaches the conclusion that passengers — if they are not to be deported from the United States — must be carefully checked before they embark. He talks the matter over with a respected doctor, who is concerned for the health of the community in Fiume, and the two of them board a ship, sparking a sharp protest from Cunard. Yet La Guardia has the immigration regulations on his side, and he warns the captains he'll refuse to issue them the necessary certificates if they don't comply. From then on, all passengers embarking at Fiume are carefully examined. From 1903–1906, around 90,000 people undergo inspection. Passengers from this port are (proportionally) the least frequently deported from the United States.

The ladies of Fiume consider the inspection a fascinating spectacle and watch it from the gallery of the upper deck. One day, La Guardia is informed the Archduchess Maria Josepha will be paying a visit. In order for her to see the event, however, it would be necessary to detain the passengers for 72 hours, even though they're already on the ship's manifest. Fiorello refuses.

It's an unheard-of decision. La Guardia knows that pressure and a tremendous uproar will rapidly ensue. He waits out the most sensitive period at the home of some discreet friends, and the ship sets sail without waiting for the Archduchess.

After three years working at the Fiume consulate, once everything is operating smoothly, Fiorello decides to seek out a new calling. He signs on to a British ship sailing to America. He gets his ticket for free, in exchange for helping the ship's doctor vaccinate the passengers.

In New York, he quickly learns shorthand, gets a fairly good job for $20 a week, and takes the interpreting exam for Ellis Island.

His very first steps on the island lead him to Frank Martoccia.

Frank, actually Francesco, was born in Italy and is a veteran interpreter: he speaks Italian, English, Spanish, French, German, and even Polish. He's just as outgoing and cheerful as Fiorello, and is glad to give him advice. This is valuable, since an interpreter's duties on Ellis Island are not only grueling, but also ambiguous, as their role is by definition two-sided. But in this case, this ambiguity or duality is particularly acute. The interpreters know the lot of the immigrant well: before arriving from Italy, Francesco was a hairdresser in his home country. Fiorello's father was born back in the Kingdom of the Two Sicilies, and his mother came from a family of Sephardic Jews who settled in Trieste after their expulsion from Spain. Aside from that, Fiorello himself learned much about emigration as the consul in Fiume. Some of the interpreters are common people and Commissioner Williams laments in one of his reports that although some of these employees really do speak foreign languages, they don't know how to read or write in them, while others, of course, can read and write, but can't cope with the spoken language.[64]

All the interpreters are servants of the American government, yet they still belong spiritually to the countries they've left and the communities they've abandoned; they feel torn by their obligations to the government and its laws on the one hand, and their sympathy for the newcomers on the other. This is a terrible burden, for so much depends on their interpreting. Canny testimony before the Board of Special Inquiry can save a person, while naïve testimony can ruin them, especially since the Board adjudicates hundreds of cases every day and is always rushed.

Besides, some laws are so dubious they are hard to follow. Such is the case, for instance, with contract work.

A group of inspectors works on the island to ensure no immigrants have come to the United States as a competing labor force. They interrogate strong, healthy men. Martoccia knows — and can convey to La Guardia — how much depends on the foreigners not being too truthful when asked if they already have work. He recalls *thirty-four common laborers were deported because one of them was honest about coming here as a contract laborer, and unwittingly involved all the others in his group.*[65]

In La Guardia's opinion, the law is contrary to common sense. Everyone knows people emigrate to work.

> It is a puzzling fact that one provision of the Immigration
> Law excludes any immigrant who has no job and
> classifies him as likely to become a public charge, while
> another provision excludes an immigrant if he has a job!

Fiorello, like Francesco, thinks you can never be too cautious as an immigrant in front of the commission.

> In answering the inspectors' questions, immigrants had
> to be very careful, because if their expectations were too
> enthusiastic, they might be held as coming in violation

of the contract labor provision. Yet, if they were too indefinite, if they knew nobody, had no idea where they were going to get jobs, they might be excluded as likely to become public charges.[66]

Interpreters can't give advice or be partial. But at a key moment, they can use a pause or a look to give the immigrant something to think about. They can relieve the pressure by keeping calm and toning down a question or an answer. In a word — they can be sensitive. That's necessary not only for those undergoing investigation, but for the inspectors too, since most of them are decent people, La Guardia thinks, and they want to do the right thing.

Meanwhile, Commissioner Watchorn, whom Fiorello respects greatly and who gave him a good salary right from the start ($1,200 a year, specifically because of his much-needed Croatian), as a former union activist, is a staunch defender of the law. He of course immigrated himself years ago to work in a mine, but the law was not in force back then, and besides, he found work on his own — well, maybe with the help of his fellow Methodists.

La Guardia, who thinks the law is peculiar, does allow himself to consider (possibly under the commissioner's influence) that the act limiting importation of labor also limits exploitation in the mines, steel mills, car factories, textile plants, and slaughterhouses of America.

When Fiorello starts working at the island, Francesco Martoccia is already exhausted and — he acknowledges — running out of patience. He feels this especially on the short ferry ride from the Battery, when he must mingle with the crowds of people going to Ellis Island in hopes of seeing their loved ones who are being held there for questioning or treated in the hospitals. They are mainly Italians. They recognize Martoccia as their countryman, and, seeing his service uniform, seize him *by the coat, by the arm, and even by the neck,* and follow his every step, begging him to find something out for them, arrange something, explain something. And in the detention rooms on the island, Martoccia hears questions asked in the faith that someone speaking their native language will surely be able to help:

> Have you seen my son? Have you seen my daughter? Do
> you know him, my Giuseppe? When is he coming for me?[67]

This is what awaits an interpreter on Ellis Island, Martoccia warns La Guardia, who will write years later:

> Our compensation ... for the heartbreaking scenes we
> witnessed, was the realization that a large percentage of
> these people pouring into Ellis Island would probably
> make good and enjoy a better life than they had been
> accustomed to where they came from.[68]

Robert Watchorn's Ten Dollars

It is almost impossible to tell if Robert Watchorn is tall or short. In the aforementioned portrait he sits in a chair, while two pictures taken by Augustus Sherman, with the commissioner standing in clear light and sharp focus, are even more confusing.

In the first, Sherman has posed Watchorn and his deputy Joseph Murray next to a man who is unnamed in the photo. The only note on the print reads *Russian Giant*. The giant, exceedingly elegant in a waistcoat, top hat, and huge shining boots, is placing his arms protectively around the shoulders of both officials, while his pale hand is surely not much smaller than the commissioner's left lung, over which it is suspended.

In the second, Watchorn and Murray stand next to a man described as *Burmese*. The fellow is so tiny he would fit in the commissioner's desk drawer, and is just as smartly dressed as the giant.

Burmese

(Both the giant and the dwarf maintain their dignity, just like Perumall Sammy, with his extra limbs. We don't know if they were allowed into the United States, but none of the three seems mentally or psychiatrically impaired and certainly would not be a social burden in a country so enamored of world records.)

Robert Watchorn's sometimes large and sometimes small appearance perfectly reflects his situation. In this job every decision undergoes immediate contradictory assessments.

The commissioner forbids religious Christians from approaching Jews on the island and pressing religious texts translated into Hebrew or Yiddish into their hands. He explains that the majority of Jews have fled to the US from discrimination, including on religious grounds, and the missionaries' interest must upset them, especially inside a government institution. He wins the gratitude of Jewish organizations, but one of the Christian associations complains about him to the White House.

He rids Ellis Island of the lawyers who fleece immigrants of their last pennies in the promise of sorting out hopeless cases. The purge began back under William Williams; from 1904 to 1908, 205 such lawyers are evicted. For this the commissioners can expect no one's gratitude.

Robert Watchorn shows great respect for William Williams' organizational directives, but he abolishes his predecessor's requirement for immigrants to present $10 along with a ticket to their destination in the United States. In his view, many able people are deported only for lack of money — as a potential social burden — when they deserve entry for other reasons. The ethnic organizations are appreciative, but his superiors are hesitant, because they feel the commissioner is loosening the straitjacket of the inspections.

Additionally in April 1906, during Robert Watchorn's term, 1,000 immigrants are deported from Ellis Island as contract workers. The deportations cause despair among the rejected, anger among manufacturers needing cheap labor, and praise from the unions.

It is hard to reject Watchorn's reasoning when he complains to his government superior: *A saint from heaven actuated by all his saintliness would fail to give satisfaction at this place.* As a matter of fact, he repeats Williams' words that the millennium on the island is impossible.

At the end of his term, he tells a reporter from the *New York Times* with distinct relief: *I'm out of it.*[69]

William Williams' Return

The first action William Williams takes after his return to the island (on 28 May 1909 at 8.20 am on the *Ellis Island*) is to elevate Byron H. Uhl to the position of his deputy ($4,500 a year) in place of Joseph Murray, who naturally loses his position.

For Williams is returning victorious. He will be the only commissioner in the history of Ellis Island to come back for a second term. He thereby is fulfilling the wishes of President William H. Taft. Taft visits the island just as Theodore Roosevelt (currently relaxing on safari) did previously, and is similarly immense and satisfied, in a loose-fitting coat and broad-brimmed hat, his hand stretched out in greeting. The commissioner, whom we see to his right, seems somewhat heavier-set than in the photo with Roosevelt, more dignified, wearing a top hat.

Uhl's promotion is entirely deserved; the new assistant commissioner is 36 and has worked at Ellis Island for 17 years, nearly half his life. Peter McDonald is longer-serving, since he began at Castle Garden, but his experience is limited to luggage traffic, while Uhl, as he has worked his way up the clerical ladder, has had a hand in everything. His scrupulousness combined with uninterrupted practise is much needed by Williams, who's had nothing to do with the station for five years. Byron Uhl's unflagging labor also makes him worthy of promotion. He lives in Rutherford, New Jersey; he leaves home every day at 7.25 am, starts work at 8.15, finishes at 5.35 pm and returns home to his wife and children at 6.20. To the minute.

Among the old employees welcoming Williams are Francesco Martoccia and Augustus Sherman. The latter is also getting a promotion — from senior clerk to chief clerk. He is still the station's official photographer, and as a recognized artist he enjoys a privilege — he keeps a cat in his office.

Also still working at Ellis Island are two Emmas, Corcoran and Oosterhoudt, both competent and meticulous secretaries. Corcoran assists Uhl; she has a buzzer on her desk connected to the commissioner's office and a bell connected to his deputy's office. She stores the staff files, since they fall under Uhl's remit; she calculates there are 540 people working on the island.[70] When immigrants and their interpreters come to Uhl's door and must wait their turn there, Emma Corcoran sees their gestures and eyes, hears their exclamations and whispers, and can tell right away if they're fighting on behalf of a child who's meant to be deported. But Emma also recalls funny moments. When President Taft wants to question a family from Wales himself, Uhl invites Emma to take notes. *[A] man and wife and ten children and they were pretty fine looking people too*, recalls Emma years later.

> And I remember Mr Taft, oh, he was a huge man, and he sat
> there laughing and nodding his head, and the other thing I
> noticed that he said was he asked them if he sang because,
> you know, Welsh people are supposed to be singers. But I
> don't recall what they said. I think they were too petrified to
> say anything. That is the way immigrants were usually.

Emma thinks the immigrants are the bravest people in the world.

> Can you imagine starting out with ten children and no
> money or maybe twenty-five dollars or something like
> that, and arriving in a place where you couldn't speak
> the language, you couldn't understand the word that
> was said and just in the hands of the enemy, so to speak.
> And I guess I think it must have taken a lot of courage
> and it was very sad when they had to go back, very
> sad. Everybody felt sorry when they had to. You know,
> people there did too, but the law was the law.[71]

Emma, sensitive to the sounds of the island, has noticed the floor where immigrant examinations take place is always quiet. People wait for questioning in deathly silence. But once they've got all these trials behind them and they go down to the ferry or the train ticket counter, they regain their voices. At the counters, the currency exchange, the telegraph office, there's chatter, noise, life.

For Emma Corcoran, working on the island has many charms. October is her favorite month, for then she departs the island at sunset, which is beautiful over the bay. But she also loves summer, when she and her colleagues eat lunch on the roof. There's a perfectly good staff restaurant, but she and her colleagues never go there.

The second Emma, Oosterhoudt, probably doesn't go to the roof; she's hard at work preparing information for appeal cases. Sometimes she has 50 of them a day.

Dr Safford has already left the island. He's working at the immigration station in Boston, closer to his native Kittery; he still can't part with the smell of ships and the sea. Dr Salmon hasn't abandoned his passion either, and Ellis Island's doctors find his articles in renowned medical journals with increasing frequency. In these articles he considers the relationship between immigration and the occurrence of mental illnesses, how to diagnose insanity in immigrants, the pros and cons of deportation in certain cases, and how it should proceed. American psychiatrists, who evidently don't hold the doctor's eccentric lifestyle against him, are beginning to consider him an authority.

Robert Watchorn is relaxing in England. Despite his relief at leaving, he had expected a nomination for a second term and is disappointed not to get it.

> I was emotionally exhausted, and so I took an ocean
> passage to London, with the idea of making a possible
> American business connection there. I had been

there only a few days when I met a dear friend who was a popular preacher in New York. One morning, immediately after breakfast, we set out from the Hotel Victoria for a stroll along the Thames embankment. We had not gone far when a Victoria Hotel bellboy came after us with a cablegram for me. It read: "We understand you are open for a business position and we offer you a place in our organization. Answer."[72]

The telegram's sender is 70-year-old Lyman Stewart, chairman of an oil company from California, *a rigid old-time Calvin Presbyterian, a very strict Sabbatarian, an uncompromising antialcohol, antitobacco, antigambling advocate. He was devoted to missionary work at home and abroad, and liberally financed both.* Watchorn, who in his day evicted missionaries from Ellis Island, accepts Stewart's offer; it marks a new chapter in his life.

John Baptiste Weber is finally happy. He dreamed of having a son at the United States Military Academy at West Point, but he's had five daughters. So he begins dreaming of a son-in-law from West Point instead, and finally his middle daughter marries an officer, a real military man, a captain at the Port of New York, who even gives orders at home. The colonel now has grandchildren and the whole family celebrates Thanksgiving at his estate in Lackawanna, near Buffalo. There, grandpa is always in good humor and when his daughters put a song on the turntable called "Raindrops," he sneaks out of the room, then returns in a raincoat, which he wears all through lunch.[73]

Maud Mosher apparently lives in Chicago. She crops up from time to time, publishing lively and emotion-filled stories of her experiences on Ellis Island in the popular magazine *The Coming Nation*.

Now the person looking after girls who need help is petite, blue-eyed Cecilia Greenstone from Białystok, who even at the age of 13 demonstrated remarkable presence of mind when she came to the rescue of her family's small cigarette factory. Her father had gone to Łódź on business without taking proper care of the accounts, and when an unexpected inspection arrived, Cecilia took such a long time showing them around the factory that her hastily summoned siblings were able to fill in the tables and smuggle the ledgers over to the office.[74] She sailed to America in 1905 and by lucky coincidence

became a secretary and interpreter for Jacob Schiff, a banker, financier, and philanthropist supporting Jewish organizations. She also caught the attention of Sadie American, founder of the National Council of Jewish Women, who sent her to Ellis Island as a social worker. Cecilia knows five languages, and despite her acuity and resourcefulness, she has gentle eyes and a round oval face — some already call her the island's little angel.

How to Find a Victim

The matrons and other social workers are meant to help victims of human trafficking, but how can they spot them? A 17-year-old Jewish girl from Poland coming off the Ellis Island ferry in the company of a handsome, well-dressed American man appears happy and in love.

They present themselves as a couple and declare they are traveling to Montana. Their papers raise no suspicions and neither Maud Mosher nor Cecilia Greenstone would have the slightest cause to ask the girl any questions. So the couple leaves the island down the right or left side of the Staircase of Separation, followed by the eyes of those unlucky souls going down the middle path. We know what the remainder of this 17-year-old's trip looks like thanks to the so-called commission report of Senator Dillingham, *Importing Women for Immoral Purposes*, presented to the United States Congress in 1909.

They really are traveling to Montana. The girl (anonymous in the report) expects her traveling companion, who is not actually her husband, will marry her soon, as he promised.

Instead, he places her in a hovel and forces her into prostitution. The towns, brothels, their owners, and the girls joining her in misery (Japanese, French, and Jewish) keep changing. The man stops offering marriage when he learns she's pregnant. He forces her to prostitute herself until she has the baby, then he takes all her money and confiscates any clothes she could wear in public. Soon after giving birth the girl must return to her slave labor, though she hasn't yet recovered and is so weak she struggles to walk. She finally lands up in a paupers' hospital, while the procurer moves on to new victims. We don't know what happened to the child.

The report includes many similar cases. Over two years, the Dillingham Commission collected and analyzed data from the police, courts, various organizations, and its own agents (one of the female agents ended up badly beaten while gathering information) and interviewed many witnesses. Their research covered cities such as New York, Chicago, San Francisco, Seattle, Portland, Salt Lake City, Buffalo, Boston, and New Orleans.

The report's authors open with this sentence:

The importation and harboring of alien women and girls
for immoral purposes and the practice of prostitution by
them — the so-called "white-slave traffic" — is the most
pitiful and the most revolting phase of the immigration
question.

While the Ellis Island staff can spot trachoma or ringworm, no
person bears the mark of future unhappiness. That comes to light
beyond the island, often when little can be done to help.

Just as in the case of the 17-year-old Jewish girl from Poland,
trafficked women and girls, unaware of their fate, arrive in the company of a presumed husband or brother, or with an invitation from an
American citizen, who declares responsibility for her life in the United
States. Japanese girls are often met by a man with whom they've
entered into a marriage *per procura* — in accordance with the customs
of their country. Sometimes these girls' future routes can be found on
ships' manifests, because the destination addresses given are known to
be suspicious, such as the French Club on West 29th Street. But the
pimps operate flexibly. When inspectors notice 25 female passengers
have sent their luggage to that club, the address vanishes from the
ships' manifests and another takes its place.

The commission traced 65 immigrant women from Europe who
arrived in New York in January 1908.

The results were as follows: Thirty were found to be
living under proper conditions; 9 were traced to the
address given on the manifest, but had moved; 5 could
not be found, as no address was given on the manifest; 8
more could not be found, because the numbers given were
not correct; 9 addresses given were tried, but the girls
could not be located, the people of the house having never
heard of them; 3 of the girls found were living under very

suspicious conditions, namely: one Irish girl was booked
to a Greek, a Russian girl was booked to a man alleged to
be her uncle, but later found to be no relative of hers —
the man was a typical Jew pimp, and refused to give the
girl's present address; a Polish girl, 19 years of age, came
with a man who married her just before she sailed, but
who already had a wife in this country.

The Dillingham Commission presents a list of the most dangerous
convicted human traffickers. It describes the system of recruiting and
exploiting slaves. It offers data on prices: from $300 to $3,000 per girl.
It adds that the cheapest are Japanese girls and the most expensive
Chinese ones, because the Chinese Exclusion Act makes them more
attractive by virtue of being so rare in the United States. It notes that
when traffickers and pimps are punished with fines for their actions, the
punishment in fact falls on the unfortunate trafficked women, who have
more money extracted from them.

All concerned in the exploitation of immigrant women
under the system above described seem to share in the
profits except the immigrant girl herself. Although she
earns the money at the cost of her body and soul, she is
rarely able to retain anything.

The commission obtains a great deal of information, yet is disin-
clined to give numbers on the extent of the traffic, because *the nature of
the business precludes, of course, exact statistics.*[75]

It cites only case data from the New York City night court. Over
four months in 1908 and 1909, the court penalized, sent to workhouses,
or reprimanded 581 women born abroad. The largest number were
Jewish (225), French (154), German (69), Irish (29), and Southern
Italians (26).

It is to this court that the interpreter Fiorello La Guardia is transferred. He is happy to have a night job because now he can study law during the day. Each night he assists in 30 to 40 cases. They are very brief. But it sometimes happens that a police patrol brings an entire wagonload of prostitutes to court. *To me it was clear that this was a dirty trade.*[76]

Over a decade later, Edith Abbot of the University of Chicago becomes interested in the fate of a few girls who sailed to the United States alone, were cleared at Ellis Island, and never arrived at the addresses where they were expected. Emilia Anderson's aunt waited for her in vain in Chicago; for Maryana Pajakiewicz and Theresa Olshefski, it was their cousin in New York; for Rozalia Kazewski, her married sister in Chicago; for Maryana Kucynski, her aunt and uncle, also in Chicago. Searches turned up nothing.

One response sent from Ellis Island read:

> Beyond passing a successful examination and leaving for
> her destination, we have no further knowledge of this
> girl. I hope she will not fall into evil hands.[77]

Franciszka Jagielska, No Bells

On 6 December 1912 the *Königen Luise* — two masts, two chimneys, built in the Vulcan shipyards in Stettin — sails into the Port of New York. It has 225 first-class cabins, 235 second-class, and 1,940 berths in steerage. It belongs to Norddeutscher Lloyd and sailed from Bremen under a German flag.

The steerage passengers and their luggage take the ferryboat *Ellis Island* and disembark at the station.

If there were any balance in this world, at this moment bells of every size would ring out — on the ferry, on the wharf at Ellis, in the hands of the watchmen and on the secretaries' desks. The ferry would be draped with banners, at least as beautiful as the ones 20 years ago when its first patron, Annie Moore from Ireland, set foot at the station.

Franciszka Jagielska steps off the ferry. All we know about her is what's on the manifest, but that's enough to be sure — she is the same Franciszka Jagielska whose husband sent for her, threatening that *in America a man can get lots of wifes for not much money.*

Origin: *Russia, Polish*
Last place of residence: *Dulsk, Russia*
Age on day of arrival: *42*
Marital status: *Married*
Height: *5' 1"*
Whether in possession of money: *No*
Whether ever before in the United States: *No*
By whom her passage was paid: *Husband*
Where her husband lives: *Pa., Pittsburgh* (the name of the city not entirely legible)
Whom she is joining: *Husband*
Able to read, write: *No*
Polygamist, anarchist: *No, No*
Deformed, crippled: *No*
Physical, mental health: *Good*
Complexion: *Fair*
Hair: *Blond*
Eyes: *Blue*
Distinguishing marks: *None*

Yet no one greets Franciszka Jagielska either with bells or banners. Maybe her husband Józef has come from Pittsburgh. Let us hope Franciszka was allowed into the United States. She does not have the deposit of $25 introduced recently by Williams, but her husband has surely brought some money. On the other hand, she's not under threat of a literacy test, because it has not yet been introduced.

Twenty years ago, Józef Jagielski was waiting for a young woman, in truth already a mother (*until you send me a letter back and I will send you the ship ticket and you will come to me along with the children*); he welcomes a mature woman who has probably by now become a grandmother. What about the children? What happened over the years? Will they be together? We will learn nothing more.

Fiorello and Tammany

Before being transferred to night court, Fiorello is an interpreter at weddings between immigrant women and men already settled in the United States. They take place at New York City Hall. The metropolis's authorities have entrusted this duty to Tammany Hall, an organization founded in the 18th century as a social, fraternal, and democratic organization (it took its name from a famous leader of the Lenape Indians and in the first period of its existence used Native American dress and symbols). In time, however, it degenerated into a mafia, buying votes and controlling city authorities and institutions. The corruption that went along with arranging relationships and fixing documents brought Tammany a great deal of income. Fiorello La Guardia, taking part in these peculiar ceremonies, gained some new and interesting experience, as his biographer Alyn Brodsky described:

> Alderman Big Tim Sullivan, boss of the East Side,
> controlled the "wedding chapel," situated in the
> basement. He and his Tammany cronies liked to
> punctuate the granting of the marriage license and actual
> ceremony with dirty jokes, repulsive references to the

anatomical features, apparent or assumed, of the bridal pair — understood, if not by them, then certainly by their interpreter — and filthy comments about immigrants in general, unless, of course, they were Irish. ("Dago," "guinea," "wop," "kike," "bohunk," and "Polack" were the epithets of choice.)

Their comments were interspersed with drunken guffaws as bottles of whiskey were passed around and cigar smoke all but obscured the proceedings. The state legislature had given these sleazy aldermen the right to perform marriages, a grift they turned into a tidy racket that yielded annually some thirty thousand dollars. Invariably on hand to partake of the disgusting fun and games were other aldermen and City Hall functionaries who seemed to have nothing better to do than go down to the "chapel" for a few laughs — and a few drinks. Usually the officiating alderman — sometimes even Big Tim himself — would not only make a mockery of the proceedings at the expense of the bridal couple, he would demand a fee in excess of the legally established two dollars: "No fee, no wedding, your little bitch goes back on the next ship." Should a groom protest this extortion, the alderman would shout something along the lines of "Get out o' here! Don't ever let me see your face again — you cheapskate — where the hell do you get off to get married?" The alderman's cronies would roar in drunken laughter, adding a few choice remarks of their own, while Fiorello could do little more than stand by, powerless against these "red-faced, cheap, 'tinhorn' politicians" ... and try to find words that might allay the poor immigrants' understandably negative feelings about their new country.[78]

He decided the day would come when he'd lay Tammany Hall low.

Colonel Weber in Transit

John Baptiste Weber stops by Ellis Island to visit his old colleagues and have a look at how life is proceeding at his old post. He has come to New York City to sail to Japan. The trip, which he has long been planning, is as wonderful as he expected. The colonel finds the journey so extraordinary that he shares his impressions with the readers of *The Buffalo Sunday Times*. His correspondence takes the form of letters to his daughter. He writes about rickshaws, the imperial palace, enchanting girls in kimonos, a woman with black teeth, houses with no chimneys, a rope woven from the hair of 200,000 Japanese women hanging in a temple, earthquakes, and theaters where the actors shout, run, stomp, and grapple in fights so ardent he can't tell if they'll be able to get back up off the floor.

General Maresuke Nogi, a count, samurai, and one of the main commanders of the Russo-Japanese War of 1904–1905 (two of his sons perished in battle), sends an elegant carriage to collect the colonel and listens with interest to his stories from Russia. The colonel might very well amuse him with the anecdote about hiring an imperial carriage to ride to the *pristav*. John Weber feels sympathetic to the general, who reminds him of William Tecumseh Sherman, the famous Union commander in the Civil War.

Two years after this meeting, Nogi and his wife commit *seppuku*. They do so on the day of the funeral of the Emperor of Japan. The general did not wish to outlive his lord, but also felt compelled to expiate his guilt — too many soldiers died under his command.

In the year of General Nogi's death, 1912, Colonel Weber, having well and truly caught the travel bug, visits Trinidad, Uruguay, Panama, and Brazil. He observes the Panama Canal and describes its colossal lock in detail. In his correspondence from Brazil he complains the company operating his ship has run no emergency drills, particularly for abandoning ship in lifeboats. The letter turns out to be prescient — about two weeks later, the *Titanic* goes down.

A few days after that disaster, 20-year-old Teresa Duffy-Gavin from Ireland disembarks at Ellis Island. She's sailed to New York on the *Celtic* — she'd intended to take the *Titanic*, but couldn't get a ticket.[79]

Commissioner Williams on Poisonous Leaven

While the former commissioner is enjoying his pleasant travels, the current commissioner — William Williams — is caught between Plymouth Rock and Ellis Island as though they were Scylla and Charybdis. According to the different wings of public opinion, he is either betraying his own heritage (the right wing), or the ideal of the United States as a second homeland for everyone on earth in need of adoption (the left wing).

Williams' critics are attacking him much more aggressively than they ever did Watchorn.

The commissioner is being disloyal to his class and status by demanding cabin passengers be inspected, even in first class.[80] Williams explains criminality is profitable, so it's precisely in the cabins, not steerage, that human traffickers and their victims travel, along with fraudsters and swindlers of other types. Yet in the view of his right-wing critics, this move against first class offends the dignity of its actual and potential passengers, honest Anglo-Saxons whose consciences are clear.

William Williams is betraying democratic ideals because immediately after taking over the station he returns to the idea of a financial requirement for immigrants (the $25 Franciszka Jagielska didn't have). A left-wing political cartoonist mocks the commissioner the way Soviet propagandists later would, as imperialism's guard dog. Williams is a goblin with four teeth in his mouth, sitting on a wall, swinging his legs in shortish checkered trousers. He and plump President Taft stop Columbus from reaching the gates of America: *Pay as you enter, Christopher!* [81]

Perhaps an even more painful betrayal of the American ideal of equality comes when the commissioner writes of the mentally disabled:

> Not only are they more likely to become a public charge
> on the community, but they are also quite likely to join the
> ranks of the criminal classes. In addition, they may have
> feebleminded descendants. Many immigrant children who
> are feebleminded or mentally backward may be found in
> the public schools of our large eastern cities … Now is the
> time to take greater precautions to differentiate between
> the good and the bad immigrant … this will be possible
> only when parasites who come here with no purpose of
> becoming productive forces shall be held back and they
> shall not fill up our congested cities.
>
> … The admission of mentally defective immigrants
> strikes at the very roots of the nation's existence … It is
> the duty of the officers of the Public Health Service at
> Ellis Island to safeguard the country against the admission
> of these lumps of poisonous leaven … [82]

Commissioner Williams evidently believes mental illnesses and mental disability are hereditary, and such tragedies are therefore beyond the power of society to prevent. At the time, this is a widely held view. Almost all doctors dealing with mental illness are eugenicists. This naturally affects Ellis Island. Protection from immigrants with dubious mental faculties is in any case a necessity and demands legislation.

Even Dr Thomas Salmon, surely innocent of any prejudice, claims the new immigrants' mental health condition is concerning. When he was still at Ellis Island he examined the statistics on psychiatric wards in New York State. He found they held a disproportionate number of patients born outside the United States: newcomers from outside the US made up 26 per cent of the state's population, but as high as 46 per cent of the mentally ill in New York hospitals.

Dr Salmon presented the following calculation: deporting 59 immigrants for psychiatric reasons in 1905 saved the state of New York nearly $90,000. He based his calculation on the cost of treatment, upkeep, and the expected lifespan of the ill. At the time this was an enormous sum. According to Dr Salmon, it cost less per annum to test immigrants for mental illness as they came in, and, additionally, deporting the ill was a prophylactic measure for the United States.[83]

Yet how can they handle the sifting (not to say "selection") of the mentally ill from the well? Physical defects are easy to catch, the staff at Ellis Island have excellent experience in that area. Mental illness is enigmatic and often hidden. But new diagnostic tools are being developed in this field of medicine as well. Progressive doctors in the great European metropolises are making use of intelligence tests. The French psychologist Alfred Binet pioneers this method. His work comes to the United States thanks to Henry H. Goddard, who began his career as a football coach, and Latin, history, and botany teacher in southern California. In time, after his PhD, he became director of research at a school for mentally disabled youth in New Jersey.

While working at the school, he translates Binet's scale into English and distributes tens of thousands of copies in the United States.

This news must interest William Williams, not only as commissioner of an island of immigrants, but also as a member of the enlightened University Club. Williams therefore invites Goddard to Ellis Island in 1910, hoping he will help with diagnoses.

Henry H. Goddard, despite his progressive research methods, is a radical eugenicist and would gladly implement widespread sterilization for the mentally disabled. But fearing societal criticism, he only proposes segregation, ideally in special colonies.

Introducing intelligence tests to the island has an immediate effect — the number of deportations soars.

Half of all Jewish, Italian, and Russian immigrants fail the tests. They are ruled *feeble-minded*.

In 1912, the *New York Times* reports not thousands in savings — as Dr Salmon previously predicted — but millions. That year sees over 56 per cent more deportations ordered than the previous one. The number of mentally ill in New York State's hospitals drops from about 2,300 to 573. The paper quotes the finding of the State Hospital Commission that New York State has rid itself of nearly 5,500 patients since 1904. Almost 3,100 were deported, and about 1,500 were sent elsewhere in the US. If they had remained in New York they'd have cost the state nearly $1.1 million a year.[84]

Commissioner Williams should be happy. So should Thomas Salmon, now observing Ellis Island from the outside (he's become medical director of the National Commission on Mental Hygiene). And so should Howard Knox, who has just started working at the island as a psychiatrist and is also a supporter of eugenics. He writes that the tremendous labor of Ellis Island's doctors *helps to maintain the high physical and mental standard of our race.*[85] Yet they are not happy. They increasingly doubt whether these screening tools are beneficial or if they've inadvertently thrown the baby out with the bathwater, sinning against America by rejecting human material that is perfectly valuable, if inefficient. If so, they've also sinned against the men and women they've driven to despair by dividing families, condemning relatives to isolation, and ruining lives.

This gloomy mood also takes its toll on a holiday that should be joyful for all. A tree arrives at Ellis Island every Christmas. Clergymen of various nationalities and Christian denominations, in particular the Italian Gaspare Moretti, the Irishman Anthony Grogan, and the Pole S. Cynalewski, organize the celebrations and the matrons give out presents.[86] But from the start everyone knows this will be a somber occasion, because the men and women gathering under the tree aren't those who've gained entry to America, but those whom America has detained for repatriation or investigation. Father Moretti, popular and well-liked on the island, has such sympathy for his countrymen that instead of offering easy consolation, he delivers an expression of bitterness:

> I have spoken at Ellis Island before, but never was there
> a time when I felt so bad as now. There are so many
> detained here. You have crossed the ocean, endured
> hardships and dangers to come to the country discovered
> by your fellow countryman. You have found the door
> closed. You have had your hope in the land of liberty
> shattered. To those who will finally get in, I would say,
> you must live to be a credit to your country and the land
> of your adoption.[87]

Sensitive doctors are making their voices heard in American social and medical journals. Their main sentiment: that a mechanically applied test cannot decide a person's fate.

The experience of Ellis Island increasingly suggests that an immigrant who can't count or name all the days of the week can have surprising levels of common sense and self-assurance. One common story goes like this:

An inspector asks a Polish woman if she would sweep stairs by starting at the bottom. "Did this American think me so stupid and silly that I would not know how to sweep stairs?"[88] she declares. That pride clears her way.

Fiorello and the Girl from the Mountains

Fiorello La Guardia recorded in his autobiography:

> A young girl in her teens from the mountains of northern
> Italy turned up at Ellis Island. No one understood her
> particular dialect very well, and because of her hesitancy
> in replying to questions she did not understand, she was
> sent to the hospital for observation. I could imagine
> the effect on this girl, who had always been carefully
> sheltered and had never been permitted to be in the
> company of a man alone, when a doctor suddenly rapped
> her on the knees, looked into her eyes, turned her on her
> back and tickled her spine to ascertain her reflexes. The
> child rebelled and how! It was the cruelest case I ever
> witnessed on the Island. In two weeks' time that child
> was a raving maniac, although she had been sound and
> normal when she arrived at Ellis Island.

He also noted he always suffered greatly when he was assigned to
interpret for people suspected of mental illness. He suffered then and
suffers years later at the memory. He felt then and feels now that over
50 per cent of the "mental" deportations were unfair. They happened
because of immigrants' unawareness or doctors' ignorance and inability to understand the arrivals' disparate norms and standards.[89]

Could association with people petrified in fear and helplessness,
unaware of what fate has in store for them, drive a person insane?

In January 1914, in his apartment in the Bronx, the 40-year-old
interpreter Julius Stierheim, employed at Ellis Island station since
nearly the beginning of its existence, composes a suicide note that he
and his wife Josephine sign together. The note, in German, addressed
Dear Doctor, to Josephine's brother, includes some requests: for

forgiveness; to cover the expenses with the money stored in the desk in a black wallet ($165 in cash); and not to hold any kind of ceremony. Before the letter and the detailed will attached to it are found, four bodies are discovered. In one room, nine-year-old Gladys; in the second, 12-year-old Edna and her mother lying in their beds, as well as Julius — on the floor, half-dressed, but with his glasses still on. All have died from a gunshot in the mouth.

The cylinder of the revolver next to the interpreter's body is missing four bullets. Julius Stierheim, popular among the staff at Ellis, had lost weight in recent years. He talked about being afraid and took sick leave more and more frequently. Alongside the requests and instructions in the suicide note, the couple confessed to a fear of insanity. Graphologists ruled his wife's signature authentic, so the decision was a joint one. The *New York Times* declared in its headline:

> Ellis Island Interpreter Wrote That Fear of Insanity
> Drove Him to Quadruple Slaying.[90]

Doctor Knox's Cubes

Howard Knox is 27 when he starts working at the island in 1912 and already has a degree of medical experience — a brief stint practicing in a mental hospital in Worcester, Massachusetts, and at military hospitals at two forts. He seems to have a taste for the military: in photos from Ellis he's usually seen in a round uniform cap with the brim pulled low over his forehead. His professional mien conceals an exuberant temperament — Knox racked up four wives (following in the footsteps of his mother, who had four husbands — the second, a doctor, influenced Knox's choice of profession). He plays on the same baseball team as his sons and also boxes.

Elegant cufflinks on snow-white cuffs poke out from under his uniform, and we can make out a white strip above his cloth collar. There's no need anymore to worry about a surprise from Dr Thomas Salmon, who used to forget his collar from time to time and, when asked what held his cuffs together, would reply: *the law of attraction.*

Dr Knox is convinced maintaining the elevated level of the American race demands he employ more rigorous diagnostic tools than those used thus far on the "mentals" at Ellis. Such tools could also aid communication.

> In diagnosing mental enfeeblement in the higher and
> more refined grades, the most important test after all is ...
> the ability of one human being to take the measurement
> of another by conversing and associating with him. This
> intuitive ability can be very highly developed in persons
> of strong personality and physique ... The ability to take
> this mental measure must be founded on the experience
> of ... many positive cases and the examiner must be a

broadminded, big souled man with a keen insight into the frailties and shortcomings of the human race in general, including himself.[91]

Dr Knox is an opponent of the compasses and calipers beloved of racial researchers; as early as 1919, the Smithsonian Institution[92] calls for the regular anthropological measurement of immigrants. Knox hates holding tools up to skulls and noses. He's convinced craniometry ought not interfere in the study of the mind.

Howard Knox invents his own measuring tools — five cubes, four large and one small. They're made of polished wood, smooth and pleasant to touch, and don't rouse fear.

A test with the cubes can take place wordlessly. Howard Knox places the four large ones in a row, picks up the small one, and jumps it one by one along the four cubes, first from left to right, then right to left. Then he skips one cube, but on the way back, he touches it again.

The immigrant is meant to watch this and do the same. There are no traps in this test stemming from differences in culture, knowledge, or experience. It only demonstrates coordination and perceptiveness.

Another of Knox's tools is a jigsaw puzzle — a flat wooden head in profile. The shape has to be assembled from a few pieces. The head is human, universal, hatless. Everyone knows one like it. If it were a crocodile or an automobile, for instance, you might fear the image would defeat some test subjects.

We have another jigsaw puzzle too — a hand-drawn picture of a ship divided into ten regular squares. You might now think this would require some knowledge. But everyone knows a ship. They've all arrived on a ship, spent many days in the presence of one.

In developing his tests, Howard Knox did his utmost to find the common denominators of his subjects' awareness.

Nevertheless it might happen that an immigrant watches and simply wordlessly moves her lips, like one old woman from Macedonia.

It takes some time before the examiners realize she is praying and let her go off to the dormitory. The next day she wakes up alert and calm, and passes every test.[93]

Fiorello and Uhl Watch from the Gallery

Fiorello La Guardia is leaving Ellis. Not because he sympathizes too closely with these outcasts; his sympathy inclines him to help, not to run away.

Thanks to his night court assignment, he's finished his daytime law studies and intends to open his own practice. So he goes to the assistant commissioner, Byron H. Uhl, to inform him. He fears Uhl may be displeased, or even upset, by his departure. They've grown close during their time at Ellis, despite being so different: one sweet as sugar, head in the clouds, always ready for a change of scene, constantly in motion; the other reserved, engrossed in regulations, rooted in Ellis Island.

La Guardia hands Uhl his resignation letter and, to smooth over any potential unpleasantness, asks him *if he thought I was doing right*.

> He smiled, stood up, took me by the arm and led me to the door of an adjoining room. He pointed to two of the employees sitting there. Then he took me out on a sort of balcony around the main hall and pointed to three or four of the inspectors. "Fiorello," he said, "they are all lawyers. They are discouraged and unhappy, and they are too old to start practicing now. You are doing the right thing. Best of luck to you."
> I had two weeks' salary from my job at Ellis Island, amounting to a total capital of $65. I rented office space at $15 a month in the law offices of McIllheny and Bennett.[94]

The gallery where Uhl and La Guardia stood for a moment really is a wonderful observation point and New Yorkers in the know like to come there, as they might to the theater, though according to set rules. You have to write an application to the commissioner. After receiving approval for your visit, you arrive on a government boat from the Battery, which runs every half-hour — from 9.00 am to 2.00 pm. Anyone wishing to watch immigrants being processed from the gallery of the main hall must enter the station building under the northwest tower, two levels up. Visitors may also view the dining room and the dormitories, but they're closed at lunchtime. The Railroad Rooms are also worth a look.

> Apply to any guard ... Interesting scenes may often be witnessed as a result of the meeting of people who have been separated for some time.[95]

Liberty

Green, as though soaked for centuries in sea fog.

Nobody knew what it was. One man said, "Don't you know? That's Columbus." ... So we thought it was Columbus. For years I thought that, recalls Estelle Miller, from the village of Bilche Zolote in Galicia. She was 13 when she first saw the Statue of Liberty.

Listen, this don't look like Christopher Columbus. That's a lady there. That's the opinion of the cabin-mate of the Greek Theodore Spako, who sailed to Ellis Island at the age of 16.[96]

> Yeah, they looked. But then, I don't think anybody knew what it was, you know. It was just, you know, a lady out there with her hand up, you know ... But at that time I

didn't know really what was going on, you know. I was
young, didn't know.

Anna Wittman from Germany wasn't so young anymore, she
was 20.[97]

Ten-year-old Edward Corsi, now spending his 14th day on the
steamer *Florida*, coming from Naples with his whole family, has a little
sister named Liberta, and he knows what that word means. He keeps an
eye out for the statue, but he doesn't believe it's really there, especially
since he can barely see it in the hazy air. But his younger brother
Giuseppe is convinced the skyscrapers of Manhattan are mountains.

> "They're strange," he said, "why don't they have snow
> on them?" [98]

Betty (Bianka) Dornbaum Schubert is sailing to join her mother,
whom she hasn't seen in such a long time she doesn't know her at all.
They pass the statue.

> Yes, and I remember saying to my grandmother, "That
> is not my mother." And then, of course, I looked at it
> all ways and started wondering ... what did my mother
> look like? Because I see, I knew a statue because I knew
> in Europe I saw a statue. But I thought, well, I wanted to
> probably think good thoughts, so I thought, "Well, maybe
> that's her, in honor of her," because they told me she was
> like a queen. So naturally that's the attitude I took. Then,
> when ... I saw all these other people that came to pick up
> the immigrants, they didn't look like rich people to me. So
> I started, it was very difficult rethinking everything. But
> I saw my mother ... [S]he was a very beautiful lady. And
> she had a fancy big hat on with a feather.[99]

Paul H. Laric from Slovenia arrives at Ellis Island aged 14 and probably knows who this woman is, since he's so unhappy she has her back turned to him. He spots her through the window of the Great Hall as he and his parents wait in the inspection line.

> The Statue of Liberty was, uh, facing the other way. She was showing us her back as if, uh, sending us a message. ... So, um, finally we were on the ferry back to New York and we could see the side and face of the Statue of Liberty and things brightened up.[100]

On 30 June 1916, shrapnel strikes the right arm of the Statue of Liberty. A German saboteur has blown up the Black Tom munitions depot on the New Jersey coast, just past Bedloe's Island. It's the first terrorist attack to graze America's greatest symbol. The wound is slight; the arm of Liberty — or, if you prefer, of Christopher Columbus, a mother waiting for her orphan daughter, a lady, a woman — is still held high. But nonetheless the torch is temporarily closed to visitors.

Part III
Becalmed

Military Advantages, Commissioner Howe

William Williams' successor — or really Byron H. Uhl's, since he is acting commissioner for a period after the Republican Williams' departure — is Frederic Clemson Howe, a lawyer and political writer. He presents himself to the public as a reformer whose primary vision is to unleash human beings' inherent potential. He was born in Pennsylvania and is 46 on the day he takes over his post.

> During the summer of 1914 I received a letter from President Wilson[101] tendering me the position of United States Commissioner of Immigration at the Port of New York ... The subject of immigration did not interest me greatly, and I knew very little about it. But Ellis Island is a principality. It lies in lower New York harbor, opposite to the Aquarium, which in earlier days was Castle Garden. The Commissioner has a force of six hundred men under him, and in normal times as many as five thousand immigrants passed through the island in a single day. There are two big hospitals and a fleet of boats. The Commissioner is a presidential appointee and responsible to the President alone.
>
> The appointment made an appeal to something in me which has always been fundamental, something which stirred me in the university, led me into the social settlement, urged me into politics, impelled me to work for parks and playgrounds in Cleveland ... I hesitate to give a name to something that has been instinctive in me; whether it should be called the spirit of reform, or

humanitarianism, or sentimentality, or the dreaming of dreams, or the seeking of visions depends entirely on the way one looks at life.

Ellis Island was an opportunity to ameliorate the lot of several thousand human beings. It was also an opportunity to do the work I liked to do. No doubt I thought I wanted to do this work for the sake of the immigrants. Probably I wanted to do it to satisfy my own instincts ... [Ellis Island] was a storehouse of sob stories for the press; deportations, dismembered families, unnecessary cruelties made it one of the tragic places of the world.[102]

Howe's arrival at the island coincides with the outbreak of war in Europe, which for the station means a certain phase of peace and repose.

In 1914, still nearly 880,000 immigrants sail into the Port of New York. But by 1915, the island is emptying out. The ferries unload 178,416 passengers. In 1916 and 1917, there are even fewer, though still a six-figure sum. In 1918, it drops to five figures for the first time in the station's history.

The warring nations — Austria-Hungary, Germany, Russia, Serbia, France, and the United Kingdom — have provided the United States with a large number of immigrants. Now the largest emigrant ports, Hamburg and Bremen, find themselves under British blockade, while the UK emigration port of Liverpool has limited its traffic. The Atlantic Ocean is growing more dangerous. The Mediterranean ports continue operating at first, but German U-boats prove increasingly threatening for departing ships, and once Italy joins the war in 1915, traffic nearly halts. Emigration from the Austro-Hungarian and Russian empires has also ceased. Potential immigrants are stuck in the trenches.

For more than a decade, the island has been constantly jammed with people. Commissioner after commissioner has ordered the expansion of dormitories, cafeterias, hospitals, laundries, waiting rooms, storage rooms, and offices. Before long they found each expansion too modest. Staff numbers increased, but it was a constant race against time.

On the one hand, Howe might be disappointed, because Ellis Island is no longer so mighty a principality as when President Woodrow Wilson nominated him. The days of 5,000 arrivals a day are long gone, and personnel must be reduced too. But on the other hand, the island, which after a period of heavy use finds itself in what one can only assume is a transitional state of rest, might now make a better testing ground for a reformer. The magazine *Survey*, dedicated to social issues, notes that Commissioner Howe has the advantage over previous commissioners of Ellis Island.

> The great falling off of immigration since the war began,
> has given him time for experiments and a small group
> with which to experiment. All former commissioners
> have been so buried under the administrative detail of
> dealing with a million immigrants a year that they had no
> imagination for additional work.[103]

Just after taking over as commissioner, when the wave of immigration is still accelerating, Howe attends an official lunch given by the Department of Labor. Invited to speak, he enthusiastically tells of his plans, prompting the big, *Jove-like* clerk from the Statistics Bureau, Ethelbert Stewart, to rise from his seat.

> Stuttering badly, he began:
> "I have been moved by Mr Howe's fresh enthusiasm.
> Many of us felt as he feels when we entered the service. I
> am reminded of a story about a man who was committed
> to an insane asylum." His stutter grew worse. "When he
> arrived, the attendant began taking everything from him
> — his keys, his knife, finally his watch. The man resisted.

Pointing to the wall, the attendant said: 'But you don't need a watch here — there's a clock.'

"'Is the clock right?' the insane man inquired.

"The attendant assured him that it was.

"'Well if it's right,' he said, 'then what in hell is it doing here?'"

Then Stewart sat down. Every one gasped. I did not understand the significance of the story, but every one else apparently did.[104]

Since Frederic Howe doesn't understand the anecdote, its impact surely weakened by Stewart's strained delivery, he doesn't enquire as to its point and his enthusiasm remains unabated.

One of his ideas is to make the island a warmer place — not physically, but spiritually.

It's insufficient just to follow procedure. The unfortunates undergoing torturous processing, especially the detained, deserve more empathy. If we must hold people, let the station not be a prison but a place of temporary confinement. He eliminates the separate women's and men's day detention rooms. He sets up benches and playgrounds on the island's lawns and allows detainees — adults and children — to spend time there. To the accusation that maintaining the lawns costs considerable government money, Howe answers that live babies are more precious than live grass. Women detained on the island as alleged prostitutes enjoy the same freedoms as the other detainees who are not under suspicion. Sporting competitions are held. On Sundays, national groups of immigrants hold concerts. Enrico Caruso comes to the island at the Italians' invitation and sings on their holiday. In the evenings, silent films play in the Great Hall. A school is organized for the children of detained families, as well as courses in hygiene, childcare for infants, and tailoring and technical workshops. A library is set up, collecting books in many languages from various institutions and sponsors, particularly the New York Public Library and the American Red Cross.

It's just as well that Cecilia Greenstone from Białystok has returned — the little angel of the island who is indispensable for tasks such as these. Everyone was concerned for her — she got lost between the United Kingdom and Latvia (then under Russian rule) as an American delegate for port issues in Riga. Russia, which has long watched nervously as masses of people flee its territories through the major German ports, has resolved to take control of this migration while also reaping the economic benefits. To this end, it has expanded the port of Riga and asked the Hebrew Immigrant Aid Society (HIAS) in America[105] for a consultant to assess both how the emigration port is set up and how its traffic is organized. HIAS sends Cecilia, who is sharp, experienced, and speaks fluent Russian. So, on 25 July 1914, this petite, blue-eyed 27-year-old boards the Russian passenger ship *Kursk*. The captain knows he will have the honor of transporting an official guest of the tsar's government, and bows welcomingly to Cecilia's father, not realizing the delegate is the young lady on his arm.

By the time they reach the port of Libava (today's Liepāja), war has broken out between the United Kingdom and Germany. The ship is rerouted to Liverpool. Cecilia has rubles with her that nobody wants. She sells the elegant razors she brought as a present for someone. She manages to return to the United States amid the crush of military mobilization, and sees firsthand what it means to ride in steerage.[106]

She's pleased with Howe's reforms, which are even more justified given that the war has made deportation impossible, so many are held on the island for a very extended period. When a German U-boat sinks the *Lusitania* in spring 1915, President Wilson bans repatriations to the United Kingdom and France. He also halts the deportation of 60 Russians who were meant to be sent to Arkhangelsk on a munitions ship.

Howe continually takes new steps to ensure positive coexistence between the detained nationals — as well as between those nationals and the staff, meaning America. Complaint and suggestion boxes appear in the corridors (though in reality only the literate can put in their wishes and concerns), and proposals of any kind are decided on a democratic basis. In practice this means each department at Ellis sends a delegate to a weekly staff meeting, which government representatives and immigration experts may also attend.

> I posted a notice in a dozen languages that any immigrant
> and any official could come to me directly. I posted other
> notices explaining to the aliens their rights.[107]

Flowerpots are set up in the Great Hall, and flowing down from the ceiling are two American flags, large as volleyball courts.

Military Advantages cont., Nathan Cohen and Paula Pitum

According to the Italian interpreter Frank Martoccia, who still works at the island, the most tragic case he's encountered there was the odyssey of Nathaniel Cohen.

Cohen is a mysterious figure. Information about him is scarce, but gives us room for imagination. He roamed the oceans against his will and was rescued by the First World War.

We don't know whether Martoccia met Cohen personally. We don't even know if he saw him, but years later, recalling the case, he still finds it upsetting.

> He was insane, and try as we might we could not
> establish his nationality. As a result he was shipped back
> and forth, again and again, between South America and

the United States.

Although we had but few facts to go by in this case, we did manage to find out he had been born thirty-five years before in Baush, a little village in the province of Kurland in Russia. As a boy he had left home and gone to Brazil. Three years previous [to his arrival at Ellis] he had landed in America, married, and gone into business in Baltimore with several thousand dollars. All seemed to be going well with him. Then his business failed, followed closely, as happens all too often in life, by other catastrophes. His wife ran away with another man, and Cohen lost his memory and his power of speech, and he had to be taken to an insane asylum in Baltimore.[108]

Cohen therefore becomes a public charge, subject to deportation. Since the journalists of New York develop an interest in him, today we can work out the sequence of his journey, which was paid for by the passenger shipping companies, particularly Lamport & Holt, which had the misfortune of bringing the sick man to the United States in the first place. Cohen sails:

— from the United States back to Brazil, which, however, does not wish to accept him,

— from Brazil to the United States (Ellis Island), which also refuses him,

— from the United States (Ellis Island) to Russia, which sees no reason to care for him,

— from Russia to the United States (Ellis Island), another refusal,

- from the United States (Ellis Island) to Brazil,
  another refusal,

- from Brazil to the United States (Ellis Island).

This time, Cohen goes to the hospital at Ellis, and a strange turn of events takes place. The Knights of Pythias[109] organization decides to take on this poor Jewish wanderer, whom *the New York Times* wrote about on 9 June 1914. The Knights have discovered he once belonged to their order and they place him in a refuge in Green Farms, Connecticut, sharing the cost of supporting him there with a Jewish charity.

The war also aids Paula Pitum, a nine-year-old Russian Jew who sails to New York in July 1914 on the *Bavaria* with her mother and two siblings. For two years, her father, Chaim Pitum, has been a peddler in the town of Olean, New York. He has a horse and wagon worth $200, and a supply of goods worth another $150. In a word: he's doing well and can send for his family. But when little Paula is examined at Ellis Island, she's ruled retarded, meaning a potential public charge. As a result, her entire family except her father receives an order of deportation. An intervention from her mother's brother, also working in Olean and wealthy enough to act as guarantor for everyone, is of no help.

Immigrant organizations appeal to the Secretary of Labor and achieve some success — the United States will accept the family, but without Paula. On 30 July the child is escorted on to the *President Grant* of the Hamburg–American line. Then fate intervenes — the outbreak of war sends the ship back to New York.

In the first week of August, the immigration authorities in Washington permit Paula entry into the United States, but only temporarily until the year's end, on the guarantee she stays in a designated facility for the mentally disabled.

But on 15 December the authorities receive word that Paula is going to elementary school in Olean, a violation of the conditions set with her family.

The school medical inspector in Olean certifies Paula's physical condition has greatly improved, she's making progress in English, her father is a diligent worker and ensures good conditions for the family, their house is kept clean and cozy, and the children are well-dressed and look happy.

Yet the clerk at Ellis Island dealing with Paula's case must abide by his superiors' rulings, which the Pitum family has violated. (If that clerk at Ellis is Byron Uhl, then he abides by the rulings not because he must, but because he wants to; he likes having everything tied up neatly.) So the case returns to Washington, where officials turn to the company enforcing the guarantee to give their opinion on Paula.

The company checks the doctor's certifications and concludes that the care Paula has enjoyed for the last six months was certainly more beneficial than that which the girl would have received in an institution for the disabled. So the authorities renew Paula's leave to remain in the United States, once again for a year.

All of Olean now knows of Paula's case. Neighbors and more eminent citizens declare they won't let her be taken from the town. For the time being there's no need to make an official visit to Washington, because as long as war rages on the seas, the girl will remain with her family. The last report concerning Paula to reach Ellis Island before America's entry into the First World War concerns the schoolgirl's progress and is dated 26 July 1916.[110]

The clerk who received this piece of paper must have immediately put it in a drawer, otherwise it would have been blown off his desk by the terrifying blast from the Black Tom wharf in neighboring New Jersey.

Black Tom, Sherman's Cat

Pandemonium breaks out on 30 August 1916 at 2.00 am. The doors of the Great Hall suddenly fly off their hinges. Glass rains from the windows. The ceilings crack. Dr Frederick A. Theis, who's spending the night on the island, sees on the wharf, on the New Jersey side, a column of flame casting its glow on the water, reaching as far as the Statue of Liberty, and approaching Ellis.

He hears a series of explosions, and after each one colorful flares burst in the sky as though it were the Fourth of July, not late August. Each explosion shatters windows more than a mile around (as far as 14th Street in Manhattan) and each flare hurls hot steel scrap into the Bay and on to the waterfronts of New Jersey, New York, and the island.

Dr Theis cares for the mentally ill. He, the other doctors, and the nurses wrap the patients in blankets and lead them outdoors on to the tennis courts, which are sheltered from the direction of the explosion.

> When we had them out of doors, they presented one of
> the most extraordinary spectacles I have ever seen. As
> the five-inch shells flared over the Island like skyrockets,
> the poor demented creatures clapped their hands and
> cheered, laughed and sang and cried, thinking it was
> a show which had been arranged for their particular
> amusement.

The detonations seem endless, while the sea, which before beat back the flames, is now actually carrying them further. Barges have broken loose from Black Tom wharf and drift helplessly into the bay.

> Suddenly I saw that the barges, which had been moored
> by the usual hemp rope, had caught fire and were
> exploding as they drifted toward Ellis Island.

It turns out they are loaded with munitions.

It was then that we who had to care for the patients first realized to what extent our own lives were in danger. Fortunately the heroism of those who manned the tugs of the Lehigh Valley Railroad saved us. They towed the two flaming barges out to sea, where they sank amid concussions which sounded like the end of the world ...

We bivouacked on the tennis court for the rest of the night, vainly trying to pacify the insane who were disappointed that the show was over. At 7:00 A.M. we cleaned up and returned the patients to the hospital.

There were 600 people on the island that night.

The miracle was that no living thing was injured, except a cat.[111]

This is Augustus Sherman's beloved black cat, named Toto. As Ellis Island's only victim of the great disaster, he is carefully tended to by a "people" surgeon. His wounded paw is placed in a splint. The cat becomes a hero, though we don't know what he looked like. Toto's owner exclusively photographed humans.

Byron Uhl, making an initial tally of the losses, discovers yet another injury in Augustus Sherman's circle. Shrapnel has reached a statuette of the mother of the Gracchi decorating the clerk's desk, striking her in the heart.

The next day, as the damage is carefully surveyed, a rabbit belonging to one of the nurses is found. It looks like a Christmas pudding — a jar of molasses has spilled all over it — and it is now sitting on top of a box of combustible material that's been blown on to the island, licking its fur clean. Unlike Toto, the rabbit is unwilling to accept any help.

We remember these funny stories, yet the situation is very grave. Photos from the area of the explosion in New Jersey show bent telegraph poles, tangled rails, craters and mounds of earth, muddy lakes with immobile wheels sticking out — clearly were vehicles flipped over then sank into the ooze. We can see entire sawmills' worth of scattered timber, heaps of stone and concrete rubble, roofs torn off, walls leaning. On Ellis Island, the ceiling of the Great Hall has collapsed. The panes of the countless windows have all shattered. Doors have been blown off. The cafeteria and some offices are wrecked. In the infectious diseases hospital, the explosion destroyed bathrooms, ripped out fittings, and bent pipes backward. It all looks like the aftermath of an attack, and for America the explosion really does sound the signal of war. The public is convinced it was German saboteurs who set fire to the gunpowder and ammunition supplies stored at Black Tom wharf in preparation for being loaded on to ships bound for Russia. America has not yet joined the war but is favoring Russia, the UK, France, and Italy.

At Ellis Island only the cat was wounded, but in New Jersey at least three people died, while dozens (hundreds, according to some sources) sustained injuries.

The press reports material losses exceeding $20 million.[112]

Meanwhile in France, the Battle of Verdun is still ongoing. Dr Thomas Salmon, the ambitious psychiatrist, is developing an interest in *shell shock*, a neurosis linked to incessant gunfire.

Commissioner Howe's First Objection

The press applauds his reforms, Caruso sings, children run around on the grass, but Commissioner Howe pays for his success with a feeling of total exasperation. Now he understands exactly what Ethelbert Stewart was getting at with his joke about the clock. He laments in his *Confessions* that his superiors in Washington don't answer his correspondence, that reform projects are neglected; that unidentified documents concerning the fate of people detained in immigration stations are piling up on the desk of the hopeless and incompetent Commissioner-General of Immigration; that the Assistant Woman Commissioner sent to him on the island has a New England morality, is suspicious of everyone and everything, and tells unbelievable fairy tales; and that he's finally realized how badly these stingy Republican officials have damaged America.

> In a generation's time, largely through the Civil Service reform movement, America has created an official bureaucracy moved largely by fear, hating initiative, and organized as a solid block to protect itself and its petty unimaginative, salary-hunting instincts.

Washington bureaucracy is the worst of all, but — as the commissioner's *Confessions* reveal — the clerks at Ellis Island resist his ideas too. We may assume that at the forefront is the meticulous and conservative supporter of the professional hierarchy, Byron H. Uhl, who after two years as acting commissioner (1913–1914) has to swallow the nomination of a Democrat, Howe.

But even among the immigrants Howe tries his best to meet halfway, there are some he can't stand. These are the arrogant, self-assured, demanding British.

> The British gave the most trouble. When a British subject was detained, he rushed to the telephone to communicate with the consul general in New York or the ambassador at Washington, protesting against the outrage. When ordered deported, he sizzled in his wrath over the indignities he was subjected to. All this was in effect a resentment that any nation should have the arrogance to interfere with a British subject in his movements. All Englishmen seemed to assume they had a right to go anywhere they liked, and that any interference with this right was an affront to the whole of the British Empire.

Yet in spite of everything:

I was happy in my work of humanizing Ellis Island.[113]

Job and Piast the Wheelwright

In April 1917, the United States joins the war.

Now, alongside the immigrants awaiting investigation, Ellis Island holds the interned crews of German and Austro-Hungarian ships, plus *enemy aliens* scooped up from various places in the United States and held as potential spies or saboteurs. America calls them *Huns*. The

American military is requisitioning more and more of the island's equipment and buildings. The Navy takes over the large luggage room and dormitories. The Army takes the hospital buildings and unwell immigrants are offloaded to 28 different clinics in the New York metropolitan area. The island does not have enough hospital beds in any case, so the Great Hall transforms into the largest hospital room in America, as one military newspaper writes. It now holds 260 beds for wounded soldiers.

In March 1918, the first hundred wounded American infantrymen arrive at Ellis Island. These men, mutilated, with missing limbs, deafened, and blinded, have a marvelous work of architecture over their heads — a self-supporting ceiling by the Italian master Guastavino Jr, built after the Black Tom explosion. Covered with shimmering mother-of-pearl, it is fire-resistant and broad and tall as a basilica. The Guastavinos,[114] both father and son named Rafael (the father is no longer alive), were outstanding specialists in vaulted ceilings, and this one, soaring over the rows of bunks and bandaged heads, is simultaneously mighty and full of the fresh air these victims so badly need.

In 1918, as Rafael Guastavino Jr is hanging his ceiling above the Great Hall, just under 29,000 immigrants land at Ellis Island — the lowest annual total in the station's history so far.

Such a small group shouldn't spark fear, but they're subjected to the most thorough vetting of any so far. The current battery of tests is augmented by one for literacy.[115]

Naturally no one demands the immigrants know English, unless they are English themselves. They are each to read a short passage in their own language. All these passages are taken from the Bible and every group is assigned a different one.

Let us try to imagine the soundscape of the island. The clink of plates, the calls of seagulls who smell food, the water splashing on the side of the ferry just arriving at the dock, a groan from a hospital room, a nurse's whisper. In one of the rooms still left for civilians in the east wing of the main building, someone is reading effortfully, in a monotone:

> This our bread we took hot for our provision out of our
> houses on the day we came forth to go unto you; but now,
> behold, it is dry, and it is mouldy ...

This is from the Book of Joshua, for Jewish immigrants. Only that much. But someone who doesn't find the letters a struggle and can recognize the next words by sight might be tempted to read on:

> And these bottles of wine, which we filled, were new;
> and behold, they be rent: and these our garments and our
> shoes are become old by reason of the very long journey.

Who chose these texts? Jews have an eternal journey, Arabs — the desert wind. If an Arab arrived at the island after 1917, he or she would have to read a passage from the Book of Job:

> While he was yet speaking, there came also another,
> and said, Thy sons and thy daughters were eating and
> drinking wine in their eldest brother's house: And behold,
> there came a great wind from the wilderness, and smote
> the four corners of the house, and it fell upon the young
> men and they are dead; and I only am escaped alone to
> tell thee.

The text for Poles suggests whoever chose it from the Epistle to the Hebrews knew the legend of Piast the Wheelwright, who found his hospitality to strangers magically rewarded:

Let brotherly love continue. Be not forgetful to
entertain strangers: for thereby some have entertained
angels unawares.[116]

Howe's Second Objection, Ellis as a Dumping Ground

Commissioner Howe took over the island when it was a mighty immigration station, though in a relatively dormant state, to be sure. Now
Ellis is a massive field hospital, internment camp, and military base, all
of it subject to martial rules. Howe sought to introduce humanitarian
reforms in the spirit of faith in his fellow man, yet the war demands
mistrust of foreigners from enemy countries, even if they are ordinary
civilians long since domiciled in the United States, with no relation to
the politics or ideology of their countries of origin.

> The Department of Justice and hastily organized
> espionage agencies made [the three islands] a dumping
> ground of aliens under suspicion, while the Bureau of
> Immigration launched a crusade against one type of
> immigrant after another, and brought them to Ellis Island
> for deportation. No one was concerned over our facilities
> for caring for the warring groups deposited on us. The
> buildings were unsuited for permanent residence; the
> floors were of cement, the corridors were chill, the islands
> were storm-swept, and soon the ordinary functions of
> the island became submerged in war activities. Eighteen
> hundred Germans were dumped on us at three o'clock in
> the morning, following the sequestration of the German
> ships lying in New York harbor. The sailors had been

promised certain privileges, including their beer, which was forbidden by law on the Island.

... [I]ncoming trains from the West added quotas of immoral men and women, prostitutes, procurers, and alleged white-slavers arrested under the hue and cry started early in the war ...

I became a jailer instead of a commissioner of immigration; a jailer not of convicted offenders but of suspected persons who had been arrested and railroaded to Ellis Island as the most available dumping ground under the successive waves of hysteria which swept the country.[117]

Dr Salmon, the Meaning of the Nail in the Horseshoe

Today it's hard to understand how isolated Commissioner Howe feels at Ellis Island. He can certainly rely on the community-minded enthusiasm of Cecilia Greenstone from Białystok, the experience of Peter McDonald the baggage handler (almost 70 but still working), the dependability of his cheerful secretary Emma Oosterhoudt (the other Emma — Corcoran — left the island in 1916), the sharp eye of Augustus Sherman, and the now gray-haired interpreter Frank Martoccia. But what about the professional loyalty of Byron Uhl? That is no longer certain. Most of all, he could use Dr Thomas Salmon at the island, even collarless, with his cuffs held together by the laws of attraction. The doctor's eccentricities wouldn't matter now, because his knowledge of shell shock is in such demand at Ellis Island. In any event, Dr Salmon has changed — he now sports a carefully trimmed moustache, an impeccable suit, and the knot of his tie rests elegantly between the round flaps of his shirt collar.

Yet if asked about shell shock, Dr Thomas Salmon would sharply object. He is among the doctors fighting to have that expression expunged from popular and medical consciousness, since it suggests a long-lasting disability and sparks a paralyzing fear in its sufferers and their caregivers.

> No medical officer should use the term "shell shock" either in reports or in conversation, nor should nurses and hospital corps men be permitted to use it.
>
> It is not a medical term but a piece of military slang … It is not permitted in the British or French armies, nor in the armies of our enemies.
>
> To discontinue using the term "shell shock" shows a desire to preserve manpower, to be accurate and clear in medical nomenclature and to follow regulations framed after thoughtful consideration; to continue using it shows clinical slovenliness, disregard for regulations, and indifference to the preventable wastage of manpower. This is a little thing but so was the nail, for the lack of which the horseshoe, the horse, the rider, and a kingdom were lost.[118]

The above is an excerpt from an order to the United States Public Health Service from the chief surgeon of the United States. It was Thomas W. Salmon who prepared the text.

"Shell shock" ought to give way to the phrase "war neuroses."

One month after the United States joins the war, in May 1917, Thomas Salmon sails to the UK to observe methods of treating victims of these neuroses, and in December, now promoted to major, he becomes chief consultant in psychiatry for the American Expeditionary Force in France. His popularity is growing. He visits hospitals and also wins over the powerful and influential; he lunches with Mrs Vanderbilt and travels with Isadora Duncan to see the house the dancer wants to convert into a hospital for war-traumatized nurses.

His work is evident in the treatment of psychologically wounded American soldiers. Psychiatric wards are set up in war hospitals, expert-prepared diagnostic tests are published, medical personnel are trained, home rehabilitation plans for veterans are developed.

In February 1918, the National Committee for Mental Hygiene passes a resolution declaring Major Salmon owes his achievements to the *meekness of Moses, the patience of Job, the wisdom of Solomon, and the valour of David.*[119]

Does Salmon smile ironically to himself? Perhaps not; he likes a good literary metaphor.

Commissioner Howe Burns His Papers

The war is over. Fear of the Huns has receded and an even greater fear has arisen — the "Red Scare." The map of Eastern Europe (for Europe extends to the Urals, as we often forget) has turned red — the color of Bolshevik revolution.

No one suspects Commissioner Howe of Bolshevism, though of socialism — certainly.

He's given plenty of cause to do so. In the winter of 1914–15 he persuaded the island's employees to search the Battery for homeless paupers camped out there. The result of this initiative shocked everyone: they found 750 people freezing in the cold. They took them to Ellis Island and gave them a bed and warm coffee — for five cents a day, Howe assured. All winter long at 7.30 am every day, a ferry took the needy to Ellis Island.

He also came up with a labor exchange in New York, run by immigration service employees specially for immigrants.

But immigrants aren't the only ones struggling to find work. For instance, a whole multitude of oyster divers and traders are losing their jobs, especially on Staten Island, one of New York's five boroughs. Twenty-foot-long rakes for scraping crustaceans off the reefs lie abandoned in country lanes. The Methodist chapel in Sandy Ground, a settlement that has prospered off oysters for a century, is sinking into poverty — where the faithful once brought dollars, they now bring cents. The inhabitants of Sandy Ground must seek other work. One got a concession for hauling trash, another left to become a school janitor, while Jacob Finney got a job as a porter at Ellis Island.[120]

It goes without saying Commissioner Howe's actions don't prove he's a socialist; after all, a committed Republican might have had similar ideas. But if, alongside these social ideas, he is liberal toward deportation, sanguine about enemy aliens, dismissive of immorality, and finally a crusader against dishonest contractors taking advantage of immigrants, this all starts looking a little pink. Even before Howe, commissioners fought with contractors and largely won without putting their own positions at risk. Yet Howe's reform attempts now reinforce the idea he's an enemy of American enterprise.

Byron Uhl's loyalty to Commissioner Howe does indeed turn out to be limited. He too thinks Howe is pink, if not red.

The Red Scare means Ellis Island increasingly acts as a deportation station, not only removing from America new immigrants who can't pass the rigors of inspection, but also all sorts of undesirables apprehended within the United States.

In February 1919, a wave of the Scare brings a large group of Industrial Workers of the World (IWW; its members were known as Wobblies) activists to Ellis Island.[121] They're sent from Seattle on a train nicknamed the Red Special. Howe is attending the Paris Peace Conference at the request of President Wilson (who was his professor at Princeton). The decision about the Wobblies' fate falls therefore to Uhl, who with little hesitation severs the group's contact with their lawyer. He wants to deport them quickly via measures introduced in the 1918 Immigration Act to ease the deportation of anarchists and subversive elements.

Yet Commissioner Howe is opposed. He returns from Europe, examines the group's situation, and concludes that, legally speaking, all detained aliens are meant to be interviewed before a ruling is made on their case. As a result, the majority of the Red Special's passengers are freed.

That summer, the United States is rocked by strikes and bomb attacks, the Red Scare intensifies, and the seemingly mild-mannered Fiorello La Guardia — since 1916 a congressman representing New York City — joins the ranks of Howe's opponents. La Guardia will serve seven terms in Congress, with one interruption; he wins under the banner of fighting Tammany, he declares he joined the Republicans because he

couldn't stomach Tammany Hall, he warns New Yorkers the *Tammany men* are killing their city. Fiorello's familiarity with Ellis Island means he's extremely astute on this issue, so Howe must have found his voice particularly vexing. La Guardia declares in Congress they ought to cut Frederic Howe's salary from $6,500 a year to $2,500, since the commissioner *is very rarely at his station, unless he goes there for the purpose of defending a detained anarchist.*[122]

Fiorello might dislike Howe's views, but isn't he being too hard on the commissioner? A possible reason for this could be Fiorello's friendship with Uhl.

Even if the tension between Uhl and Howe might affect the tone of La Guardia's remarks, it likely wouldn't change his basic assessment. Fiorello is an ardent Republican, an ardent American patriot, an ardent defender of the United States. He might feel for contract workers or a child questioned excessively harshly at Ellis Island, but he has no sympathy for subversives and enemy aliens. When it comes to patriotism, Fiorello is more than just talk.

When America joins the war he enlists in the Air Force, trains, and is sent to supervise a training camp in Foggia, Italy (coincidentally the very town where his father Achille was born). There he immediately introduces essential regulations, such as boiling the water, washing the fruits and vegetables, and installing mosquito nets — meaning, to general astonishment, the camp is free of malaria. When military failures lead to a breakdown in the Italians' morale, he bucks them up with speeches at rallies in Rome, Genoa, Naples, Milan, Turin, Florence, and Bari. He lifts their spirits and scolds them for eating too much, drinking too much, fooling around too much, and not working hard enough (as an Italian himself, he's allowed to give them a piece of his mind). The *New York Times* writes *President Wilson and the United States could not have chosen a better representative in Italy than this brave soldier.* Then on a training flight, Fiorello loses control over his plane in strong winds and is injured; he'll never fully recover from the crash.[123]

But let's return to Ellis Island. Howe is losing control of the station too, yet no one is inclined to lend a hand. He really does spend too much time away from the island. Now he's back at the Peace Conference in Paris. While he's gone, foreigners whose safety he'd assured are being deported. For these men and women, returning home can mean repression and imprisonment.

Howe is so bitter he burns his personal documents from his work at Ellis Island, which he was collecting to write a book, and informs the president of his resignation.

Not long after, Uhl testifies to a Congressional commission on Howe's activities as commissioner, saying the station's employees weren't happy with him.

> So far as I received their individual opinions … they
> were all of [the] opinion that the conduct at that time was
> utterly improper.[124]

Augustus Sherman's Italian Soldier Boy

Augustus Sherman's oeuvre has long warranted a huge exhibition, one that might distract the wounded soldiers filling the Great Hall of Ellis Island in the final years of the war from their awful memories of the battlefields. They could see the Russian giant, the Burmese dwarf, the Ruthenian woman with transparent eyes, and the loveliest children Sherman's lens ever captured — two Dutch siblings, plump and motionless, like puppets whittled from white wood, squeezed into thick, tight-fitting clothes, large hard clogs, and round caps. The boy, perhaps five years old, gazes fearlessly into the lens, his arm protectively around his little sister, perhaps three, who is on the verge of tears.

Yet Augustus' work remains a private matter for himself and an administrative matter for the island, with no one casting an artistic eye over it. Something entirely different decorates the walls of Ellis Island: instructions and custom-made posters. The latter are meant to support the new immigrants' education as patriotic Americans.

If an arrival is Polish, they might spot two colorful profiles: Tadeusz Kościuszko and Kazimierz Pułaski, Polish patriots who fought in the American War of Independence. A caption reads in Polish:

> They fought for freedom in America. Will you help
> America fight for freedom in Poland?

The Poles would also notice another poster in their language:

> Eat Less
> Wheat — meat — fats — sugar
> So we can help our brothers
> Fighting in the Allied Armies

But some appeals (and assurances) in English are meant to speak to everyone:

> Be Loyal
> Many Peoples, But One Nation

The first two posters, born of military necessity, are no longer relevant. Time to take them down. The latter ones surely stay up.[125]

One of the final mementos of the war is the Italian soldier boy photographed by Augustus Sherman. He's fifteen and has an ageless little face, wide eyes, and a stiff neck; he holds his hands at his hips and is straining as hard as he can to look heroic. His name is Enrico Cardi and, as is written on the photo, he received the French Croix de Guerre, was wounded thrice, captured three German prisoners, and was nicknamed the "Little Corporal." He was adopted by an engineering unit of the US Army as an honorary sergeant.

He prompted such tremendous interest at Ellis Island that the vaudeville star Elsie Janis actually wanted to adopt him. All efforts were made, but it turned out Enrico had stretched the truth — he wasn't an orphan at all; he had parents in Italy. And anyone caught lying to the immigration service goes back where they came from. So in 1919 Enrico sets sail for his unwanted homeland.

In April 1919, the Navy moves out of Ellis, and, in June, the Army departs from the island's hospitals. They leave them in perfect order to the satisfaction of the staff, as Howe admitted while still commissioner.

The end of the war is also farewell to the island for the barber Miji Cogic, an immigrant from the Austro-Hungarian Empire. He came to the US on 8 August 1914 and lived at Ellis Island for five years, awaiting his inevitable deportation. We no longer know the accusations against him, but his industriousness is remembered. He gave a perfect shave and earned $495 in savings. That was his money and the United States didn't feel it had the right to deprive him of it, though according to careful calculations, Cogic's stay at Ellis Island cost the federal government $2,046. That money ought to be reimbursed by the Austro-Americana Line, which he took from Trieste. But the Austro-Americana Line has gone out of business, just like the Austro-Hungarian Empire.[126]

The Great War never speaks its final word. As the last war-neurosis patients are departing the island, suddenly yet another victim arrives. Her stay on the island is kept discreet, but the *New York Times* gets word it's Hannah Chaplin, the mother of Charlie. Apparently she's mentally ill; she suffered during the bombings in England; it's rumored her actor son negotiated with the American authorities at length to bring her to the US, apparently promising he'd cover all the costs of treatment. She sailed over on the *Celtic*, but her name was left off the passenger list. Byron H. Uhl was unwilling to share any details with the press; he only said Mrs Chaplin was already on her way to Los Angeles.

Peacetime, Paula Pitum

The Pitum family's hardships come roaring back to life.

In 1919, Paula Pitum is 14; she's been in the US for five years and still lives in Olean. Now that peace has come, Europe's ports are open and deportations are possible. She must report for questioning. She is still in the United States illegally.

> Her mind and body had improved during the five years in America. There was no question of her becoming a public charge. The very fact that she was afflicted had endeared her not only to every member of her family, but to practically every resident of the little city of Olean. The entire town went "to the bat" for her. It seemed a travesty that she might be snatched from her mother's protecting care and sent back to Russia where she had no relatives or friends — she, who so needed her family. The hearing day found all the Pitums again in distress.

The father was the first to testify. He told of the care which Paula had been receiving ... He also testified as to his own financial progress and the sacrifice all were making in the hope that the little girl might be left in America ...

"Have you ever declared your intention of becoming a citizen of the United States?" the immigration inspector asked Pitum.

"I am a citizen," was the reply, and Pitum produced his citizenship papers ... "She has no one to go to in Russia," he went on pathetically. "She might better be thrown into the ocean."

Chaim Pitum not only showed his certificate of citizenship, but also testified he'd purchased Liberty Bonds and War Savings Stamps. For now, Paula returns to Olean.[127]

The Soviet Ark Leaves Port

The military has departed Ellis Island but it's hard to say the station is back to normal. The specter of the *reds* still haunts it. In November 1919, a new wave of undesirables reaches Ellis Island. Now, with Howe gone and a new commissioner not yet nominated, Byron H. Uhl is in charge of the island's administration.

This means deportations are taking place much more energetically. On the frosty evening of 21 December, a steamer named the *Buford* leaves the Port of New York. It was built nearly 30 years ago as the SS *Mississippi* and is now known colloquially as the "Soviet Ark." It has taken onboard 249 deportees, mainly anarchists, and is to meant to deposit them in Russia, but is sailing for Finland because the British are still blockading Russia's ports following the revolution.

The *Buford* leaves port in New York to the applause of the public and the lamentation of divided families. Onboard is the famous anarchist and feminist Emma Goldman, who allegedly contributed indirectly to the attack on President McKinley by influencing the views of his assassin, Leon Czolgosz. She's accompanied by her close friend and fellow traveler Alexander Berkman.

Emma Goldman, a rousing rally speaker, author of radical pamphlets, repeatedly imprisoned, brave and independent — as even her fiercest opponents must admit — is 50 years old when she departs for Soviet Russia. We see her in a photo by Augustus Sherman. She peers gravely and patiently through wire-rim glasses; she is passive, motionless, heavy-set, wearing a conventional blouse with an appliqué design at the neckline. If there were an exact opposite model of the image of a fiery rebel, this would be it. And yet:

> Who was the most interesting radical ever to pass,
> eastbound or westbound, through the gates of Ellis Island?
>   The answer permits no arguments. For human
> interest, one person stands out — Emma Goldman.

This opinion comes from Edward Corsi, the Italian immigrant who passed the Statue of Liberty as he arrived on the *Florida* in 1907. Years later he will rule on the island.

During Emma's interrogation before being loaded on to the "Soviet Ark," she declares the American deportation procedure to be worthy of the Spanish Inquisition or the tsarist secret police. She adds that under the cover of the law against anarchism, they can smother any criticism of a corrupt administration, any attack on government excess, any expression of solidarity with a newly born country.

We reached Finland, recalls Emma Goldman,

> without knowing where we were, having crossed the Baltic

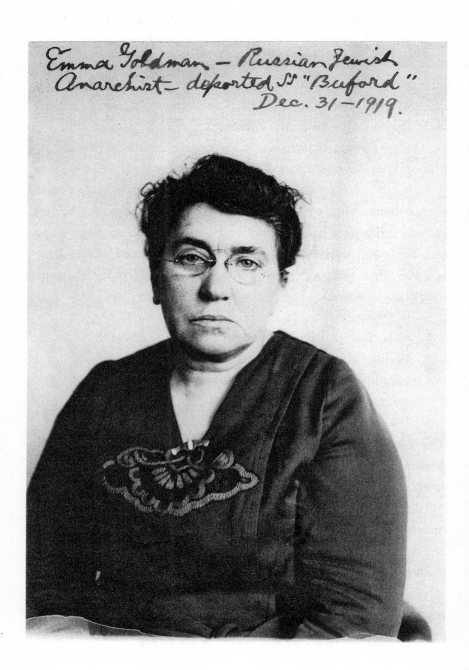

Emma Goldman — Russian Jewish Anarchist— deported SS "Buford" Dec. 31—1919.

Sea which was still underlain with German mines. We were placed in sealed cars on a Finnish train, each door manned by a guard, just as Trotsky went through Germany ... We were received in Russia with military honors. It was a grand ovation. None of us knew for sure that we were nearing Russian soil until we were so informed. The Russians in our party fell down to the ground and kissed the snow. The band played. We were cheered. It was magnificent.[128]

As Emma Goldman feels the warmth of her welcome in Soviet Russia, Acting Commissioner Byron H. Uhl composes a report to the authorities in Washington. It concerns the station staff's deportation activities. In January 1920, those arrested in the United States for subversive intent numbered 4,000, of whom 600 ended up at Ellis Island.

The document is so painstakingly detailed that we can only hope Byron Uhl sped its preparation with his skill in the Pitman shorthand method, still popular in the United States. The press has just reported that one Nathan Behrin has broken the all-time Pitman speed record — 350 words per minute (the test lasted two minutes).

The bulk of the information Byron Uhl passes on to his superiors is: clerk (name here) devoted his entire time to deportation cases, inspector ... devoted his entire time to these cases, interpreter ... devoted his entire time... After dozens of English, Slavic, Scandinavian, German, and other names, the same formula follows, ad nauseam: *devoted his entire time ...*[129]

Byron Uhl's rigorous reporting is the final act of these devotions. Even conservatives are now criticizing the detentions and arrests as excessive, and the zeal for deportation is cooling. In 1920, about 25 people described as anarchists are being held at Ellis Island. Little by little, Ellis is returning to normal, though it is the poorer for one important person: Peter McDonald the baggage handler, who swore to work at the station to the day he died, and kept his word.

Part IV

Pitch and Toss

Josephine, a Bad Experience

People come and go. One who goes is that ardent caregiver to the wronged, the utopian socialist Cecilia Greenstone; it's likely the era of deportations at the station has made her uncomfortable, and in any case she's decided to start a family.

With ships sailing into New York once again full of immigrants — now exhausted by poverty, the journey, and also by war — Ellis is in desperate need of girls to help — girls such as 16-year-old Josephine Friedman. She got a job at Ellis because her mother, who's separated from her husband, is an orderly in the hospital. They're poor. Josephine earns money before by assembling paper bags and tending to elderly people.

> I was frightened because ... they took me up to this
> building and told me what I had to do. I had to, when
> the boat would bring in these patients who were ill ...
> take them into this room and wash their hair and some of
> them had never seen a bathtub and they were afraid to get
> in the water. And you had to scour the tub good and ...
> put [their clothes] in a bag where they were sent down to
> be fumigated ... [A]nd then they would be brought back
> and ... they would be so wrinkled and I used to feel so
> sorry, I was wishing I had an iron that I could iron their
> clothes for them.
>
> [S]ome of the patients were, would get very nasty
> if you try to take their clothes from them. They thought
> you were stealing their clothes. And then they found out
> why. Some of them had money sewed in their hems. The
> bills. And even in the seams they had the money rolled

up and sewed in the seams of their clothes. And, uh, one person wouldn't take his hat, her hat off. She wore like this bed cap and then we found out why. It was, she had all the money sewed, her bills sewed in there.

They didn't know how to use the toilets. And, and, they didn't know. They would go and they wouldn't know what to do and then they would be ashamed to call you to find out. So you used to, I used to have to go in after each patient and make sure that it was flushed properly ... And they were all poor people. And they thought the streets were paved with gold.

[W]e had one lady there who was ... almost seven feet tall and she couldn't fit in any of the beds. And they had the white metal beds there ... and I had to take two chairs and put a pillow and put her feet through the posts and put each foot on the pillow. But she was from England and ... she thought that was wonderful that I found a place for her feet.

It seemed that they were afraid to talk ... They liked potatoes. Every one of them liked potatoes. You couldn't give them enough potatoes ... One woman ... wanted an onion one day. And I didn't know why she would want to eat the whole raw onion. So we found out that a lot of them like raw onions.

[T]his one little German girl and I became friendly ... and I bought her a Hershey bar for the first time. She had never seen a Hershey bar. And she was just so thrilled with that candy, she wouldn't eat it she would, she just enjoyed it so much. Then there was another Armenian girl who came in who had been abused by the Turks. They had burned her with cigarettes, burns all over her breasts and her arms and they had become infected.

And I know one night I was taking care of a little
infant who was born on the ship and it died. And I was, I
was such a child then myself that it was like a baby, taking
care of a little doll ... It had pneumonia and, uh, it didn't
live through the night and it was quite a shock for me to
have, the doctor told me prepare for burial. And I didn't
know what to do. I had to bathe it and wrap it up in a,
and I don't know if they buried the baby to sea or they,
I don't what they did with it. Quite a bad experience for
me for a couple of days.[130]

The Mercy

The ship that took my mother to Ellis Island
Eighty-three years ago was named "The Mercy."
She remembers trying to eat a banana
without first peeling it and seeing her first orange
in the hands of a young Scot, a seaman
who gave her a bite and wiped her mouth for her
with a red bandana and taught her the word,
"orange," saying it patiently over and over ...
A nine-year-old girl travels
all night by train with one suitcase and an orange.
She learns that mercy is something you can eat
again and again while the juice spills over
your chin, you can wipe it away with the back
of your hands and you can never get enough.[131]

An End and a Beginning

The children who died in Josephine's care were not buried at sea but did have to depart over the water. It's forbidden to dig graves on Ellis Island. Bodies must be shipped to one of New York's cemeteries, generally the paupers' plots at Mount Olivet in Queens or on Hart Island.

But there are a number of steps to follow first. If a patient dies in the hospital, the head nurse must summon the doctor on duty to fill out the deceased's medical forms with the appropriate information. The body is covered with a shroud and an identification tag is attached to the toe before it is taken to the morgue. If the cause of death is infectious disease, the body is wrapped in a sheet that has been soaked in disinfectant solution and then wrung out, and the tag is attached not to the deceased's toe but to this cocoon. The funeral parlor signs a receipt for the body, passes this document to the hospital registry, and then is responsible for all subsequent activities related to burial. At the family's request, they will arrange a religious service with a priest, pastor, or rabbi.

Edward J. Scully's funeral parlor, which buried the dead in the days of Commissioner Watchorn, reported to him in 1909 that the average grave for an adult in the United States was eight feet long, eight feet deep, and two feet wide, and that Scully dug his graves to these measurements. His contract with Ellis was — he assured Watchorn — the first contract in the history of the immigration service to guarantee the deceased a wooden coffin with white metal screws, linen upholstery, and a lacquered surface.

A contract drawn up around fifteen years later with the undertaker Thomas M. Quinn requires him to shave, wash, and dress a corpse (in the clothes handed over to him), place it inside a proper coffin with six handles made by a reputable coffin-maker, bury it in an individual grave, and place information on the grave including the name and age of the deceased, plot number, and the letters USPHS (United States Public Health Service). Any additional services must be paid for. Preparing the body for waterborne transportation, which requires special permissions and embalming, costs $69. A hermetically sealed coffin — $25.

Over the course of its existence, 3,500 immigrants died at Ellis Island station, including 1,400 children.

Around 500 successful births took place. The mothers were women detained for deportation or questioning. Although children born in the United States automatically obtain American citizenship, the majority of newborns at Ellis Island were refused that right, which their parents had looked forward to with hope; instead, they received their father's or mother's citizenship.[132]

Commissioner Wallis on Cruel Laws

In 1919, the number of newcomers at the Port of New York is even smaller than in the previous year: just under 27,000. But in the next, it grows radically, once again reaching six figures — over 225,000 people.

Byron H. Uhl is still in charge of them, though no longer as acting commissioner. He will be deputy once again. The new commissioner is the Democrat Frederick A. Wallis from Kentucky (President Wilson, a Democrat, is still in office).

Frederick Wallis must follow the immigration laws, of course, but he doesn't mince his words about them, particularly the literacy test, which Congress implemented over President Wilson's veto. In the commissioner's view, this barrier actually harms America's interests, since it closes the door to hardworking people but opens it to educated criminals, as well as frequently dividing families. Such a law treats immigrants as a mass, not as individuals.

> [W]e have managed to pass laws bearing no relationship to our needs, such as the literacy test, and then, to make matters still worse, their application is made as inhumane and cruel as it is possible to imagine ... Our present immigration system ... is simply criminal.[133]

It might seem Wallis is taking over the station during an easy period: the military has left, the wounded have been taken away, the Red Scare is passing. Nothing could be further from the truth — it is not a good moment, and not because the immigration laws are inhumane; they have never been humane.

A prying reporter from the popular Newspaper Enterprise Association calls upon his readers to go to Ellis Island and see what takes place there:

Immigrants herded like cattle in the ill-ventilated, fetid detention-room.

No separate quarters provided for mothers with babes in arms.

Vermin on the walls and floors of detention-rooms and in dormitories.

Immigrants forced to sleep indiscriminately two in a bed or on the floors.

Only 1,100 beds, tho the overnight population averages from 2,000 to 3,000 and often is as high as 4,500.

No mattresses for beds — only blankets spread over strips of steel; bunks built in tiers, three high.

Only six bath-tubs for the use of all the women and small children.

No bath-tubs for men; thousands forced to use sixteen shower-baths.

Lavatories so inadequate that they are a menace to health.

Many wash-basins on upper floors without a water-supply.

Only two pumps, with low water-pressure, inadequate against fire.

Many immigrants forced to wait weeks because affidavits and even money sent by relatives had been lost.[134]

Even if the journalist was sensationalizing and we are better off dividing his numbers in half, that's still plenty. Or maybe he isn't exaggerating, since Commissioner Wallis accepts the criticism and himself describes to the press conditions on Ellis of *filth, inefficiency, and red tape.*[135]

It's not so long since the station's modern equipment, health service, tight organization, and efforts to improve the lot of detainees were being praised. What happened?

There's been a break in institutional memory. Over the years of the war and the chaos just after, the island was full, but not with the regular immigration service. The importance of meticulous Commissioner William Williams' procedures is now clear, as is the value of the island's former seclusion.

That seclusion was first violated after the great fire of 1897, when the station had to relocate to Manhattan. It took some time after the return to the island to restore order and morale. The First World War once again disturbed its luxurious solitude. The station needed to send immigrants into New York to free up space for the Army and Navy, the wounded, enemy aliens, and subversives awaiting deportation. Furnishings have aged and crumbled, procedures have grown lax, new employees are replacing the old.

Yet the need for old experience has not passed, for immigrants are still arriving in steerage, travel conditions have changed little, throngs of people are coming down the gangways in worse condition than the throngs before the war, some — Armenian survivors of Turkish atrocities,[136] Russians fleeing the revolution — require immediate medical care, psychological care, or care of any sort, while any given ship might be bringing typhus. Years ago, America feared infectious cholera from Hamburg — now it fears lice, a fear that is all the worse because lice have many homelands.

During the largest of the typhus scares, a 30-year-old cobbler's journeyman, Nicola Iacocca, sails from Italy with his new bride, a 17-year-old cobbler's daughter named Antoinette. Nicola has been living in the US for some time, but when he travelled to Italy on a visit, the two of them fell in love.

Lee Iacocca, Nicola and Antoinette's son, recalls years later:

> My parents' voyage to America wasn't easy. My mother
> came down with typhoid fever and spent the entire trip in
> the ship's infirmary. By the time they reached Ellis Island,

she had lost all her hair. According to the laws, she should have been sent back to Italy. But my father was an aggressive, fast-talking operator who had already learned how to manage in the New World. Somehow he was able to convince the immigration officials that his new bride was merely seasick.[137]

Nicola Iacocca must have had truly remarkable powers of persuasion. This is a time when finding a louse on an immigrant's collar would mean ships being held long hours for disinfection, leading to complaints from the steamship companies, which lost time and money during the stoppage. The United States Public Health Service and the local Department of Health in New York do what they can to prevent people and luggage entering the country before undergoing delousing, but there is a lack of space. The medical services and the passenger lines search for appropriate facilities all over the metropolitan area. There are fortunes to be made here. The New York health commissioner, Dr Royal S. Copeland, organizes a delousing facility in the Battery and sends 30 officers to chase 200 immigrants into it before they take the ferry to Ellis Island according to procedure (in a word, he wages a guerrilla war against the station commissioner); Copeland is soon elected senator. The crisis on the island gives impetus to new measures to limit immigration. This time they take the drastic form of quotas.

Weber, Williams, Watchorn

The three longest-serving island commissioners, John Baptiste Weber, William Williams, and Robert Watchorn, are in good health and could certainly provide insight into resolving the crisis at Ellis, but evidently the domestic immigration authorities have no intention of consulting them. In any case, the three Mr W's have plenty to keep them busy.

Colonel Weber is nearing 80. He has abandoned travel and has probably relegated his automobile to the garage, especially since American intersections are getting more dangerous. His loving grandson Dyas Carden recalled his grandfather, who loved to invest in the latest trends, haggling over the first car by the Pierce-Arrow Motorcar Company.[138] The manager, an acquaintance, demonstrated the car and took the colonel for a spin. *What do you think of this new form of transportation?* he asked. *Well, it's very interesting,* replied John Weber, and asked the manager if there was any way for the vehicle to go backwards.

No, came the reply, *we haven't figured that out yet, but it's coming along. We'll have a reverse gear in the next ones.* So the colonel held off buying one for a couple years. He was actually stingy. When someone spent too long on a long-distance call, he would always glance meaningfully at his watch.

Now the colonel — happy to finally have a grandson at West Point — spends much of his time collecting books for his library in Lackawanna, where his favorite residence is located, known by the Native American name *SHA-MO-KIN*. He is also writing his memoirs, devoting them primarily to his service in the Civil War, his grim journey to Russia, and his fairy-tale impressions of Japan. He drinks gallons of coffee as he writes and is constantly having more water put on to boil.[139]

Commissioner William Williams unfortunately has no instinct for writing, apart from legal opinions, statutes, and regulations, so we know little of his personal life. When the United States joined the war, he moved to Washington and, as a colonel, oversaw supplies of material for the Army. Now he's returned to his legal practice and his Manhattan club, though, we don't know what he thinks of the modernizing steps the University Club taken — for instance, admitting women on some Thursdays between 2.00 and 6.00 pm (crowds of them flock in), or holding movie screenings.[140] Nor do we know if Colonel Williams plays chess, though a brilliant chess player has just arrived in New York: eight-year-old Samuel Rzeszewski, a child prodigy and son of a wealthy mercer from Łódź. In simultaneous competitions he's defeated the best adult players in Europe and naturally had no trouble getting into the United States. William Williams' club invites Rzeszewski to a tournament in their building, even more impressive than the mansions of Łódź's factory owners, and assigns him 20 opponents. Is William Williams one? How many of them lost?

Robert Watchorn, like John Weber, is writing his memoirs. We know from Watchorn himself that while he was still commissioner, H.G. Wells and Mark Twain encouraged him to do so.

During one visit to Ellis Island, Wells asked Watchorn how long he would remain in post, and suggested:

> When you are entirely free, come back to England for a
> while and be my neighbor, and there write the story of
> your life's work, not as any other person may suggest,
> but just in your own natural way, just as you have so
> captivated me ...[141]

Watchorn never took him up on this offer, but he remembered it. Twain had a different influence.

> Samuel Langhorne Clemens, better known as "Mark
> Twain," conducted a school (in what is generally known
> as the Bowery section of New York City, which is on the
> East Side and is peopled very largely by the wage-earner
> class) especially in the interest of the stage. Plays adapted
> from his own writings were taught to the children of that
> section and he took a deep and earnest personal interest
> in the lessons they were required to learn ...

That, I fancy, was the reason that the inimitably humorous Mark Twain invited me to attend a rehearsal of one of his plays, *[The] Prince and the Pauper* ... Mrs Watchorn and our son Ewart attended several such rehearsals and in due course Ewart was favored especially by Mark Twain on several occasions and became a special favorite of his. Mark Twain facetiously remarked occasionally that it was quite the proper thing that the commissioner of immigration at Ellis Island, through which station fully 100 per cent of his "dramatic artists" had entered the United States, should become acquainted with their remarkable talents by attending both their rehearsals and public performances. We approved of the suggestion and on several such attendances were greeted cordially by our host and shown to reserved seats in his private box. The performances were all surprisingly fine and we never doubted that in due course the stage at large would be open to many of them.

After meeting Twain, Watchorn thought that

I believe the paramount justification for writing my life story is that it may have some inspirational value to boys born to hardship, but who have been blessed with an undaunted desire for self-reliance.

The former commissioner can peacefully tend to his writing; he has plenty of time.

Life's pursuits no longer concern him. All is vanity, especially since the death of his beloved son Emory Ewart, with whom he attended Mark Twain's play rehearsals. Ewart died of war wounds; he was a volunteer in the First World War, a pilot in the trans-Alpine forces.

Robert Watchorn is very rich. Ever since the hotel bellboy approached him in London with a cablegram from 70-year-old Lyman Stewart, he's done such a fantastic job running a series of oil companies that he can offer $485,677.50 to the Bible Institute in Los Angeles. And that's only one of his donations to that noble cause.

He makes many donations in Ewart's memory. He first commemorates his name by funding an organ for the First Methodist Episcopal Church in Los Angeles, choir stalls for the Protestant Episcopal Cathedral in the same city, chimes for the tower of the First Methodist Episcopal Church in Redland, California, as well as a duplicate set of chimes for the Protestant Episcopal Church in La Crescenta, in the same state.

Ewart's memory demands ever more from his father. Watchorn must direct his devotion and attention to his old homeland. When Ewart returned from the war in Europe, he told his father the English would understand Americans better if they were familiar with Lincoln's life and ideas. So, in Alfreton, Derbyshire — whence Watchorn set off with his home-made chest — the Abraham Lincoln Library is built.

Sharp-Eyed Ludmila Foxlee

Ludmila Foxlee, who comes to work on the island at the age of 35, is not afraid of lice — she isn't afraid of anything at all. Her maiden name is Kuchařová, her father is Czech, her mother Austrian. She and her family sailed to Ellis Island in 1894, when she was nine. *I knew the hardships of the slow, third-class trains across Europe, the misery of steerage.* She married John Foxlee, an English immigrant who's interested in art, but has a practical side too and loves country life — in 1917, he purchased a farm in Montvale, New Jersey.

Ludmila enjoys singing in Czech and English; she also knows German and is conversational in Russian, Polish, Serbian, and Croatian.

She refreshes her memory of steerage in 1919, crossing the ocean en route to Czechoslovakia. For two years she's worked for the Young Women's Christian Association (YWCA) in America. Her social-minded zeal caught the eye of Edith Terry Bremer, director and founder of the YWCA Immigration Bureau; they work together and will become life-long friends.

Ludmila sails to Europe in a cabin on a French ocean liner, but she descends to steerage to see what's changed so many years on. Supposedly shipping companies are increasingly replacing steerage with proper cabins including hygienic facilities, their hands forced by civilizational progress. But on this French liner, steerage has changed little from when Ludmila and her family came to the US. An elderly passenger invites her to see her bunk, separated from the others only by a curtain, while the woman's modest luggage slides around on the floor.

Many immigrants who've already settled into the US are heading for Europe on this French ship. They've set out to see their old countries of Poland, Czechoslovakia, or Hungary, which have now become independent since the war, and assess what this change means for themselves and their families. American Ludmila's work in the newly founded Republic of Czechoslovakia is connected to these changes as well, and serves both the state sending the emigrants and the one receiving them; but this new situation might make the division of labor less obvious than in the days when only America was receiving. The President of Czechoslovakia so highly values Ludmila's work that in 1928 he grants her the Order of the White Lion, reserved for foreigners who've offered outstanding civil or military service to Czechoslovakia. (Another recipient was Dwight Eisenhower in 1945, and in 1999 Lech Wałęsa.)

The tips Ludmila brings back from Czechoslovakia are telling examples of her practical nature and her determination to use her sharp eye to help others. So anyone wanting to visit Czechoslovakia should know that:

They may be robbed.

They will not receive precise information.

It's very likely their baggage will be lost.

From Antwerp, they must travel to Czechoslovakia via Luxembourg and Germany. From Le Havre or Cherbourg — via Paris and Strasbourg. From Rotterdam — via Oldenzaal and Hanover.

Many Czechoslovak residents of the United States ... take with them no proofs of their residence in the United States ...

When a family intends to [return to their home country] with all their children, an official birth certificate issued by the State Bureau of Vital Statistics should be obtained for each child. A baptismal certificate issued by the church is not sufficient proof of the American birth of a child. While the parents may plan to settle permanently in their native country, their American-born children may wish to return to the United States when they reach maturity. Then they will need the certificate. Because this paper is very important it should not be left in a consular office or any other office, even if an official insists that it be left with him. An American birth certificate has the same value as a certificate of naturalization. American-born children should travel on American passports ...

The illiterate resident going abroad should understand that he must return to the United States within six months of his departure; and that he needs a statement from his employer, his bank, from any organization of which he has been a member to prove that he did reside in the United States.[142]

Ludmila's first encounter with Ellis Island at the start of her work there has echoes of Maud Mosher's first day. Like Maud, Ludmila Foxlee observes each stage of processing. She enters the detention room, where women sit waiting for interviews.

The room has a view of Manhattan and the ships in the Bay, but Ludmila notices that not a single one of the women looks out that way, as if they had a windowless wall before them. They're aware of nothing but being locked in. She also notices the men detained in the hospital are very surprised to be there. They are convinced they're healthy. A person who can walk and work is healthy. They had always worked like normal people, and now the doctors are trying to locate some kind of illness in them.

At this time, 29 aid organizations are working at the island, including the American Red Cross, the Daughters of the American Revolution, the Belgian Bureau, the Bulgarian Society, the Clara de Hirsch Home for Immigrant Children, the German Society, the Greek Society, the Hungarian Relief Society, the Polish National Alliance, the Slavonic Immigration Society, the Society for the Protection of Italian Immigrants, and the National Institutes of Immigrant Welfare.

The reformist era of Frederic Howe is gone and the social workers are treated coolly at the island because they get in the way of administration, slow down procedures, and force changes to various decisions. Ludmila Foxlee is under no illusions as to the divergent interests of the immigration station's mechanisms and — as we would now call them — the defenders of human rights. This was also Matron Maud's experience. Ludmila recalls:

> Caution and complete knowledge of the immigration
> law preserved us from trouble. It was our safeguard from
> inspectors who resented our presence.

She works in a dark space on the ground floor, where *mice played around our feet, and everything seemed covered with grime, gloom, and ugliness*. It has no windows or ventilation, bare bulbs hang from the ceiling, and there are only two telephones for arranging countless interventions.

Maud wrote after her first day: *And I — I had to stay*. But she left the island after five years. Ludmila thinks she won't be here long, but she stays 13 years.

The First Quota, a Mad Dash

When 3 June 1921 arrives, the Port of New York becomes the finishing line for a peculiar type of boat race. Years later, Edward Corsi notes:

> Imagine the ships, bulging with human cargo, racing
> through the Narrows and into New York harbor, actually
> colliding with one another in their hurry to be at Ellis
> Island before the last minute of grace.[143]

On 30 August 1921, the *New York Times* reports the SS *Gdańsk* (Gdynia–America Line) has been halted at sea and will not enter the port before 4.00 am. The Polish quota for August is already exhausted. The ship holds 173 Poles. It will be cheaper to keep them at sea and wait for the September quota than to send them back to Danzig.

A more memorable incident at the island is when the Red Star Line's *Lapland* arrives a day late. Onboard is the wife of a Polish miner from Pennsylvania. She went to Poland to visit family and on the way back, at the end of the voyage, gave birth to a baby. She has the right to enter the United States, but the infant does not, because the Polish quota is already exhausted. The Ellis Island commissioner points out to the inspector that the baby was born on a British ship, and the British quota is large. *British quota exhausted yesterday*, replies the inspector. The commissioner discovers that the unlucky mother embarked at Antwerp and suggests using the Belgian quota. *Belgian quota ran out a week ago*. The baby is finally allowed into the US because the ship was late: they had every reason to believe that if they'd landed on time, the child would have been born a citizen of the United States.[144]

On 2 July 1922, the *New York Times* reports:

> [T]he race of a dozen ships ... to be counted under the new quota, was subjected to climactic interference, the heavy fog yesterday causing several to remain outside the bay ... Only six finished the race in time to be examined yesterday, discharging 1,300 newcomers ... The Latvia of the Baltic–American Line from Baltic ports, 56 passengers; Cunarder Aquitania, from Southampton, 412; Argentina of the Phelps Line, from Trieste, 76; Vasari, of the Lamport & Holt Line, South America, 98; Presidente Wilson, Phelps Line, Naples, 614; Vestris, Royal Mail Line, Hamburg and Southampton, 65 passengers.

Luckily, the newspaper continues, Assistant Commissioner Byron H. Uhl has decided the ships that didn't make it into port yesterday will be accepted today, on Sunday, because the next Tuesday is a holiday — the Fourth of July.

So we see clearly ships are racing to get their passengers to Ellis Island before their respective quotas fill up. The quotas, in turn, are a new method of restricting the wave of immigration, which has once again surged. The literacy test is expected to restrain it, but in the event it's not a great success. In 1921, nearly 561,000 immigrants arrive in New York, more than twice as many as the previous year.

America has not shaken off the Red Scare, while the World War has left many Americans with negative feelings toward Europe, even an aversion, and these feelings combine with anxiety about unemployment. Underpinning these fears is a view, amplified in the press, that Ellis Island isn't up to the task of gatekeeping. The fact of the matter is that the magnates of the most highly developed industries still require foreign labor, but lack sufficient influence in Congress.

President Woodrow Wilson vetoes the quota bill, but his successor, the Republican Warren G. Harding, signs it.

Therefore in May 1921, the 67th Congress of the United States enacts a quota law. It comes into force on 3 June and is meant to expire after one year, but is extended until 1924 — when the next, even harsher, quota law comes into force.

From now on, each nation is issued a cap on entries to the United States. The cap amounts to 3 per cent of the total members of that nationality living in the United States in 1910. As we know, the number of "worse" immigrants — poor people from Europe's southern and eastern regions, as well as Jews — has been growing year after year, so setting a point of reference 11 years in the past demonstrates clearly whom the law's authors support and whom they do not. They want more people from the old immigration countries — Germany, Scandinavia, or the United Kingdom — and fewer from the new.

Nationality is determined by country of birth. As of 1918, Poland is one of these countries. Yet how were Poles counted in America in 1910, before Poland regained independence?

The law further demands the quotas be filled gradually. No more than 20 per cent of the annual share can be used up in a single month.

The shipping companies persistently flout this law. Over the first month the quotas are in force, passenger ships bring to the United States, and primarily to New York, 10,000 immigrants beyond the limit. This recurs in the months to follow. The immigration authorities refuse to let the passengers in. The ships must turn back.

Gertrude Slaughter, one of the first female doctors at Ellis, witnesses and describes this:

> A greatly magnified tragedy was a shipload of 500
> immigrants from southeastern Europe who had disposed
> of their homes and all their possessions to start life

anew on American shores, only to find that they were
above the quota and were forced to return. The ensuing
demonstration of these excitable people is one of my
most painful reminiscences of service at the Island. They
screamed and bawled and beat about like wild animals,
breaking the waiting-room furniture and attacking the
attendants, several of whom were severely hurt. It was a
pitiful spectacle, but officials were helpless to aid. Again,
it may be asked why they were permitted to leave their
native port without a determination of the quota. Again,
however, the Island was culpable in the eyes of those who
were blind to the facts. Still the officials were forced to do
their duty.[145]

Meanwhile Commissioner Wallis adds that *the suffering we see at
the Island daily ... is indescribable and ... would melt a heart of granite.*[146]

He submits his resignation, but the Secretary of Labor asks him
to stay on until October, when the new president will be able to name
a successor.

The quotas are more than a source of despair for immigrants and
frustration for sensitive officials. They are also a subject for vaudeville,
applauded first in Paris at the Théâtre des Champs-Elysées, then at New
York's Century Theater, and on tour throughout the US. The play is
titled *Within the Quota*, suggesting its authors won't take issue with the
new immigration law. And sure enough, everything goes swimmingly
for this immigrant. The composer Cole Porter and the librettist Gerald
Murphy open their piece with a ballet scene portraying their hero
landing at Ellis Island, then being thrown into America's deep end. The
newcomer meets an heiress, a cowboy, a starlet, a tax collector, a modern
liberated woman, a sheriff, and others. Finally fate places in his path the
personification of hope, success, and beauty, luring this immigrant into
a brave new world: the movie star Mary Pickford. She welcomes him

with an embrace, whisks him away to Hollywood, and turns him into a leading man. This vaudeville was performed 63 times in the US — a great success in those days. It took its final bow in March 1924.

La Guardia in Mourning

Immigration opponents increasingly raise the alarm about immigrants taking Americans' jobs. But they're also reminding people of the ancient plagues the poor bring with them. One such specter is tuberculosis, which for years (alongside trachoma) has headed the list of infectious diseases strictly banned in each subsequent Immigration Act. The staff of Ellis Island take extreme care not to let the disease into the United States, using appropriate procedures and expensive diagnostic and sterilization equipment. But from time to time this entire control mechanism encounters unexpected circumstances.

A country girl from Poland named Basha (as recorded in a Red Cross report from 1920), with a cough that worries her doctor, refuses to undress for an X-ray. She is detained on the island but digs her heels in, acting sad and sullen. She behaves so oddly the doctors start to wonder if she's insane. She doesn't want to listen to anyone, doesn't want to speak to an interpreter. She finally confesses what's worrying her. She thinks the X-ray machine is a camera, that — since she's meant to remove her shirt — they intend to photograph her for indecent purposes. She finally agrees to an X-ray, provided a matron will be present. The X-ray reveals no illness; Basha is admitted to the United States.[147]

The fear of tuberculosis is well grounded: it has no treatment yet. In 1921 it kills La Guardia's wife and daughter. Fiorello's efforts — buying a large, well-lit apartment in a more elevated, airy neighborhood where it's easy for the sick to breathe, and seeking out the best medical care — are no help. In spring, his daughter, not yet one year old, passes away. La Guardia attends her funeral alone because her mother, Thea, is too weak. When Thea dies in the autumn, she's 26 years old.

Yet Fiorello's despair is not focused around immigrants who've infected America with their diseases. When a journalist from the *Evening Mail* asks him whether he could do more with the city's budget, he responds:

> Could I? Could I? Say — first I would tear out about
> five square miles of filthy tenements, so that fewer would
> be infected with tuberculosis like that beautiful girl of
> mine, my wife, who died — and my baby ... Then I
> would establish "lungs" in crowded neighborhoods — a
> breathing park here, another there ...[148]

Yet he cannot change those hypotheticals into reality. He is no longer a congressman. And in September, between the deaths of his baby and his wife, he loses the race to be mayor of New York. Tammany Hall-connected John F. Hylan wins again. Fiorello is exasperated, tired; he feels old.

Jacob Auerbach, In the Belly of the Whale

The United States now demands passports. Before 1921 they were only required of Chinese and Japanese laborers.

To that end, Jacob Auerbach has gone to Warsaw. Once he's got his passport, he goes to the consul for a visa. He's turned 17 and although he grew up somewhere outside Brest-Litovsk in today's Belarus, in a shtetl so small it never appeared on any maps, he knows how to speak

English. By a strange twist of fate Jacob had a teach-yourself-English book at home, whose author, Alexander Harkavy, a Jew from nearby Novogrudok (Navahrudak), used the Ollendorff method to explain English pronunciation to his patient pupils. Jacob shaped his mouth and tongue in front of a mirror and learned the words and expressions by heart. His ambition he inherited from his grandmother, who was such a grand lady she refused to walk to the bathhouse, so his grandfather constructed a bathtub for her out of wood. They had to bring water from far away, because the shtetl had only five wells, and they heated it on something hard to pronounce in English — *what they call a pripetchok* — and when Jacob was little, his grandmother put him in the bath next to her.

Jacob took a horse and wagon to the station. He was dressed like a high-school student, in a black mandarin-collared jacket sewn from his mother's wedding cape. His suitcase held a spare shirt, two changes of underwear, socks, and a small embroidered bag with his tefillin. The whole shtetl walked behind the wagon and blessed Jacob on his journey, until the driver impatiently urged the horse faster. He sailed to Ellis Island *as a naïve youngster* aboard the SS *Algeria*.

> We walked up a ramp into ... the ship and were
> swallowed in its bowels like Jonah inside the whale.

He spends the night onboard just off Ellis Island. New York is in shadow, but the New Jersey coast is aglow. He sees an ad for *Lipton's Coffee — Lipton's Cocoa — Lipton's Tea* and it reminds him of *Mene, Mene, Tekel, Upharsin*, God's ominous warning to feasting Belshazzar. He thinks of the shtetl, *where the only artificial illumination was a crackling wood fire or a stinking kerosene lamp.*[149]

Foxlee, On Clothes

Ludmila Foxlee is interested in clothes. She likes trying things on, dressing up in different outfits, and decking out other girls.

Yet she is absolutely not flighty. She's so level-headed, and maybe even high-minded, that she's offended when a New York reporter — in her view — accuses her of being flighty, and she makes up her mind never to speak to the press again. She enjoys dressing up not only because she has a feminine affinity for it. She's astute and compassionate enough to immediately grasp the significance of a change of clothing for immigrants. Besides, it's long been known that every day piles of used clothes with long European lives behind them form in the corners of the Battery and the large train station on the neighboring New Jersey coast, ultimately abandoned in favor of American dresses or suits brought to immigrants by their loved ones.

Among the crowd of newcomers Ludmila spies a beautiful Slovak woman who appears young and healthy, but is walking laboriously, as though every step pains her. It happens the floor-length, stiff, heavy peasant skirt she has spent the crossing in chafes at her hips. This costume and its ungainliness will certainly dismay her family waiting on the shore. Ludmila can offer a storeroom full of American dresses, coats, and hats donated by charity organizations, and her charge — now dressed lightly, fashionably, and comfortably — immediately moves more easily, with a bolder look in her eyes.

A journalist described this situation with wonder and added that Ludmila rouged the immigrant's cheeks. This is a lie — for a Slovak girl the very suggestion would be a tremendous affront, and Ludmila would never have gone so far. Changing someone's clothes is not for the sake of coquetry; it's a serious matter, equipping someone for their new journey.

There are also immigrants who've brought their best garments, carefully protected over the whole journey, to don in celebration before they land, just as they would in the old country for weddings, for important feasts and church fairs, for funerals, in times of great hope or great change, for great meetings or great partings. Augustus Sherman still tracks down and photographs these wonderful costumes, but they're a less common sight at the island since the dreadful war; the world has grown poorer, plainer, and lost a great deal of its dignity. These days the norm is home-made peasant clothes or shoddy factory-made ones, worn out from the long crossing and the arduous cart and train journeys to the port that preceded it (or sometimes dramatic escapes, if for instance one was an Armenian in Turkey).

Ludmila recalls:

> To see a lovely woman among the many who passed my desk gave me pleasure. Jan P., twenty-five, Slovak, and Suzanna, twenty, his wife, arrived on the SS Majestic December 21, 1927, and were detained temporarily because they lacked transportation money. The man had an innocent young face that made him to appear about eighteen, instead of twenty-five. His wife was as tall as he; she was clothed in a light tan cotton dress with a very wide skirt and she wore a kerchief over her head. She had a long, narrow face with an aquiline nose, a strong, large mouth with large, heavy teeth beautifully shaped. Her abundant blonde hair was tightly done into braids that were attached in a stiff formation on her head. Her large eyes were hazel and her complexion lovely.
>
> We found a complete wardrobe of modern clothes for her, but we were horrified when we discovered that her feet, then encased in huge, heavy felt boots, were about size twelve and our storeroom had no shoes of that size. The change that the American clothes wrought in her appearance astonished us. Her features took on a new

dignity when her head was freed of the shawl. Given a
pair of pendant earrings, and clothed in a finely draped
dress of soft material, she made a splendid modern Juno.
She was delighted with her American clothing, but
decided to go about in her old dress until she could buy
a pair of shoes to go with her new outfit. She and her
husband went to Ohio to a friend to work on a farm.[150]

All this must have made Foxlee sympathetic — after all, following
hours of work at Ellis she herself tends a farm.

Suzanna's case differs from that of Prakseda, a Polish woman who
arrives on the *Berengaria* with a four-year-old daughter and is in the final
days of pregnancy with another child. She gives birth at Ellis Island and is
frightened of leaving to meet her husband; the baby's father is Prakseda's
brother-in-law, who came to help her with the harvests — after all, she
didn't have a man at home. She admits to Ludmila she was powerless in
his arms. She cares for her children, she's eager to learn, and in the end
her husband is moved by his wife's ordeal and understands everything.
He can't wait to see her and both children. Ludmila makes sure Prakseda
looks her best for him, and finds her a lovely city dress instead of her
heavy linen petticoat and tight-fitting vest of plain wool.

On the other hand, a different Polish woman, Emilia, has been
robbed on a train in winter and needs warm clothes. Ludmila has a
plush coat for her with a large collar, very old-fashioned, but Emilia is
about 70 and couldn't be happier with the coat.

The introduction of quotas does not lift any of the restrictions
established by previous Immigration Acts. The experience of the
war, which forced millions of Europe's women to grapple with fate
and accelerated their self-sufficiency, has not altered the requirement
for immigrant women to be married or engaged. The shipping companies organize eye-catching events in New York, which are reliably
promoted in the press. On 3 July 1922, the *New York Times* reports on

the *King Alexander*, which has docked in New York with 700 women of 16 different nationalities. Of them, 231 are *picture brides* — women engaged based on a photograph. They come mainly from Turkey, Romania, Armenia, and Greece. Setting out to meet what the paper calls *the matrimonial special* are 50 motorboats and tugs, and, onboard, fiancés with boxes of candy and bouquets. Three confess their woes to the reporters — their young women fell in love with other people during the crossing.

The *Times* article sticks to a light-hearted picnic tone, but it's easy to imagine what horrible disappointments could arise from such an idea, even if we exclude the likely role of human traffickers in the whole business, and remain only in the realm of honest private aspirations.

Ludmila Foxlee, like Fiorello La Guardia before her, accompanies immigrants during their marriage vows and is yet again convinced of the great significance of attire. This time she has in mind not ladies' dresses, but men's suits.

One bride is Polish. She exchanged a photo with a young man, saw

him at the port, everything was agreed, but the girl is late to the ceremony. It must be rescheduled, so Ludmila directs her to a home for Polish immigrants in the city, for the night. Yet the next day the man running the shelter informs her the wedding won't take place. The photo that won the young woman's heart showed a Polish legionnaire in uniform. The man who came to get her in America was an ordinary civilian; the girl felt swindled. She swore she'd repay the full cost of the journey and got a job as a housekeeper. The immigration authorities left her in the US.

> After that we persuaded the inspectors to release the girls to us so that the betrothed couple could think things over a little.[151]

One day Ludmila takes off her city suit and puts on a Slovak peasant costume. She ties a scarf around her head and conceals her hair beneath it, leaving her high forehead exposed. A close-fitting but shapeless jacket with ornamented fasteners flattens her breasts and broadens her waist. Her ruffled floor-length skirt is edged with a strip of lace. In this get-up, borrowed from an immigrant woman, Ludmila looks no different from the Slavic women August Sherman photographed. Her stance and smile show she feels comfortable dressed up this way, and maybe she isn't playing dress-up at all but hearkening back to her previous life. Doctor Safford would surely, without a moment's hesitation, have counted this peasant Ludmila as belonging to the races of East-Central Europe.

Maybe it's a game, maybe something more. Who is the Slovak woman who came to America and dresses up as an American; who is the American woman from the Czech lands who dresses up as a Slovak; who are they at all — regardless of how they dress up? Who is Ludmila? As she looks at the immigrants, she feels for them — not only because they are suffering an immigrant's tribulations, but most of all because they've abandoned their country.

> I was sorry for old persons transplanted to a new and strange environment ... There was nothing for these old persons to do and no place to go. No wonder they soon began to yearn for their native village in which they knew everybody and everybody knew them; where, if they

stepped out of their cottage, they could enjoy the sky, the trees, the song of birds, the rushing water of a mountain brook.[152]

The Radiator Vanishes

The island's shape does not escape the changes constantly taking place there. Not long ago, it looked from above like a radiator: two strips of water lay between three strips of land. Now the lagoon between the second and third islands is filling up with earth, or actually hot ash from the furnace of the electrical plant. The filling-in is going slowly, but we can already see the two younger islands will gradually unify and form a wide interior space, surrounded by the existing hospital buildings. Covered with fertile soil, this could become a park, garden, or sports field. There's likely no need for buildings here. In fact, the new commissioner — Robert E. Tod, a New York banker, sailor, and philanthropist, who arrives at the island without fanfare in October 1921 on President Harding's nomination — demands a range of investments, but the authorities refuse him the funding. America wants a respite from immigrants.

Paula Again

Yet from some things there is no respite. Paula Pitum is on her way back. She's been back before, anyway. In 1921 Washington ordered her to be examined at Ellis Island and deported if she was found developmentally retarded. The tests determined she was, but Washington hesitated and let her stay in America. Nonetheless she's been kept in limbo.

The girl's status — or rather the young woman's now — is still unclear. It's no wonder Byron H. Uhl, the assistant commissioner at Ellis Island, insists that her case be brought to a conclusion one way or the other. Maybe another man would rather let sleeping dogs lie, but not Uhl, who prefers order. He writes to Washington and requests instructions. Washington replies he must wait because Congress is considering legalizing residency for mentally disabled immigrants. Not long after, Uhl states in a letter to Washington that, given the failure of the aforementioned legislation to pass, Paula should be deported immediately. Washington approves and the girl is once again at Ellis Island.

Meanwhile in Olean a storm is gathering. One of Paula's neighbors writes a letter to the commissioner at Ellis:

> In the winter her mother broke her arm and Paula kept
> house, cooked and did everything just as well as anyone
> could. We have here in Olean a very prominent citizen,
> who has a daughter that is afflicted the same way as
> Paula, and if anyone were to say his daughter were
> feeble-minded he would be very indignant. Our country
> boasts of liberty and justice to all, and you as a high
> official would want to maintain that standard, and see that
> justice was done for the little girl.

A legal hue and cry ensues. Paula's case reaches the United States Supreme Court, which orders a judicial review. In 1925, the authorities in Washington issue the following directive to Ellis Island station: Paula has the right to stay permanently in the United States on condition her family pays a $3,000 bond and reports to Ellis Island on the girl's progress — every six months.

When was her final report? We don't know.[153]

Foxlee, On Money

Ludmila Foxlee realizes the scene unfolding before her every day, and in which she herself is taking part, is exceptional, and though she's very busy, come evening she notes down her activities and observations. We already know how closely she observes immigrants' clothing. She dedicates no less attention to their money.

Five dollars.

The German boy Emil D. has sailed to Ellis Island, sick, hungry, with a large head, a thin neck, dark circles under his eyes, and not yet six months old. He's spent two months in the hospital.

> When Emil emerged from the hospital he reminded us of a round, ripe apple; clear, white skin, fat legs with firm flesh ... His father was ... grateful for all that was done for his family. I was pleased by the fact that I was also able to claim for him $5 which he found in a corridor ... This money was turned over to the Treasury, and when no one came forward to claim it, it was given to Mr. D. One of the clerks in the Special Inquiry office said he would never forget Mr. D. because he turned the money into the Treasury.

Eleven dollars.

> Just as I began to believe that I was completely hard-boiled ... I came across the case of an Austrian family of five children going to their American citizen father in a Pennsylvania town, all of whom except the oldest, a girl, were afflicted with trachoma. Of course, the father could not afford to pay $11 a day for treatment ... $2.75 per day per person ... The Austrian family was deported.

Twelve dollars.

Many a foreign-born person, when he has to deal with
American officials, feels helpless as a small child. Mytro B.
from Perth Amboy, New Jersey, was sent to us ... by the
Law Office to help him make arrangements to attend the
funeral of Wasyl B., his nephew, who had been brought
to Ellis Island because he had entered the United States
unlawfully, and had died in hospital. I had to go from
office to office to learn at last that it was necessary to put
in writing a statement to the Commissioner that he, Mytro
B., possessed no means to pay for his nephew's burial, but
that he wished to attend the funeral ... Eight [relatives]
wanted to go, but we finally persuaded Mr. B. to make the
number six and to pay $12 toward the cost.

Ninety dollars.

The 36-year-old Pole Wiktor L. is detained at Ellis Island because
of a weak heart. He spends a month in the hospital waiting for decision
after decision. Each test shows he's healthy and can stay in the US. Yet
he makes up his mind to return to Poland. Because he doesn't qualify
for deportation, he has to buy himself a ticket, but he only has $30.
Ludmila reaches an agreement with the Polish consulate, which obtains
a discount on a steamer for Wiktor. Yet the Pole must raise $90. They
determine together that he will work for a while at a hardware store he
knows in Reading, Pennsylvania, and in the autumn he'll sail back to
Poland on the *Pulaski*.

Fifteen hundred dollars or more (bond for three people).

Three wrestlers from Germany arrive at the island. The oldest,
the massive Paul F., has earnest brown eyes and his ears are completely
cauliflowered. The middle one, Fritz K., world champion in Greco-
Roman-style wrestling, gets nervous easily, his hands shake and you

have to hold them to keep them still. One of his ears droops like a piece of tripe. The youngest and smallest, Alois K., has small ears; he explains to the inspector at Ellis Island this gives him a great advantage in a match. Ludmila calls them *our three Behemoths*. It's not hard to notice that the mighty Paul F. is very worried. The manager from Chicago who invited them hasn't shown up with the bond the immigration authorities require. Paul is prepared to make a down payment on the bond — a pearl necklace, a present for his wife. Yet Ludmila has a better solution. She calls Madison Square Garden, the site of all kinds of sporting tournaments, and secures not only a contract for the *Behemoths*, but the bond as well. They leave the island and send Ludmila a fruit basket. *Ellis Island had its light moments,* she notes.[154]

Sir Auckland, Madame Lalande, and Countess Cathcart

If we were to judge conditions at Ellis Island based on two documents — a report by the British Ambassador to the United States, Sir Auckland Campbell Geddes, and a letter by a French lady, F.M. Lalande — we'd find it just as hard as trying to work out former Commissioner Watchorn's height from Augustus Sherman's photos of him standing next to a dwarf and next to a giant. Ambassador Geddes visits the island just after Christmas 1922 in the company of Commissioner Tod, whom he considers *a sympathetic, kindly, energetic and efficient man, who holds office for patriotic reasons. Any country might be proud to point to him as one of its officials.* And yet after this tour Sir Auckland would prefer Sing Sing prison to being held at Ellis Island awaiting deportation. He writes of the *diabolic* extended appeals process in detention cases, rooms with locked doors, beds like *wire cages*, the prison-like atmosphere, crude conditions for the medical inspection, and especially the stench. He discusses the smells of Ellis Island in a vein recalling the literary passion of Dr Safford, so sensitive to the aromas of decks, holds, and rigging.

> As a result of the presence of chronic dirt, the buildings
> are pervaded by a flat, stale smell. This is quite distinct
> from the pungent odour of unwashed humanity. Both are
> to be met at Ellis Island. Indeed, the compound smell of
> old dirt and new immigrants is so nearly universal there
> that I should not be surprised if it were no longer noticed
> by the members of the staff. After leaving the island, it
> took me thirty-six hours to get rid of the aroma, which
> flavoured everything I ate or drank.

In Geddes' view, Ellis Island's problem is not merely the chaos at the station or the state of its cramped and aging facilities (though he praises the food and the meal distribution, as well as the hospital's organization and equipment), but rather the immigrants.

> If they were all accustomed to the same standards of
> personal cleanliness and consideration for their fellows,
> Ellis Island would know few real difficulties, but they are
> not. Those who pass through the immigration station
> range from the highly educated and gently nurtured,
> now fallen into straitened circumstances, to the utterly
> brutalised victim of poverty and oppression in some
> scarce civilised land ... They all, lady, prostitute,
> mechanic, rabbi, and what-not, are frightened, nervous,
> shy and strange to their surroundings. They are quite
> ignorant, too, of what is expected of them and have no
> conception of what is going to happen next ... The units
> in this heterogeneous mass of humanity obviously dislike
> some of their contacts with one another and yet like sheep

follow where any leads. Like sheep, too, they have to
herded and, by hurdles, kept from straying.

Geddes attempts to imagine himself in the place of those condemned to the lower bunks. He's heard *there have been cases where the
different calls made by nature on the upper berth-holder are responded to
without his or her rising from the "bed"*.

He notes the sterilizing equipment is inefficient and doctors don't
change their gloves as they examine men for possible venereal diseases.

> I saw one nice, clean-looking Irish boy examined
> immediately after a very unpleasant-looking individual
> who, I understood, came from some Eastern European
> district. I saw the boy shudder. I did not wonder.

Ellis Island should be unburdened of about half the people inun-
dating it, concludes Sir Auckland. Before laying eyes on the island, he
thought it might be possible to segregate the arrivals here according
to nationality. Now he's convinced under present conditions this is
impossible, though he still thinks it would be desirable.

Sir Auckland's notes on Ellis Island grate particularly on the island's
staff, coming as they do from a representative of the United Kingdom,
for let us remember the words of former Commissioner Howe:

> The British gave the most trouble ... All Englishmen
> seemed to assume they had a right to go anywhere they
> liked ...

What's more, Sir Auckland's views attain international notoriety.
They are published by the UK Parliament[155] and provide fodder for the
British press, which bemoans British subjects at Ellis Island being made
to endure the humiliating company of less civilized peoples. Shortly

before this, Commissioner Tod, who has already made up his mind to resign, tells a *New York Times* reporter that if he split up the island among the nationalities it served, it would look like a honeycomb,[156] meaning the British have no chance of separate quarters.

In Ellis Island's wired-in beds, fierce enemies are oftentimes bunkmates. Now they will be citizens of a shared country that they've chosen for themselves; they are already preparing themselves for it, willingly or otherwise. Louis Adamic, an immigrant from Slovenia, spends the night in an upper bunk.

> The bunk immediately beneath mine was occupied by
> a Turk, who slept with his turban wound around his
> head. He was tall, thin, dark, bearded, hollow-faced,
> and hook-nosed ... I thought how curious it was that I
> should be spending a night in such proximity to a Turk,
> for Turks were traditional enemies of Balkan peoples,
> including my own nation. For centuries Turks had
> forayed into Slovenian territory. Now here I was, trying
> to sleep directly above a Turk, with only a sheet of canvas
> between us ...[157]

Tod's successor is Henry H. Curran, a New York lawyer, Yale alumnus, and Republican politician who — it is said — resembles stony-faced Buster Keaton. Since returning from the war in France, he prefers to be addressed not as "Judge" but "Major." Though he's universally considered a poor speaker, he strikes back at the British view of Ellis Island, pointing out that immigrants from the United Kingdom aren't so choice themselves, and besides, masses of them are trying to get into the United States, in excess of the quota. The British — he adds — are once again kicking the dog guarding Uncle Sam's gate.

This colorful comparison is not accidental; Henry Curran, before he came to Ellis Island, tried his hand at literature in his spare time. The

protagonist of his stories for *Scribner's Magazine*, Van Tassel, is a young man from a good home who's taken up politics and gets in the way of Tammany Hall. He's probably an alter ego of the author, who was previously elected to the City Council and also lost a race for mayor; he was crushed by Tammany's candidate. Now that controversy has broken out around Ellis Island, Curran sees his expectation of rest at the island was sorely mistaken.

In the midst of this storm there's one ray of sunshine: Madame F.M. Lalande (we don't know her given name). She's an educated Frenchwoman, no longer so young, who's had the chance to see the island up close (she was detained there for ten days) and has an entirely different perspective from the British ambassador. She presents her impressions and observations in a lengthy letter to Commissioner Curran. She lists numerous instruments to support immigrants' health, comfort, education, and even their spiritual needs, such as services by various churches. She sees no dirt, the tablecloths are changed daily, sheets three times a week. The men and women tending to the immigrants are unimpeachably polite.

Finally Madame Lalande adds:

> This statement is not solicited, but if it can make emigrants understand and appreciate what U.S. does for them [sic], you are welcome to publish it (in any and all of the eighteen languages understood at Ellis Island).[158]

Sir Auckland surely exaggerates, particularly given the British sense of superiority, but Madame Lalande — expressing a typically Gallic sympathy for the New World (Lafayette, the Statue of Liberty) and love of knocking the English down a peg (for Waterloo) — surely exaggerates more. She is probably trustworthy as far as the menu goes, but the sheets? Perhaps an educated woman of a certain age who arrived in a cabin is assured of better conditions. Commissioner Curran accepts years later that he's seen many prisons, but none as bad as the dormitory on his island, thereby agreeing with Sir Auckland Geddes' assessment that he'd prefer Sing Sing to Ellis Island. Curran fought long and hard for government funding to finally convert the bunk beds into ordinary ones.[159]

While Madame Lalande comes to the commissioner's aid, another lady wreaks havoc on the island. Vera, Countess Cathcart, arrives alone at Ellis, thoughtlessly declares she's a divorcée, and additionally guilty of having an incident with the Earl of Craven, and the inspector places beside her name a threatening letter *D*: *D* for *divorced*, or maybe *deportation*? One way or the other, Byron H. Uhl is able to treat that *D* as a condemnation: deportation for *moral turpitude*.

Yet Uhl is overruled. It's no different from when he wanted to deport Isadora Duncan and her husband Sergei Yesenin (a morally and ideologically suspect couple). Commissioner Curran, maintaining his stony (some say wooden) countenance, declared *immorality* could be anything — from *murder to a glass of beer* — and suggested to the senior clerks that *you can make your choice*.[160]

He leaves the island after three years, just as relieved as his predecessor.

Watchorn on Britain, America, and the European Federation

The slight tension between London, Washington and New York provoked by Sir Auckland Campbell Geddes' report might have touched the heart of former Ellis Island commissioner Robert Watchorn, an American born and bred in an English mining village. Yet Watchorn has thought so long over his place between two homelands and their relationship with one another that his deliberations are immune to passing emotions.

He feels deep gratitude to America:

> She not only welcomed me cordially, a poor English pit lad,
> but she threw around me all the safeguards provided for her
> own children, and she withheld nothing from me that I could
> rightfully acquire. Whenever I hear unfriendly comments
> about my adopted country, I always think of these lines:
>> Woodman, spare that tree!
>> Touch not a single bough!
>> In youth it sheltered me,
>> And I'll protect it now.

He doesn't want to call the Britain he left the "old country," nor America the "New World." He considers these appellations meaningless. These days England and America are closer to one another in pedigree than ever before, for a country's age is determined by industry, trade, and transportation, not history.

Both Britain and America are as old as the steam engine. Recognizing this equality gives them the opportunity to work together for extraordinary benefit.

Europe, seeing these benefits, will rapidly see that if it wishes to catch up to Britain and America, it must form a federation of its countries.

It has been said that the sincerest form of flattery is
imitation, and, if federation were ever to come into being,
America would no doubt find in the United States of
Europe an inexpressibly high compliment.

Yet there's a fear Europe won't risk the enormous expense of so
uncertain an enterprise.

One way or the other,

Britain and America have nothing to fear from any source,
for just as they can defend themselves in war, so they can
compete with the rest of the world in the ways of peace.[161]

The Second Quota, the Death of Annie Moore

In 1924, the United States Congress passes a second quota act that
limits immigration even further. The first act allowed in 357,803 immigrants per annum — the latest one, only 164,667. The first set out that
each nation could send 3 per cent of its population already present in
the United States in 1910. The new law says they can only send 2 per
cent, based on the year 1890. The clock has been turned back 20 years,
meaning the quotas are even more biased in favor of the old, "good"
immigration — British, Irish, German.

These rules earn the vehement opposition of Congressman
Fiorello La Guardia. Before voting on the bill, he warns Congress: *You
can not escape the responsibility of the vicious, cruel discrimination against
Italians and Jews mainly* ... Fiorello also asserts that all he has heard
in the House is *expressions of fear for the future of the Republic unless we
slam the door in the face of races which have a thousand years of civilization
back of them and open the doors only to Anglo-Saxon stock.*[162]

Yet he convinces few.

The perceived superiority of the old Anglo-Saxon immigration over the new so vexes him that when the *New York World* asks a number of congressmen about their heritage, he replies:

> I have no family tree. The only member of my family who has is my dog Yank [a German shepherd]. He is the son of Doughboy, who was the son of Siegfried, who was the son of Tannhauser, who was the son of Wotan. It's a distinguished family tree to be sure — but after all he's only a son of a bitch.[163]

The writer and illustrator Hendrik Willem Van Loon presents the new situation. Two weary Pilgrims holding bundles walk tentatively along the shore; in the background, the *Mayflower* is at anchor. A serious-looking Indian blocks their path. *You can't come in*, he says. *The quota for 1620 is full.*[164]

A few weeks after the second quota law is proclaimed, in New Jersey an eye-catching demonstration takes place. The Ku Klux Klan

You can't come in. The quota for 1620 is full.

is marching. The procession displays threatening paraphernalia — white robes, hoods, burning torches, and crosses. This time the organization's members are directing their energy not so much against African-Americans as against Jews, Slavs, Italians, Asians, Latin Americans, and all immigrants alien to the former Protestant, white America. Jews, who hold in their own memory or their neighbors' the pogroms in Kishinev (Chi in u) in 1903, Białystok in 1905, Proskurov (Khmelnytskyi) in 1919 and elsewhere in the Russian Empire,[165] look in terror upon the endless march of white supermen; even women march in their disciplined ranks. The year Congress passes the second quota act, the Ku Klux Klan numbers over 4 million members in the United States.[166]

The introduction of the new quotas means the beginning of the end of the great era of American immigration and a turning point in the role of Ellis Island. That same year, Annie Moore — who inaugurated the station's work when she came down the gangplank 32 years ago — passes away. Apparently she had many children, apparently she was killed in a car accident in Texas. She was only 47.

Between 1892, when she set foot on the island, and 1924, when she died, the United States accepted over 20 million immigrants. Of them, 14,277,144 sailed into the Port of New York. The enormous majority of them were sent for processing to Ellis Island.

Part V
Ebb Tide

Augustus Sherman's Absence

In 1925 about 137,500 immigrants sail into the Port of New York, over seven times fewer than in the peak year of 1907.

Now missing from the clerks observing the newcomers' movements on the stairs and in the Great Hall is Augustus Sherman. One day in mid-February he didn't come to Ellis, didn't leave his home in Greenwich Village in Manhattan. He was only 60, had been in good health, and it never occurred to anyone his sudden absence might be permanent. He was loved and respected on the island. The station staff came in droves, including Commissioner Curran, to his funeral at the Episcopal church on the corner of Broadway and East Twelfth Street.

He lived alone and discreetly. Those whose main memory of him is with his camera would be surprised to hear his oeuvre adds up to only about 250 photos. Two hundred and fifty over roughly a quarter-century. Ten pictures a year. Not even one a month. That's how many he left behind. How many he really took, how many he destroyed because he was unsatisfied with them, no one knows. It's a pity he didn't live to pose before his lens the group of 16 Chinese men who've just arrived as stowaways on the *Ecuador*, coming via the Panama Canal with a stopover in Havana, transporting illegal alcohol and drugs. They're discovered in New York Harbor and sent back on the same steamship on the long journey home.

Not only did Sherman make very few prints, he also rarely captioned them; they were evidently meant to speak for themselves. Zybszko Cyganiewicz, Enrico Cardi, and Emma Goldman are among the exceptions — to them he dedicated three words, seven words, 30 words, and a date. He broke his rule of anonymity because these models were not types, but people with stories of interest to the public; today we'd call them media-friendly.

However, we don't know the names or hometowns of the Italian beauty with the melancholy gaze and scarf draped romantically over her head; the Dutchwomen in white caps with large starched wings like nuns' cornettes; the Cossacks with ballet dancers' waists but fearsomely stern expressions, mustaches, lambskin caps, and swords; the Greek in a stiff, white, knee-length skirt sewn from dozens of canvas trapezia; or those two Dutch babies, the little brother and little sister.

There's a fear Sherman didn't sign his prints either, since those that long ago found their way into publication appeared without attribution. In 1905 *National Geographic* printed the photo of the immigrant children on the wagon labeled *Uncle Sam*, and then at least twice, in 1907 and 1917, used Sherman's portraits without giving the photographer's name. The Dutch siblings appeared on the title page of the missionary book *Aliens or Americans?*, also uncredited.[167] As if Sherman cared nothing for his rights, as if for him the pleasure of gathering his subjects was enough. Yet we'll never know what photography meant to him. He left us no reflections. The only pieces of personal information about Augustus Sherman to have survived at Ellis Island are about his cat, Toto, wounded in the paw, and the Mother of the Gracchi, struck in the heart.

Thomas Salmon's Voyage

Sir Auckland Campbell Geddes, who would have preferred Sing Sing to isolation at Ellis Island, also visited the psychiatric testing rooms and concluded: *Their equipment seemed to me effective and adequate.*

At the time Geddes is composing his famous report, the psychiatrists at Ellis have for several years had the help of a guidebook amassing the experience of their predecessors and colleagues: Thomas Salmon, Howard Knox, Eugene Mullan, and others. The booklet, published by the US government for doctors starting out their practice, is titled

Manual of the Mental Examination of Aliens and informs its readers that the methods presented therein are the result of a long evolution.[168]

Early in the introduction, it warns diagnosticians that their test subject will remain mysterious:

> The history of his family, as well as his personal history, is unknown and unobtainable. His previous environments can only be estimated or suspected. His friends and relatives, as well as himself, are unwilling to lend their cooperation and the statements which are made by them must all be accepted with suspicion, for, as experience has shown, they are more interested in securing entry of the alien than in assisting in obtaining the truth.[169]

After arming the doctors with awareness of their ignorance, the book recommends (or rather requires, this being a government document) that the testing room be quiet, well ventilated, at a temperature no higher than 70 degrees Fahrenheit, that the examination take place in the morning and be preceded by a bath, a good night's sleep, and a hearty meal, and that the number of people at the test not exceed three. The foreigner must understand the interpreter well, and the interpreter is to be calm, patient, and sympathetic. The test subject must never be told they've done something wrong.

The diagnostician should test the patient's basic life knowledge. He should be aware an arrival from southern Italy, from an impoverished home with a bed, a table, and two chairs, cannot name the objects in an American apartment. This is not mental deficiency, but lack of experience.

The guide therefore suggests exercises already well tested at Ellis Island. Alongside Knox's cubes and puzzles, these include some questions, for example:

You are in a burning house. You have two objects you can save: a mattress and a lamp. Which do you throw out the window and which do you carry out?

A woman's body has been found cut into 18 pieces. The police say it was suicide. What do you think? (The handbook says it's common to hear answers such as: *"Indeed, I wasn't there,"* *"It was a great sin for her to kill herself."*)

You're in a boat, alone, far from land. You have two boxes containing 50 pounds of bread and 50 pounds of gold. The boat is sinking; what do you throw overboard? (Bertha M. Boody, author of a book about the tests at Ellis Island,[170] writes that one doctor who asked this question of a young girl first got a wrong answer and then, after repeating it, got the right one, along with an intelligent explanation. When the girl heard "a boat," she thought of the large ship she'd arrived on, and didn't grasp the drama of the situation.)

The textbook notes subjects must not be asked abstract questions — for instance, the meaning of *charity* or *justice*.

The manual's authors inform doctors that if a subject must be deported, it is to be done with appropriate attention. The steamship company is meant to ensure them hospital care on the ship. They should be boarded when their health has improved. It's necessary to determine if they are in a condition to withstand the journey, or if someone must accompany them.

These directives would cheer Dr Thomas Salmon, who, years earlier, insisted the mentally ill should be sent back to their countries safely and respectfully.

In recent years he's lived in peace and ease, mainly treating veterans. In a letter to a friend he writes:

> If any soldier who fought in France and received
> an invisible wound that has darkened his mind now
> lies in a county jail or almshouse or is for any reason

deprived of the best treatment that the resources of modern psychiatry can provide, our national honor is compromised ...

He's also been very busy working with students at Columbia University — he's been made Dean of the School of Medicine. He resisted the appointment, but finally accepted it and — witnesses assure us — students have come to his classes in droves.

He's bought himself a boat. He brags in the letter to his friend:

I have bought a dandy little schooner, 41 feet overall ... and I am going to spend nearly all of July and August sailing.[171]

He's always enjoyed sailing. Once, long ago, he decided to spend his vacation in Nassau. He left his luggage at the hotel and went down to the quay. There he saw a boat with a crew and it happened they were keen to take on an extra hand. He sailed with them around the Bahamas, performed the most difficult duties, and at the end of his vacation picked up his bag, said goodbye, and disappeared.

He was able to describe the boats he sailed on in minute detail. He was thrilled to be made ship's doctor on the cutter *Gresham*, sailing to Newfoundland and Labrador. On the voyage he came to the view that the fishermen needed a hospital ship to rescue them in case of a sudden illness or accident. He attacked Congressional committees on the issue and before long the first hospital ship was created.

He'd have been better off not buying that dandy little schooner. He enjoys sailing alone. On 13 August 1927 his boat is found empty, knocking along the wharf, its main rope tangled in the mainsail. His body is pulled out of the water a few days later. Evidently there was a high wave.

The autopsy, performed by Dr Winternitz, Dean of the Yale Medical School, does not reveal anything specific. Rumors of suicide die down. Salmon is buried with military honors on a quiet hill in the cemetery of Dorset, Vermont. A memorial plaque is unveiled at the New York Psychiatric Institute. It reads:

Professor of Psychiatry Columbia University 1921–27. Beloved physician, teacher, mental hygiene leader whose vision guided the state and the university in establishing here this psychiatric institute and hospital.

Foxlee, On the Soviets and Odd Jobs

After seven years beneath a bare bulb with mice for company, Ludmila Foxlee is finally working in good conditions. The social workers are given a large room in the southern part of the building, with tall windows through which they can see the *Ellis Island* ferryboat with its new human cargo heading for the island. Each worker has a desk, space for papers, and access to a telephone and office supplies from the Information Bureau next door. There's so much space they are able to freely receive the friends and loved ones of immigrants detained at Ellis and offer them whatever explanation they can.

The commissioner who so values their work is — judging by the dates — 40-year-old Benjamin Mulford Day, from New Jersey, who took over from Henry Curran in 1926.

He's even given the social workers a lounge, though they don't take advantage of this luxury because they have no time. One would think that since the tide has started going out, there would be less work, but Ellis Island constantly provides them with something new. Whatever is going on in the world, in politics, in the markets or black markets, in entertainment, in exploration, and even in nature (Mount Etna), it all ends up at the island; Ellis and the rest of the world are linked like communicating vessels.

For some time, the island has been receiving victims of Amerikanskaya Torgovlya, or Amtorg[172] — a Soviet trade corporation, which in addition to its commercial activities carries out special clandestine missions. For instance, it encourages Russian immigrants to return to their homeland. These returns hold great propaganda value for the Soviet Union, and besides, people who've acquired experience in the United States can provide various useful services.

The United States is already acutely feeling the symptoms of economic depression. The Soviet economy doesn't know the concept of depression. To those abandoning their illusory hopes of a good life under capitalism, Amtorg promises good jobs and excellent careers in a truly new world.

It's a pity their recruits don't first acquaint themselves with a book by Emma Goldman, who not so long ago was sent via Ellis Island back to Soviet Russia, where she was ready to kiss the snow. She held out there for a year and 11 months. She managed to make it out to an anarchists' conference in Berlin and never returned to the USSR. She described the all-consuming terror and misery of those close to her, and confessed:

Life in Russia had become to me a constant torture; the
need of breaking my two years' silence was imperative.
During all the summer I was in the throes of a bitter
conflict between the necessity of leaving and my inability
to tear myself away from what had been an ideal to me. It
was like the tragic end of a great love to which one clings
long after it is no more.[173]

Joseph K., one of Ludmila Foxlee's charges, has also managed to
break free from the USSR. Some time ago he was fired from the Ford
plant in Detroit and Amtorg offered him a job in Stalingrad. He went,
and at first all was well. Things started going wrong when he refused
to join the Party. Joseph K. realized they wouldn't leave him in peace
and he decided to return to America. Yet he found himself trapped;
he hadn't arranged reentry into the United States before leaving for
Russia.[174] Helpless and disoriented, he traveled to Ukraine to visit
his sister, but he turned back, terrified at the sight of famine victims
being buried in mass graves. He somehow made it to Riga, where the
American consul gave him a visa outside the quota. He returned to
America without a penny to his name. Ludmila is now helping him get
in touch with American friends who can come get him or send him
money to travel onward.

Victor K., a specialist from the Pennsylvania mines, has faced
similar problems, according to Ludmila. He was poached to work in
a mine in Siberia. He left with his wife and their four American-born
children. They lasted nine months. Victor managed to send his wife
and children back to the US. But the Soviet authorities were unwilling
to release Victor himself and forced him to work another year. When
that year was out, now in Moscow, his documents were stolen. Luckily
he remembered the name of the ship and date of his arrival from the
US. The American consul checked this information and issued him a
reentry visa.

These people need help because they're arriving like fugitives, their situation is at least unclear if not suspicious, and Ludmila must lead them out on to calm seas.

Meanwhile she has trouble with Jan K., who was born in the United States and traveled to Czechoslovakia, yet now they don't want to allow him back into the US, so he's stuck at Ellis. What happened? It turns out that while Jan K. was in the old country, he was pressed into the Army. He protested, but nobody wanted to listen to *a mere, simple peasant*,[175] as Ludmila describes him. Now his documents bear a foreign military stamp. Ludmila must write to Washington on behalf of Jan's cousin, because, despite her good position at Ellis, she has no influence on the Board of Special Inquiry, which has already written Jan off.

After sorting out these matters of principle, Ludmila writes her home address on a piece of paper and gives it to some Slavic girls who don't trust the luggage room; now, reassured, they hand over their bundles to the island. She brings in a men's sewing machine, because, while the women held at Ellis Island have long been working as seamstresses, the male detainees include some excellent Jewish tailors after all. She tries to get a new ball, because the old one's fallen into the Bay yet again and the immigrants' sports teams are struggling anyway — they can barely start playing before someone new arrives or someone departs. She hunts for books in various languages, because she's noticed that those who secure entry to the US like to bring a book with them; it's the current fashion. (A memento Ludmila might possibly give people she particularly likes is a book she's written herself, a musical on Slavic themes titled *The Shepherds' Christmas Eve*; the cover shows a Russian Madonna in a headscarf with the features of an Orthodox icon.[176] This present might comfort those Amtorg escapees who'll never see their Russian homeland again.)

After leaving work, Ludmila goes to the store for a pound of liverwurst, because one German held at the island can't live without it. But there's one wish she won't fulfill — an Albanian highlander would like to have a donkey at Ellis.[177]

Haarlem House, Edward Corsi

On 1 November 1931 an American couple disembarks at Ellis Island — a 40-year-old black-haired man and his wife. As they sail past the Statue of Liberty the man recalls straining to see its shape in the fog when he was ten. This is Edward Corsi, the new commissioner of the island. Before taking over the station he wanted to go on an *incognito* private walk

around the island, taking advantage of the fact that the Ellis authorities permit visits, though, as it turns out, the zealous clerks start asking him so many questions at the entrance that he has to reveal his identity.

There were six of them that sailed to the island in 1907: his mother, his stepfather, and four children. The boys were named Eduardo and Giuseppe (after Garibaldi), the girls, Liberta and Helvetia (in gratitude to Switzerland, where the Italian republicans were able to hide out). His family lived in the medieval town of Capestrano in Abruzzo. His father, Filippo Corsi, explained to his son it was named after Saint John of Capestrano, who led 40,000 Christians to Belgrade *stopping the advance of Mahomet* ... *"He was a fighter for human rights,"* said Edward's father.[178]

Filippo was a fighter too, a student of Mazzini.[179] In Capestrano he founded the liberal publication *La Democrazia*, set up the first farming cooperative in central Italy, fought to unionize the railroad workers, and organized rallies. He had to leave the country, fleeing the police. Seven-year-old Edward, who accompanied his father, recalled a happy moment out on Lake Lugano, when their boat, as it crossed the border, took down the Italian flag and raised the Swiss one — from that moment they were safe.

In Switzerland they received word that Tuscany had elected Filippo Corsi to the Italian parliament. He traveled there to thank the voters. His election guaranteed him immunity. He was to speak in the town of Massa before thousands of his supporters, but — as his son later recounted — he only managed to utter *Cittadini!* (Citizens!), before he turned around and died of a heart attack.

Edward's mother remarried, and his entire family, thanks to support from his father's political allies, emigrated to America. They moved into a tenement on the East Side of Manhattan near Harlem, with one window overlooking a dingy street. His mother didn't want to live this way; she fell ill, returned to Italy, and there she died.

Edward's stepfather, a professional soldier with no other qualifications, became a manual laborer. He earned $11 a week, *which was barely enough keep our bodies and souls together*. They had to supply their own heating for the tenement apartment. Edward and Giuseppe collected lumps of coal from the freight yard.

> On one cold winter day we went there as usual, and crawled under a standing train of cars which had not moved for many weeks. I finished sooner than Giuseppe, and was waiting for him on the other side when suddenly the cars were set in motion. I heard him cry out sharply once, and then there was no sound. The cars moved on, and I saw him lying on the ground, one of his arms torn and mangled ... A doctor came and amputated the arm ...[180]

Now, returning to Ellis Island 24 years later, Corsi remembers how he and Giuseppe mistook the skyscrapers of Manhattan for a rock crag.

Corsi's first paid job, while still a schoolboy, was as a lamplighter. He rose at 4.00 am and put out the streetlamps in a given area. He had to finish before the city began teeming with people. It wasn't so far removed from the start of Robert Watchorn's working life, rushing to open and close ventilation doors in mine corridors.

The area had a lot of youngsters hanging around. The police didn't like them grouping up on the street and would chase them away. There was also Haarlem House, a "settlement house" for the poor, but the Italian families were afraid it might draw their children into Protestantism. Corsi went into this brownstone building, which seemed a mysterious fortress to him, to ask if the youngsters might make use of it. Of course, but he had to make sure to keep the group under control, not damage the furniture or smash the windows. This was the start of his social life in his new country. *It was as if a wide door to America had been opened to me.*[181]

Together they organized a baseball team and talked about what to change in the neighborhood. Corsi developed an interest in American history, went to college, graduated from law school, and organized a fundraiser for Haarlem House, which had grown too cramped. A new building was indeed built that focused the neighborhood's social life, assimilated immigrants into America, organized vacations for tenement children, taught English, provided medical care, helped young mothers, and held sports lessons. At Haarlem House locals also exchanged views and formed campaign groups — for instance, for the city to build more playgrounds, and for tenement landlords to treat their tenants better. The House — now run by Corsi, who also made a name for himself as a correspondent for New York newspapers — revitalized the entire neighborhood. And Corsi's favorite politician was Fiorello La Guardia, who'd gathered his strength and returned to politics. In 1923, local votes sent him back to Congress, where he'd serve five terms.

In 1931 President Herbert Hoover invites Corsi to Washington. He repeats to him what presidents have generally said to future Ellis Island commissioners: *I think you can clean up the mess down there.*

He means corruption has once again been uncovered at the island: two ordinary clerks were issuing false entry-papers in exchange for bribes. Commissioner Day had nothing to do with it, but submitted his resignation nonetheless.

Corsi notices the president has aged greatly. *The lines of his face had deepened. His hair was snow-white. He personified in his physical aspect the whole tragedy of the Depression.*

He takes the train back from Washington. On the way he lets his emotions cool off — an Italian-born immigrant probably cannot accept the position he has just been offered. Yet he's convinced an immigrant should be the one to fill it. He disembarks at Pennsylvania Station and continues on foot. Entering Times Square, he sees the news ticker on what's still called the New York Times Building (though the paper has already moved elsewhere) declaring:

President Hoover To-day Named Edward Corsi
Commissioner of Immigration at Ellis Island.[182]

Farewell, Promised Land

The United States unemployment register in 1930 shows 3 million, including 180,000 in Manhattan. Nine months later unemployment grows to 6 million, and in 1932, to 13–15 million (25–30 per cent of them fit to work). Eleven of the 25 American banks collapse. Nine million savings accounts are wiped out. National income is halved.

People pour on to the streets of New York, seeking any kind of work and any kind of income — many sell off their personal possessions. Hospitals rescue people emaciated with hunger. Photos taken in this period by reporters and amateurs show people in long lines for handouts of bread from aid organizations, or cauldrons of free soup. Typically, there are no women at all in these lines. These are unemployed men lined up, doing their best to maintain their dignity, in caps, or hats, ties, and sometimes even bow ties, yet their eyes show clearly this is an arduous time, not a masquerade. If we arranged these photos of charity kitchens in chronological order, over time we'd see fewer ties and hats, but more sunken faces. The city has lost its glow, some of the streetlamps have been turned off. Who knows if these days Corsi the lamplighter would have work before going to school?

In 1930 the number of people coming into the United States was nearly five times the number leaving it. Barely two years later, in 1932, the Depression causes nearly three times as many people to emigrate from the United States of their own free will than choose to enter. Sailing out are 103,295 emigrants. Sailing in are 35,576 immigrants (including 21,500 via the Port of New York).

In the worst years of the Depression — and it lasts a long time (only the industrial exertion of the Second World War brings it to an end) — forced internal emigration is underway all across America, from villages to towns, from state to state, in search of bread, work, hope. Farmers are abandoning homesteads they can't maintain. They leave signs reading *Evacuation Sale, Furniture All Must Be Sold* and load their essential possessions into dilapidated cars. Some families travel miles to relatives'. In many states in 1934 and 1936, the skies send down yet another misfortune — droughts and gales covering everything in gray dust.

Corsi thinks of the former immigrants to America now leaving America to return to their old countries as a defeated army.

It is an inspiring sight to watch a mighty parade, to hear
martial music, to view the gorgeous costumes and note
the uplifted chins beneath eager determined eyes. But how
different, and what a contrast, is an army in retreat! The
broken ranks, the maimed and wounded, the dying, the
desperately struggling, proceeding anywhere but toward the
original objective. Such is the contrast between the caravan
of immigration to America, and the exodus of those hapless
ones who, old and broken, defeated, discouraged, the better
parts of their lives spent in vain, often turn in refuge toward
their homelands after disappointments in America![183]

Despite this exodus, President Hoover — who took the reins of
government in 1929, the year of the dramatic stock-market crash —
would like nothing so much as to close the US border to immigration
entirely. Yet that would be too radical a step, even in a time of mass
unemployment. The Labor Department decides at least to expel as
many unwanted and illegal foreigners from the United States as they
can and sets their number at 400,000. So once again to Ellis Island — as
in the days of fearing the Huns, fearing the Reds, or fearing the lice —
falls the unpleasant tasks of jailing and deportation.

In 1930, still under Commissioner Day, it attains its annual record
for deportations. It removes 18,142 people from the United States.

Jacob Auerbach, On Uniforms

One of the inspectors who introduces themselves to the new commissioner Edward Corsi is Jacob Auerbach, who arrived from the
shtetl near Brest-Litovsk *like Jonah inside the whale* and associated the
glowing slogan *Lipton's Coffee — Lipton's Cocoa — Lipton's Tea* on the

New Jersey coast with the *Mene, Mene, Tekel, Upharsin* on the wall of King Belshazzar's palace. Today, with his new homeland mired in the Depression, he might remember that association as prophetic. Yet grimness is the last thing on his mind.

After coming to the United States he worked for a shopkeeper and studied accounting in the evenings. He became a city employee. However, he wanted to work with people, not documents, and one day he told himself: *I have experience as an immigrant. I know what it feels like. I know that this country, the United States of America, is built of immigrants. What can I do about it?*

He passed the necessary exams and got a job at Ellis Island.

> ... if a Russian were made the czar of Moscow, they couldn't have felt any more exhilarated than I was, especially the work itself, to talk to people. My job was to ask them questions, find out, check their papers, find out whether they are eligible to land, whom they are going to, and so on and so forth.

His uniform brings him the most joy. He tells the story years later:

> in Europe, look, I was a kid, I was in Europe. I saw the police down there. I, [saw] how they treated the people. You were nobody. The cop on the beat could slap you in the face for no reason at all, for nothing ... I saw how the people, the human, they treat us here. And, by the way, they were all in uniform down there. To me somebody in uniform is somebody who is very important, for good or for bad, but he is important. And I should be in uniform, wearing a uniform, and be respected? ... [A]nd getting a good salary, and having a very pleasant job. What else could a poor immigrant want?[184]

Yet the uniform that allows Inspector Auerbach to enter Marlene Dietrich's cabin to conduct the necessary interview (she declared she wouldn't stand in line) is no match for the United States Public Health Service uniform, the handsomest on the island. These are described in a directive from the Treasury Department in 1914, with precise drawings in numbered tables attached.

The beak, tongue, talons, and wings of the eagle on the cap are embroidered in gold thread like on a baroque chasuble. The belt of black Moroccan leather known as *maroquin* has a leather lining, is decorated with gold thread and attached to a buckle with Asclepius' serpent wound around an anchor. A small sword is worn for the dress uniform, and a formal civil uniform has also been thought up: a white tuxedo jacket with shoulder loops, a white shirt with a standing collar, a black bow tie and a waistcoat. There are two buttons under the bow tie, four on the waistcoat, and the tuxedo jacket is single-breasted.

Do any of the doctors at Ellis Island have such a tuxedo jacket? We don't know. In group photos they appear modest, more like soldiers than *bon vivants*.

The Health Service has its serpent of Asclepius, but the island's other employees have also had distinguishing symbols designed for them, more familiar and comprehensible. For instance:

Cooks are to wear on their arms an elegant, embroidered crescent moon,

carpenters — a framing square,

laundrymen — an iron,

messengers — a wing,

the shipkeeper — crossed keys,

the night watchman — a lantern, of the sort you'd carry into a cowshed.

When Jacob Auerbach puts on his inspector's uniform, Alexander Harkavy, author of the Hebrew–English self-teaching textbook — the book that opened the door to Jacob's new life — is still alive.

Did they meet? It's possible. Alexander Harkavy was born in Novogrudok in 1863, the year of the January Uprising, and emigrated to America after the pogrom of 1881. A writer, lecturer, and author of numerous linguistic texts, including the famous Yiddish–English–Hebrew Dictionary (1925), he enjoyed the respect of Commissioner William Williams and for a few years was a HIAS representative on the island. He died the year the Second World War broke out.

We Need to Talk, Edward Corsi

Anyone thinking back about Commissioner Edward Corsi would mention his diplomatic talents, particularly his skill at talking to the media. Corsi is the first commissioner at Ellis who understands the power of the Fourth Estate and makes every effort to win it over, with the certain aid of his own journalistic experience. When the *New York World* sent him to Italy, he conducted an hour-long interview with its 40th prime minister, Benito Mussolini, and was surprised *il Duce* didn't say a word in their common native tongue.

Just after installing himself at Ellis Island, Corsi sets up three important and pleasant events, each including a delicious lunch and a tour of the island. To the first he invites local reporters; he assures them the island is open to them and they can meet with the internees. The second he organizes for the foreign press corps, for years frequent critics of the immigration service at Ellis Island. At the third he hosts consuls from the countries that send the most immigrants to New York. These events are followed by press and radio interviews. Corsi gives these himself and encourages more important staff members to do so as well. His motto is: *We have nothing to hide!*

Unlike Commissioner Howe, who specialized in causing friction on the Ellis Island–Washington line, Corsi also takes care to maintain good communication with his superiors. His family background and life experiences place him more on the side of the immigrants than of the bureaucracy and police. He intends — within the scope of his abilities — to ease the lot of those facing expulsion. Labor Secretary William Doak, who'd like to deport as many as possible, accepts invitations to the island on several occasions and gets to know the procedures, the children's school, and the hospitals; he observes how the detainees occupy themselves and his heart softens. This means police operations hunting for illegal immigrants also soften, and the number of deportations shrinks. Corsi is so persuasive that he also receives considerable funds to clean up and improve Ellis Island. He does his best to maintain good relations at the island and, like Howe, has a suggestion box installed, open to all. He reads the suggestions and responds.

His predecessors could envy him. He has a calm atmosphere and comparatively little work. In 1933 about 13,000 immigrants come into the Port of New York. In 1934 — about 17,600.

Corsi therefore can indulge in long chats with the island's senior personnel. He's curious if anyone remembers a family from Abruzzi, two adults and four children: Eduardo, Giuseppe, Liberta, and Helvetia, who arrived in 1907. They tell him he should ask the Italian interpreter Frank Martoccia about it. But Martoccia, who still has a flawless memory and a luxuriant shock of hair now gone completely gray, replies that in 1907 under Commissioner Watchorn, Ellis accepted over a million people.

What was that like? How did the island operate in those years, between Corsi's first and second arrival?

Martoccia tells the commissioner about the chalk marks; the dervish dance that got all of Ellis on its feet, even though it was a protest against feeding them like unbelievers; the rebellion of a Gypsy caravan convinced their children had been kidnapped (they'd been sent to the hospital on suspicion of measles); the odyssey of Nathan Cohen; the stowaways; about the freaks and the eccentrics. Ellis has other long-time employees. Byron H. Uhl introduces himself to Corsi as a relic of the island, just like its first buildings. Dr Frederick A. Theis remembers perfectly the mental patients enjoying the explosions on Black Tom wharf. Superintendent Percy A. Baker recalls all the problems he had with supplies before realizing Italians don't like dried fish, Scandinavians don't want spaghetti, Greeks like sweets, and it's best not to offer tea to the English; but all the same he had to serve 9,000 meals a day.

This is all incredibly interesting to Corsi. He finds it useful not only for his book about Ellis Island, but also in his day-to-day working life. A commissioner hosts important personages and should be an interesting guide to the island — of today and yesterday. He's just been visited by Eleanor Roosevelt, currently the First Lady of New York State, soon First Lady of the United States. She comes to the island with a group of students. She wants, the *New York Herald Tribune* writes, to show them *the machinery of immigration in full operation.*

They look down on the Great Hall from the gallery and see handicrafts by the detained men; Mrs Roosevelt, herself an accomplished craftswoman, praises the colorful scarves and knitted socks. They go to the kitchen for a tasting and learn a day's meals cost a dollar, and Mrs Roosevelt notes that New York prisons cater for 26¢ a day. But after all, she corrects herself, this is not a prison.

One of the students asks how often they change the sheets in the dormitory.

"Oh, every day."

"My, but your laundry bill must be tremendous," worries the student.

"They probably have a laundry right in the place," Mrs Roosevelt replies.

They see a pencil drawing: the Liberty Bell.

The artist, an immigrant, spared no paper or effort.

Mrs Roosevelt asks if he was let into the United States.

"No, he was rejected as an undesirable."

"I'm sorry."[185]

The New Deal, Corsi and Fiorello

The space between the second and third islands is now completely filled in and covered in grass, while trees imported from Britain are being planted all over Ellis. Why from Britain? Perhaps they were a gift.

The large roof outside the main entrance has been dismantled (now that crowds no longer stand there in long lines, this protection from the rain is no longer necessary), and the space this frees up is ornamented with flowers. Inspections are gentler at the island, because for some time now they've routinely taken place before embarkation. What Consul La Guardia introduced years before in Fiume has finally become widespread practice — thanks to a series of directives by the American immigration authorities. In 1933 just under 4,500 immigrants are detained at the island, and generally don't stay longer than two or three days.

Franklin Delano Roosevelt, a Democrat, becomes the new president. America can feel the favorable winds of the New Deal.[186]

The president extends Commissioner Corsi's term. But Corsi will soon depart. He asserts everything on the island now runs itself and all that's left for him to do is sign letters and paperwork. He's leaving for an important position in the city government. He'll be working with New York's new mayor, Fiorello La Guardia, as his head of social assistance. Their friendship grew stronger during La Guardia's election campaign. Corsi supported Fiorello, taking advantage of his own popularity in the city's Italian neighborhoods as well as using his diplomatic talents. They're talents the hot-headed La Guardia lacks; he shouts in his falsetto voice, runs when he should walk, and tells his secretary to throw away excess official letters.

Corsi has recently had enough time at Ellis Island to write a book about it. He asks Fiorello for a foreword. The new mayor opens it with a compliment: *Mr Corsi has written a good book*. Good, because it not only offers an engaging look at the island's organization, but also its human side. Today Mr Corsi cares for hundreds and thousands of families in New York.

He closes his foreword with a thought:

> ... the rigidity of the immigration laws might have
> caused many individual injustices and hardships, still
> America is the land of opportunity. The author's own life
> typifies that.[187]

Today La Guardia no longer needs to answer journalists with the words: *Could I?* He's mayor of the largest city in the United States and his goals align with the president's plans. Now he *can*.

A million children live in slums strewn across his city's five boroughs. These families have an average income of $700 per annum. They can pay no more than seven dollars a month for an apartment. For that price, La Guardia wants them to receive decent surroundings. He won't rest until he forces this on the budgetary authorities in

Washington and the landowners in New York.

Public works are being launched across America, aiming to offer not only physical but also intellectual and even artistic jobs. The well-known sculptor and painter Edward Laning is commissioned to paint a mural in the dining room at Ellis Island. Murals are appearing all over America — following the example of Mexico, where powerful works by contemporary Mexican artists unite the people's power with a modern form. This idea appeals in the United States. On the dining-room walls Laning paints immigrants' lives in their chosen country. He has a space 110 feet long and 7 feet high (in some places) to work with. It's no trouble coming up with ideas, because the immigrant odyssey furnishes them in abundance. Laning frets that the dining room has six windows and tall doors, but he must compose the immigrants' heroic labors in American slaughterhouses, steelworks, forests, mines, and farms in a way that makes it all flow like a banner in the wind.

Birthday Party

On 11 April 1940 Ellis Island celebrates its fiftieth birthday. This is not measured from the day the station opened, which would make it two years later, but the date of its establishment in law on 11 April 1890.

Neighboring Governors Island fires an 11-gun salute and sends Ellis a military band with a patriotic repertoire, while the distinguished ferryboat *Ellis Island*, festooned in garlands and bunting, brings VIPs and journalists from Manhattan. Commissioner Rudolph Reimer — engineer, banker, Democratic politician, and son of a wealthy business-man who immigrated from Germany — offers the staff a free lunch (a fairly modest expense, because for years lunch has been systematically shrunk), and gives a speech recalling the historic circumstances under which the station was called into existence.

Soon after these celebrations, Commissioner Reimer retires. He is the final commissioner of Ellis Island. Now the station will be led by directors; the post is not as important as it once was. Commissioner Reimer hands over power to Director Byron H. Uhl — meaning he is left to handle the case of Maria Rasputin Saloviff. Madame Saloviff — who, she says, is the famous monk's daughter — arrived in 1937, employed as a lion tamer in the famous Ringling Bros. and Barnum & Bailey circus. She's long since overstayed her visa and must be deported.

The World War comes late to Ellis Island, as it did a quarter-century before, though initial signals have been coming for a few years, ones America ignored. Immigration opponents in Congress refuse to loosen the laws to allow entry for Jews from Germany and Austria threatened by Hitler's policies. Congress therefore maintains the hardline policy of the previous administration of President Herbert Hoover. This softens somewhat after Austria's annexation by Germany, the fall of France, and the defeat of Norway, but the United States still carefully guards its borders. Through all the years Hitler is in power, the US accepts barely 250,000 refugees of Nazism.

In the view of the historian Thomas Pitkin:

> The tradition of America as an asylum for the oppressed, long under erosion, seemed almost to have vanished. The flow was not on a scale to affect operations at Ellis Island to any marked degree, except for extra paperwork ...[188]

What does endure, however, is the tradition of fearing foreign enemies. As early as September 1939, immediately after the German attack on Poland, President Franklin D. Roosevelt authorizes J. Edgar Hoover, head of the Federal Bureau of Investigation, to prepare a list of *enemy aliens*, and in 1940 the Immigration and Naturalization Service is moved out of the Department of Labor into the stricter and more suspicious control of the Department of Justice. All foreigners applying for American visas now have their fingerprints taken.

Shortly after the attack on Pearl Harbor, by signature of President Roosevelt, all citizens of Japan, Germany, and Italy living in the United States — nearly a million people — are declared potential threats to the state, and Ellis Island immediately receives 608 temporary prisoners of America — Japanese, Germans, and Italians.

Fiorello La Guardia contributes to this. He is now not only mayor of New York, but president of the United States Conference of Mayors (and in 1942 he becomes director of the Office of Civilian Defense). The moment news comes of the attack on Pearl Harbor, he orders Japanese New Yorkers to stay in their homes. Their clubs and gathering places are to be closed. Fiorello is absolutely convinced the good of America demands vigilance. America's vigilance sends to Ellis Island the Japanese girl Sumi Utsushigawa.

Sumi Shimatsu Utsushigawa, Do Unto Others

My name Sumiko means "pure." And Utsushigawa means "reflecting river." I was born August 14, 1928 in Los Angeles, California, right in the middle of Little Tokyo. Forty-nine Japanese men were in Los Angeles at the turn of the century. My father was raised by Buddhist monks. He came to the United States and took pictures for the *LA Times* and *LA Examiner*. He was the very first Japanese photographer in Los Angeles. He went back to Japan and married my mother, and she came back on a later boat. My father loved American food. So he would cook the American food and my mother would cook the Japanese food. My father wanted to buy a home, my mother wanted to go back home because she was one of nine children. She is a Zen Buddhist. We had a Japanese dancing teacher that I grew up with ... It was about eleven o'clock that I heard that Pearl Harbor was bombed. Being thirteen, I did not know where Pearl Harbor was or what it meant. We just heard this was a war across the sea. I was really, totally American. I recall people running in and out of our second-story home. FBI agents were trying to arrest people. My father was arrested in 1942, March thirteenth. My mother, secretly, had packed him away one suitcase, and my father was so furious, because he felt she was disloyal to him. When I came home from junior high school I saw my mother sitting and I looked at the house and it was like a tornado hit it. So we just sat. So she says, "Go out and buy some sardine and spinach. We'll have it for dinner." But we couldn't eat. By May ninth we were busy trying to sell furniture, our piano for twenty-five dollars, our new refrigerator for fifteen dollars, one of my father's enlarging machines he had bought for $150, she sold for fifteen dollars. My Japanese kimono she had at a friend's basement.

In Los Angeles there were thirty women who were arrested from the women's club. In September 1943 we went to Ellis Island. They had the machine gun trained on our back. We searched for our father and I looked around, because I heard he never shaved after he was arrested so I was looking for a man with a beard. But because he wanted to have us recognize him he shaved.

You know we don't hug. You don't, all you do is see... I think we spoke from our heart not saying a word.

Five families were allowed to go to Crystal City, Texas, another detention camp. On my birthday, August fourteenth 1945, I thought my girlfriend is going to come bake me a cake. All of a sudden, all the whistle and bells, and sirens were going off Crystal City. And weeping. The first generation were weep when they realize it was really true that Japan lost. That there was unconditional surrender. I felt like oh, great! But you're hearing men crying. My father was seventy when the war ended. Whatever he had was gone. He wouldn't go back to Los Angeles.

My father and mother were Buddhist, but he gave us the gift of Christmas. I don't say I'm a Christian. I don't like that word. I like to say I follow the teachings of Christ. I also believe in Buddhism. Buddha had a lot to teach too, and so did Mohammed. All the great messengers of life have been there to point a way and they all teach the same thing, The Golden Rule: do unto others as you would have others do unto you. If you did, there would be peace. There would be no conflict. But nobody practices their religion. They wear it on Sundays or on the Sabbath. I had six children, I enjoy living a fruitful life, and God has been good to me. I feel I was allowed to go through all this experience, have a memory that I have knowing what I have gone through so that I can not only tell the stories, but also to have other people bring their awareness up. Life is really a school. You learn from it, and you got to grow from it, and become somebody, and show others how to walk the life.[189]

Enough Water Now, Byron H. Uhl

Byron H. Uhl, who introduced himself to former Commissioner Corsi as a relic of the island, is therefore performing the leadership duties not of an immigration station, but a detention station — just as it was during the First World War, as he remembers clearly.

His employees are occupied with upholding the Geneva Conventions. The Great Hall with its beautiful wooden furniture has been transformed into a day room for German families; the dormitories, reached via the gallery over the Great Hall, are occupied by Japanese and European families. When a new wave of internees arrives and conditions grow cramped, the Ellis staff make room elsewhere and the (largely superfluous) immigration service on the island finally relocates to a building in Manhattan. In 1943 the number of detainees on the island reaches 6,000. The internees demand more sports fields and more varied food. So a cafeteria opens serving German, Italian, Central European, and Japanese dishes, employing detainees on work contracts. Each group of enemy aliens is entitled to their own spokesperson. These are generally skillful and rigorous in making sure the law is enforced, and they secure a range of concessions. For instance, the German group may celebrate Hitler's birthday every year and they receive German government financial support through the mediation of the Swiss embassy.

Legalistic Byron H. Uhl would be the last person to resist the requirements of a convention signed by the United States. The reporters who visit him in August 1942 for the fiftieth anniversary of his work on the island — marked by a luncheon with La Guardia and three former commissioners: Day, Corsi, and Reimer, as well as a senior official from Washington who declares Ellis Island should change its name to Uhl Island — nevertheless find him in a glum mood. He declares he's now had enough of this water around him. He'd like to settle for this rest of his life in a little country house with a vista of green.[190]

Asked if over his years of work one particular immigrant has stuck in his mind, he mentions — doubtless to his listeners' surprise — General Cipriano Castro, ex-president of Venezuela, a despot swept out of office by a coup d'état.

Why him in particular?

He was a blackguard and a cutthroat, but I admired the little runt. The general had a body covered in scars. *He was vociferous, obstreperous ...*[191]

Uhl stays in post until November, then he and the island part ways, for the first time and forever.

William Williams, Liberty

The luncheon in Byron H. Uhl's honor takes place on 18 August. And the next day, completely unrelatedly, at a shipyard in Richmond, California, a ship is launched called the *William Williams*, belonging to the great Liberty family.

The Liberty Fleet is one of the most remarkable undertakings of the Second World War. From 1941 to 1945, the United States, wounded by submarine attacks in the world's various bodies of water, builds 2,751 transport ships in its 18 shipyards and names them after distinguished Americans.

The SS *William Williams* bears the name of the former Ellis Island commissioner, but is dedicated to his ancestor and namesake, who signed the Declaration of Independence.

Ten months after its launch, the ship is targeted by a Japanese submarine. The submarine's commander — Takaichi Kinashi, who has already torpedoed several American ships — does not ultimately sink the *William Williams*, and moves on. This attack takes place near the Fiji archipelago. The ship is towed to New Zealand and withdrawn from military service. After a renovation it's renamed the *Venus*.

In 1961 the ship is scrapped in Oakland, California.

The Liberty Fleet, built at an incredible American pace, was not meant to last. Roughly five years of performance were demanded of it. The *William Williams* aka *Venus* had outlived its usefulness at any rate.

Jacob Auerbach, On Gratitude

At the end of the war, Jacob Auerbach learns how much his family has lost. Twenty-three of his close relatives and 27 more distant ones went up in smoke at Auschwitz in 1943.

Jacob Auerbach is grateful to America for his life and the lives of his uncles, who were allowed in many years before. He intends to keep every medal and every button of his uniform as an eternal memento.

Churchill, Williams, Eight Hundred Steaks

It would seem the island experienced no problems with food supplies, either during the war or just after, yet shortages do affect the most marvelous New York institutions, including the University Club in Manhattan, where William Williams still lives and which elegantly balances the old with the new: it has set up a backgammon room, opened a fitness center (in a photograph we see a dignified gentleman training his stomach on an exercise plank), and made room for three squash courts, including one for doubles, with a large locker room, lounge, and showers.

On 18 March 1946 the club throws a celebratory lunch in honor of Winston Churchill. The council has tallied up the guests who will come from distant cities and the ingredients needed to feed them. It's decided to serve filet mignon; the cooks have requested 800 steaks, but wartime restrictions on meat are still in force in New York. Obtaining the necessary portions demands — as the club chronicle records — begging and borrowing. They succeed; the necessary provisions are secured.

No guest list has survived, so we cannot be sure if William Williams attended. Yet it seems impossible that a club resident would forgo such a significant and interesting event, especially one taking place just one floor down from his apartment. Not everyone fitted into the dining room; some of those gathered had to listen to Churchill from the lobby. Apparently his speech was superb, though its contents are now unknown, for the club strictly abides by its rules, one of which is: no club speeches are to be transcribed or recorded.

All that was written down are a dozen or so words on a piece of paper Churchill left on a table. But it's difficult to work out what thoughts he might have woven around these instructions:

> Fraternal Association
> Communism
> Great Britain Imperialist?
> Stability revolutionary?
> Loan — important ★★★

He devoted part of the speech to the United Sates and made separate notes for this:

> Strength
> Strikes
> War unthinkable
> "Dreadnought"[192]

As a memento of the event, the club hangs a wonderful portrait of its guest. This William Williams does not live to see. He dies in his apartment on 8 February 1947. Earlier he made a donation to the club; its amount was kept discreetly secret.[193]

Key Largo

According to a report in the immigration service's monthly magazine,[194] in 1949 the island's detainees have, among other things: the opportunity to work for ten cents an hour (the working day may not exceed eight hours), meals containing 4,100 calories a day (while civilian workers, American citizens, must make do with 3,300 calories), a chapel with an electric organ and a confessional for Catholics, highchairs for children, and film screenings twice a week.

So we can presume the detainees see *Key Largo*, starring Edward G. Robinson, who was born in Romania as Emanuel Goldenberg and sailed to the United States via Ellis Island in 1903 at the age of ten. The film has just come out and is causing a stir not just thanks to its actors — for Robinson's co-stars are Lauren Bacall and Humphrey Bogart — but also its topicality. Robinson (for $12,500 a week) portrays the gangster Rocco, inspired by the notorious Lucky Luciano, considered the father of the Mafia in America.

Lucky was born in Italy as Salvatore Lucania and came to the United States shortly after Robinson, also at the age of ten.

Two years before John Houston films *Key Largo*, Lucky Luciano returns to Ellis Island. The United States is deporting him to his homeland. Compared to his crimes, this is a very gentle way of getting rid of Luciano. But the gangster rendered certain services to America during the war, thanks to his influence in strategically important Sicily.

In *Key Largo*, Robinson–Rocco–Lucky declares:

> After living in the USA for more than thirty-five years
> they called me an undesirable alien. Me. Johnny Rocco.
> Like I was a dirty Red or something!

Whose Raindrop

The *enemy aliens* are leaving the island and returning home. Though not all of them; Sumi Shimatsu's father never returns to Los Angeles.

Now arriving at the island are *displaced persons*, those deprived of a place to live by changed borders and political systems; many of these are Poles. What permits the DPs into the United States is a special law[195] signed by President Harry Truman, but they come in a trickle. It's said the DPs, before they leave Europe, are *washed seven times in the waters of Jordan*.[196] And instead of proceeding quickly through the US border, they often linger at Ellis. After all, they're an uncertain element, their fates fantastical and incomprehensible. It's hard to trust the experiences they recount. The immigration inspectors are convinced these newcomers have no interest in disclosing the truth, like the poor who used to arrive from Italy or Galicia, though naturally their reasons are different. These people have come face-to-face with totalitarian systems, and who knows if they were drawn into their service. They need to be handled with caution, and the new Internal Security Act serves that purpose,[197] barring entry to the United States to members of communist and fascist parties. This means, as has so often (or really, almost always) happened, detainees facing different accusations rub shoulders at the island, and each has a different experience of waiting there.

Joseph Gallo, whose family came to the US from Sicily (*my father, may he rest in peace, is one of thirteen boys, believe it or not*), watches over these inmates and has a good rapport with them. He's 20 years old and a great lover of softball. This is a game similar to baseball, but played on a smaller field with a larger ball and lighter bat. He's organized a team on the island. They form their own league, play against other government agencies: the postal service, customs officers, lawyers. The foreigners aren't allowed into the league but they maintain the field and place bets. When Joseph's doing his rounds of the rooms in the evening, they ask him, *Hey, Joe, who's good tonight?* Gallo replies: *Well, we got a pretty good competition tonight. It's an iffy game.* Then they press him: *Do you think we're going to win?* And he says: *Look, don't bet heavy.* Because the detainees are real gamblers, which is a consequence of their boredom. Joseph has confiscated their cards but they find other ways. When there are no league games, they slice oranges in two and bet on how many seeds are in each half. Or if they don't have an orange they might stand by the window when it's raining and cheer on rain-drops, seeing which one will drip faster than the others. The Chinese especially are major gamblers.[198] At first the immigration service allows poker and other games, supposing if people are occupied they'll be happy and won't cause so much trouble. But things get out of hand.

Now and then fistfights even take place. Detainees have to be locked up. Some even have to be sent to the government prison on West Street.[199]

The well-known Czech actor and theater producer George Voskovec has a different memory of his waiting period (which in his case lasted almost nine months; he left Ellis in 1951). His wife is American, he's lived in the US for the past seven years, he applied for a reentry permit to the US before a visit to Czechoslovakia, but nevertheless was scooped up at the airport and deposited on the island because an informer claimed he was a communist sympathizer. Voskovec kills time reading American newspapers cover to cover and giving himself over to observation. He notices the ping-pong tables are constantly busy, but the players never line up for them. Good organization saves time, but here the goal is to waste time. He also notices himself growing hard-hearted.

> The people who have been here for any length of time
> know the situation and have their own tables and chairs,
> but the new arrivals give us trouble. "This table is
> occupied!" I say to them, putting on my iciest expression.
> Or they come over and start reading my newspaper.
> "That is a private paper!" I tell them. They retreat
> in confusion. I haven't a single qualm. My ethics are
> completely institutional, you see. The others who have
> been here awhile do the same. We wouldn't think of
> approaching each other's places, except very occasionally,
> to make a formal call. It's as if each of us, with enormous
> pains, had built a wall around his few square feet of
> cement floor. To break in uninvited would be like
> breaking in the door of someone's house ...
>
> Many of these people have lived a long time in police
> states. They are terrified of talking too freely — every
> friendly person seems a possible informer.[200]

After his wartime wanderings, Zbigniew Korfanty, the son of the late conservative politician Wojciech Korfanty, sailed from the United Kingdom to New York to join his wife and daughter. He's convinced he's ended up at Ellis Island due to an informer's claim of communist collaboration, but he never reveals whom he suspects made this false testimony. He is ultimately helped by an intervention from Stanisław Mikołajczyk, former prime minister of the Polish government-in-exile, who in 1949 declares under oath,

> during the war Mr Zbigniew Korfanty served in the
> Polish Army organized abroad by Gen. Sikorski ...
> and with all my power I state his political views were
> absolutely democratic and anticommunist.

Korfanty spends six months at Ellis and leaves it exhausted and with no faith in the future. He doesn't resume his legal practice. He will work as a manual laborer at a gas station and then an auto shop.[201]

Melville's Ghost

Voskovec and Korfanty leave the island, the writer Cyril L.R. James arrives. He was born in Trinidad, he presents himself as an enemy of Stalin, Hitler, and all forms of totalitarianism; a Marxist and a Trotskyist, he is an ardent opponent of colonialism, especially in his book *Black Jacobins*. All it takes is the FBI developing an interest for him to be held at Ellis Island to explain his complicated file. C.L.R. James's ultimate passion is investigating the thought of Herman Melville, particularly as expressed in his famous novel *Moby-Dick, or The Whale*, written in 1851. For the last three years James has given many talks on Melville and was just about to embark on a book about him. Exile at Ellis Island is not good for a person with duodenal cancer, which demands a special diet, unobtainable here. Yet for a person who is analyzing the fates of the crew of the whaler *Pequod*, a small community subjected to its captain's tyranny, it has its advantages.

> Melville built his gigantic structure, a picture of world civilization, using one small vessel, with a crew of thirty-odd men, for the most part isolated from the rest of the world. Here was I, just about to write, suddenly projected on to an island isolated from the rest of society, where American administrators and officials, and American security officers controlled the destinies of perhaps a thousand men, sailors, "isolatoes," renegades and castaways from all parts of the world. It seems now as if destiny had taken a hand to give me a unique opportunity to test my ideas of this great American writer.

Cyril James' internment lasts six months. James has no interest in softball, he doesn't count the raindrops on the windowpanes, he writes his book *Mariners, Renegades & Castaways: The Story of Herman Melville and the World We Live In*. His experiences on the island make him realize how alive the questions Melville posed 101 years earlier are in 1952. In James' eyes, Captain Ahab's 30-man crew is a world federation of workers. Its members are loyal to no nation. The officers are American, of course, but the crew that serves them is attached to nothing and no one, it merely does its work, and its members' relationships arise from this work.

C.L.R. James claims Melville was plagued by precisely the same issues that trouble us today. Under what conditions can modern civilization endure? Are the catastrophes that *Moby-Dick*'s author saw approaching rooted in man's destructive character, or do they have other causes? Can the human species control them? Can modern man be happy, or is he, too, condemned to eternal suffering? Will he finally destroy himself?

> It was at this time I began to be aware that what was happening to me and the others on Ellis Island was, in miniature, a very sharp and direct expression of what was taking place in the world at large.

The rebellious Trinidadian author provides his book[202] with an epigraph from Melville's novel *Redburn*. This choice suggests James's imprisonment on Ellis Island did not affect his relationship to America as the mother of peoples:

> "Settled by the people of all nations, all nations may claim her for their own. You cannot spill a drop of American blood without spilling the blood of the whole world ... our blood is as the flood of the Amazon, made up of a thousand noble currents all pouring into one. We are not a nation, so much as a world ..."

Our Mary Daley

Many detainees at Ellis Island require psychiatric assistance. The hospital here has installed a modern instrument for electroshock therapy.

Dr James Louis Baker believes that for diagnoses of schizophrenia, electroshock therapy is much less dangerous than insulin therapy, and he does not hesitate to use it. The doctor lives on the island with his family; he has a lovely apartment, four bedrooms, a large living room, a kitchen, a bathroom. It's all beautifully furnished, there's only one problem — the stove and refrigerator are shipboard models and the house's power grid, specially modified for them, doesn't work with the sewing machine, mixer, or especially the television set. Dr Baker's family would love to enjoy a TV like everyone else in New York. But a rotary converter costs almost as much as a television itself. Luckily the hospital has just bought a marvelous rotary converter for administering electric shocks. Dr Baker has found it's perfectly suited to the TV. Now, after finishing his treatments, he brings the convertor home and the whole family can watch the evening shows.[203]

Photographs from the island confirm we are now in the modern television era. At the end of the forties in the Great Hall, which now acts as a giant living room for the detainees, we see no headscarves, nor a single bundle; the women have short hair, simple light-colored dresses barely to their knees, and sports shoes; they cross their legs when they sit down.

Keeping this living room in good shape is very expensive. The whole island is more expensive than ever before, because its surface area and equipment, which expanded as the numbers mounted, now serve fewer people. Over the post-war decade, Ellis receives an average of 103,000 people annually, compared to over a million immigrants in the peak year of 1907.

The press increasingly calls for Ellis Island simply to be closed. Not only does it cost America dear, not only does the rest of the world associate it more with the end of hopes than with their beginning, it's also an anachronism.

You need only lift your eyes and see the planes aiming for New York's LaGuardia airport, one of Mayor Fiorello's greatest works. He got it built on swamp and wasteland thanks to support from President Roosevelt, providing jobs for thousands of workers. He opened it on 15 October 1939 before a crowd of over 30,000 New Yorkers.[204]

The more planes appear in the skies over the island, the fewer of Ellis's employees remember "Little Flower", the interpreter. Almost all

of those who gave Ellis its color, tone, and range, the *metteurs-en-scène* of the great performance of the island, have already gone or are on their way out.

Robert Watchorn dies on 13 April 1944. He lived to build the Lincoln Library in his native Alfreton, though, unlike William Williams, not to see the launch of his own Liberty-series ship. The SS *Robert Watchorn* left the shipyard more than two months after its namesake's death at the age of 86. Thus two old commissioners whose island welcomed people off ships with dynastic, literary, revolutionary, and divine names have bestowed upon vessels their own names — one of them traced back to Plymouth Rock, the other to "Ellis Rock."

Byron H. Uhl dies in 1944. The year 1947 sees the deaths of: the island's most influential commissioner William Williams, Fiorello La Guardia (who found time to dictate his autobiography), and Dr Victor Safford (who lived to edit his father's sailing memoir and who will lie beside him in the family grave in Maine). In 1950 the architect of the ceiling over the Great Hall, Rafael Guastavino Jr, passes away, and in 1954, so does the interpreter Frank Martoccia.

One person who dies at the island a little before Martoccia did not stand out in Ellis's history, but certainly co-created it. This is the hospital attendant Mary Daley. Eleanor Irwin Park, a dietician, recalls preparing the menu every day while Mary Daley confided in her. Mary came to America in 1918 and worked many years at the island. She learned they were going to close the hospital and declared she refused to leave. *I've never slept anywhere but on Ellis Island and I don't intend to ever sleep anywhere but on Ellis Island.* The Coast Guard — Eleanor continues — was already making their way through the hospital picking up equipment to put in storage. They saw a sewing machine and wanted to take it. Then one person who knew Mary told one of the guards: fine, take the machine, but only if you take our Mary Daley too. She was already over 80. But they let Mary stay in the hospital. She lived in the rooms there. And in November or December she died. *But she never slept anywhere as far as she was concerned, but on Ellis Island.*[205]

The hospital closure is an omen of what's to come; but meanwhile the island's other departments are still operating and maintaining discipline. The best place to see this in action is on the deck of the ferryboat *Ellis Island*, which picks up the employees in the mornings and over a half-century has racked up a million miles. One of the inspecting clerks, summing up statistical data he's collected over the years, declares everyone who misses the boat is late by no more than 30 seconds — or so they claim. He concludes archly that if they shifted the schedule back one minute, no one would miss the boat. He also points out there is no record of anyone missing the boat home in the evening.[206]

The island station seems certain to be closed down. But what to do with the detainees? A radical government decision helps answer this question. Evidently, the right moment has arrived. Stalin is dead. The Korean War has ended, the Vietnam War has not yet begun. In July 1955 the leaders of the United States, the Soviet Union, the United Kingdom, and France meet at a conference in Geneva in a spirit of détente.

The Attorney General of the United States, Herbert Brownell Jr, announces that on 11 November 1954, on the newly created Veteran's Day holiday, ceremonies will take place across the United States swearing in around 50,000 new citizens. Now, some of the detainees at Ellis can leave the island as free men and women, others will be transferred elsewhere.

On 12 November, the ferryboat *Ellis Island* takes the last foreigner from the island, the Norwegian sailor Arne Peterssen. The cheerful blond in civilian garb waves farewell and poses for reporters' photographs. He was detained a few days before for overstaying his leave at the port; he explains he'd lost track of time while partying on the Brooklyn waterfront. He returns home to Norway.

Summing Up

The statistics can now be closed. From 1892 to 1954, over 16.6 million immigrants sailed into the Port of New York. The overwhelming majority passed through Ellis Island. Over 610,000 were refused entry

to the United States. The excluded and repatriated included: nearly 220,000 likely to become a public charge, over 80,000 mentally and physically impaired, about 40,000 contract laborers, nearly 16,000 stowaways, over 13,600 illiterates, nearly 8,000 rejected for moral turpitude, and over 300 subversives.[207]

A financial assessment report of Ellis is prepared.

The value of the 27.5 acres of the island (or rather islands): $260,000.

The buildings: $5,877,000.

The ferryboat *Ellis Island*: $103,000.[208]

No closing ceremony for the island is organized. It is now merely a shell. The kitchen equipment, refrigerators, washing machines, and medical apparatuses have been dismantled. The ferryboat, after its years of distinguished service, returns to its channel between Island 1 and Island 2 and will see out its days there. Six guards remain on Ellis Island to patrol the abandoned grounds. The patrolling isn't easy. Now, in winter, darkness falls early, and in spring the island, more fertile now than in the days of the Lenni Lenape, will begin to be engulfed in vegetation.

Part VI

Still Waters

The Antiques Store, Ludmila Foxlee

Ludmila Foxlee was done working on the island even before the war. In 1937 she and her husband opened a small antiques store in the town of Madison, New Jersey. They treated it as a supplementary source of income, but Ludmila, who was always interested in objects that had more to say than modern manufactured goods, fell in love with her new occupation and dedicated more and more time to it. Maybe she also grew tired of difficult social work. In any case, she quit her job at Ellis Island. But she kept and organized all her notes. She intends to write a book about what she saw and did at the island.

If now, 20 years after leaving, she were to visit the abandoned station, she would see the largest antiques storeroom imaginable.

The crew that cleaned out Ellis didn't do so thoroughly — apparently they thought there was no point, better to write off some things immediately or shunt them into corners here and there, where they can await some eventual decision. The island is therefore full of equipment and objects from various eras. Some date back to the turn of the century, which in young America makes them very old, and possibly suitable for Ludmila and John Foxlee's antiques store.

Let's try to imagine strolling around the empty island, ideally in September, the most pleasant month in New York (so the guidebooks say), when the air is warm and lighter than in summer, the days are still fairly long, and the trees and ivy are growing saturated with the colors of autumn.

At the wharf, right beside the dormant, gull-whitened ferryboat *Ellis Island*, a stray cat basks in the sun. She was once the station director's pet, like Sherman's Toto. She went missing while the staff were leaving the island, so she was left behind, and maintains order in her own way — hunting mice and rats.

The island is empty, but full of murmurs and rustles. Branches knock in the wind against the large windows of the main building. The flower beds have lost their geometric shapes and been invaded by herbs and weeds, the original local flora hidden under the gardens' surface: salty marsh reeds, gray ivy, and low-lying grasses. Some plants are already climbing the walls, winding around the gutters, hooking on to the roofs.

The windows here, set into arches and divided into small squares, have never been monotone, but now they've turned surprising colors — they're blinded and gray, or completely black from being broken, or red with rusty damp patches, or red-gold with arabesques of Virginia creeper, or white from roller blinds that weren't taken down, or blue if they've remained whole enough and clean enough to still reflect the sky and water.

We can presume the doors to the buildings will be locked. But that would only mean anything if you couldn't climb through a window, if this place were meant to be guarded. Yet it's guarded less and less.

The doors inside the buildings, if they survive, are unlocked, and we can see corridors and enfilades stretching endlessly, steps rising, recesses unexpectedly opening up. It's very quiet inside and we can hear our steps echoing with one sound on linoleum, another on rotten wood, and yet another on a layer of tin fallen from the ceiling.

In the bright social workers' rooms Ludmila Foxlee found so pleasant, the thick corner post has gone dark with mold, but the furniture is holding up well — especially the heavy oak wheeled office chair that one could gracefully maneuver, turning from the desk toward an enquirer. A large filing cabinet also remains, a tin key still dangling from the handle of the topmost drawer and, on top, an iron fan once fired up in hot weather.

In worse, even outright desperate shape — especially from frugal, music-loving Ludmila's perspective — are the pianos in the recreation pavilion, which wasn't built until 1937. Their lids are open, the hammers are torn out, and the fingers resting on the keyboards belong to some plant that's made its home here.

In strong wind, drafts must rage through the building. If these don't bang the leftover furniture against the walls of the rooms and halls it's mainly because all these objects (except the musical instruments, which have their own inviolable shape) are designed for use on the enormous scale the multitudes required.

Here are soup ladles with a capacity of at least a half-gallon. A meat grinder like a small steam engine. A push-button cash register like a jukebox. Hundreds of thick white earthenware plates stacked up. Crude, strong crutches for the lame. A single-leg ironing board like a pedestal. Iron roasting pans like children's wash basins. Wash basins for adults like small swimming pools. White, round, sturdy, solid cast-iron sinks coated in thick enamel, still glistening. A steel washing machine with a lid, now open, with a crank to hold it shut. A snow shovel like the back door of a truck. An oxygen tank like a long-range rocket. A heavy sign reading: *No Smoking, Rauchen Verboten, Vietato Fumare,*

Palenie Tytoniu Wzbronione. Something that was once a couch and now is a moldy lump of plush, horsehair, and springs, like a giant shaggy animal in a state of decay.

In one of the hospital quarantines, plaster chips have rained down on a British traveling chest, a real antique, and the measles ward holds oak filing cabinets for patients' files. Their drawers, about a hundred of them altogether, pile high, up to the ceiling, protruding here and there like a sculptural decoration.

In one room, unneeded chairs lie in a pile. They've formed a mound, or rather the openwork structure of a mound.

The cluster of steel-plated stoves with steel doors, ornamented with the symbols of *Oil City Boiler Works, Pennsylvania*, are the hospital boilers. When they were installed, they called nothing to mind other than safe warmth. Now that the doors concealing the furnaces have been torn off or left open so we can see into their murky depths, someone from Europe might recoil in fear — from knowledge of the crematoriums.

Opening the autoclave might rouse similar feelings. In here, mattresses were sterilized to prevent tuberculosis. The doors are still untouched, but the wall the chamber is set into is already surrendering and crumbling.

Something has been tossed on to the windowsill — something small and delicate that Ludmila Foxlee would definitely bend over to inspect. It's a sewing frame with unfinished needlework, its pattern no longer discernible. Some of the threads have faded, the rest birds have plucked out.

What remains on the wall of the morgue — for we can get in here too — might be the work of a modern installation artist. Above a metal plate that glistens hazily like a ruined mirror, three pipes dangle down from a single opening high on the wall. They are enveloped in a steel hose resembling the cord of a handheld showerhead, and they stop abruptly at the bottom, because the object they were meant to lead to no longer exists. Beneath them, on a concrete slab, rest the remains of some machine. Both what has remained and what is gone were meant to cool the room properly. Someone seems to have left a wide chair here.

Did they not know what this room, or rather bunker, was for, and came here instead to rest?

For the island is not empty at all. It only seems so.

> Yes, all things sleep. The window. Snow beyond.
> A roof-slope, whiter than a tablecloth,
> the roof's high ridge. A neighborhood in snow,
> carved to the quick by this sharp windowframe.
> Arches and walls and windows — all asleep.
> Wood paving-blocks, stone cobbles, gardens, grills.
> No light will flare, no turning wheel will creak ...
> Chains, walled enclosures, ornaments, and curbs.
> Doors with their rings, knobs, hooks are all asleep —
> their locks and bars, their bolts and cunning keys.
> One hears no whisper, rustle, thump, or thud.
> Only the snow creaks. All men sleep. Dawn comes
> not soon ...
> But hark! Do you not hear in the chill night
> a sound of sobs, the whispered voice of fear?
> There someone stands, disclosed to winter's blast,
> and weeps. There someone stands in the dense gloom.[209]

There Were People Here, Shirley Burden

The photographer Shirley C. Burden was born in Manhattan in 1908, a year after the largest wave of immigrants at Ellis Island. Yet he was not in the least a part of that wave.

His great-great-grandfather was the millionaire Cornelius Vanderbilt. Burden's first wife was the actress Florence Fair, real name Fairbanks, niece of the star Douglas Fairbanks, that master of swashbuckling roles, famous as Zorro, D'Artagnan, Robin Hood, and Don Juan, and for sixteen years the husband of Mary Pickford. Shirley C. Burden does not need to work either for money or for status. But he is interested in photography and opens a studio in Beverly Hills. His workshop first specializes in artistic photographs for ad agencies and architectural firms, but in time he begins working on photo essays — publications uniting pictures and text — such as "God is My Life," about Trappist monks in the Gethsemane monastery in Kentucky, or "I Wonder Why," about episodes in the life of an African-American girl, a victim of racial prejudice.

In the late fifties Shirley flies to New York.

Through the aircraft window he sees an indistinct mass next to the Statue of Liberty. He knows it's the former immigration station. He's intrigued by this dark place. Days hurry by, finally he rents a boat and goes to Ellis Island. There's no one there. The buildings stand before him, seeming to question why he's disturbing their peace and solitude. He's read a lot of ghost stories and seen many such films, but what he sees there beats them hands down.

The days float on and he floats back to Ellis. He takes pictures or observes the buildings and equipment and wonders what tales they could tell.

> My fear of the island had vanished. The peace and quiet
> that was everywhere made it easier for me to hear my
> ghost friends. I could open doors and walk in dark places
> without a twinge, but every set-up I made I looked over
> my shoulder to see who was watching me. I never saw
> anybody, but I'm sure people were there.[210]

Bereft

Shirley C. Burden is lucky no one catches sight of him. Alongside the island's friendly ghosts are new pirates, or rather looters, who are best avoided. The station is guarded by a single man with a dog (the staff has been cut) and is completely defenseless against them. The metropolis of New York has enough paupers and vagrants to strip Ellis of its equipment, floorboards, windowpanes, metal parts, faucets, pipes, and wires — anything that can be picked up and loaded into a small floating vessel.

A few years ago the United States created the General Services Administration (GSA) — a federal agency mandated with overseeing abandoned government property. For 18 months it has been searching for a government institution or philanthropic organization to use the island for its own purposes, and has received a few proposals:

A group of importers and exporters would like to set up an international shopping center on Ellis Island.

New York City Hall would like to build homes there for the elderly, the homeless, and juvenile delinquents.

New York State would like to treat alcoholics there.

The state of New Jersey believes Ellis should belong to it (ownership of the island's territory is still not clearly defined) and wants to include it in plans for a large recreational park whose two areas — on the island and on the mainland — would be connected by a footbridge. New Jersey representatives have even taken a boat to Ellis Island and raised the state flag there.

This act by New Jersey rouses New York City Hall to aggressively seize the initiative, expediting the decision to build the social center on the island.

All these worthy desires vanish in the face of the contractual obligations. The law requires that applicants pay the GSA half the value of the island, defined as over $6 million (a sum much greater than it seems today). Added to that is the cost of repairs, renovations, modifications, and maintenance for the whole estate, which, though it stands on a small area, is in fact colossal. Besides, New York social workers aren't thrilled about exiling people to a place whose reputation is actually poor, one only an artist could get excited about.

In this situation, there's nothing to do but put the *pleasant situated island* up for commercial sale, just as Samuel Ellis did, and throw in all the buildings, rather than herring. The ferryboat too. Let the rich buy it.

No suitable buyer is found. Samuel Ellis couldn't come up with one in the 18th century, nor can the General Services Administration officials in the 20th. Despite at least 20 different companies making visits to Ellis Island, none decides to sink money into it, particularly since Ellis increasingly calls to mind a ruined, haunted fortress. Investors interested in the land itself, without the structures, have calculated that demolishing and clearing them would cost more than buying the entire thing: $8–10 million.

As these site visits and negotiations stretch on, and the Ellis property continues to fall apart, voices start calling for it to be preserved for posterity. Immigration historians declare that immigrants' children have no wish to recall their family odysseys, but the third generation is complex-free and curious. The grandchildren of the wave of 1907 are increasingly asking questions about Ellis Island.

The Maine senator and descendent of Polish immigrants Edmund Muskie, who heads a US Senate subcommittee assessing various uses the island could be put to, requests that the GSA halt proceedings to sell Ellis until the subcommittee finishes its work.

At this very moment a new, sensational proposal is made. Its authors invoke the awe-inspiring name of Frank Lloyd Wright.

A New Metropolis, Frank Lloyd Wright

When the sun sank at the back of Metropolis, the houses
turning to mountains and the streets to valleys; when the
stream of light, which seemed to crackle with coldness,
broke forth from all windows, from the walls of the houses,
from the rooves and from the heart of the town ... then
the cathedral would stand there, in this boundless ocean of
light, which dissolved all forms by outshining them ...

In place of doves, flying machines swarmed over the
cathedral roof and over the city, resting on the rooves,
from which, at night, glaring pillars and circles indicated
the course of flight and landing points.

Thousand-limbed city, built of blocks of light.
Towers of brilliance! Steep mountains of splendour!
From the velvety sky above you showers golden rain,
inexhaustibly, as into the open lap of the Danae.[211]

The author of the novel *Metropolis*, Thea von Harbou — wife of
the director Fritz Lang, and the woman whose imagination contributed
to the creation of the famous 1920s film of the same name — wrote in
the introduction to her novel:

This book is not of today or of the future. It tells of no
place. It is of no cause, party or class.[212]

Yet in America, which has become mighty enough to build *steep
mountains of splendour*, the vision of Metropolis has exceptional power.
It's remembered and quoted as a commentary on modern compositions,
such as the design for Ellis Island according to Frank Lloyd Wright.

Wright's son-in-law, William Wesley Peters, presents the proposal
to the aforementioned Senate subcommittee led by Edmund Muskie.

He does so in 1962, as a representative of Taliesin Associated Architects — a firm of the great architect's successors; Wright died three years ago, but saw fit to leave his students to finish his design.[213]

We probably cannot assume Wright worked on this in the last period of his life, when one of his greatest works, the Guggenheim Museum, was being erected in Manhattan, on Museum Mile alongside Central Park. His final visit to the Guggenheim construction site was in January 1959. The museum opened in October, after his death.

The Key — as the new Ellis Island is to be known — is a *self-contained, super-modern* city built on the bare ground of the island, since everything constructed there so far will be demolished. This multi-level and incredibly complex organism, combining vertical towers, terraces like the points of a star, rotundas, canopies, and cables, will be in constant motion like a living being. Residents of glass-enclosed apartments are to move from place to place on moving streets, escalators, elevators, and pleasure boats, 450 of which will fit in the local marina. The Key Center will be an agora surrounded by banks, stores, restaurants, and nightclubs. The huge climate-controlled domes will have space for auditoriums, churches, and exhibition halls. Public terraces will hang suspended on mighty steel cables, which will radiate out over the whole island like a golden spider web; the steel will be colored.

Taliesin foresees 8,000 residents: 7,500 permanent, 500 in a luxury hotel. Yet the project spokesmen emphasize that luxury is the idea generally. It's luxury for a higher public purpose, because the island's permanent residents are to be New York's workers and laborers, who after a hard day's work deserve proper rest.

The idea leaves Senator Muskie's subcommittee unmoved. Critics consider the project either utopian or commercial. It has no connection at all to the historical significance of the island. The Key shares the fate of its alleged prototype, the futuristic Metropolis, which begins to crumble when natural human desires are voiced.

As for Ellis, more and more people are in favor of converting the island into a memorial. This view manifests itself not so much in action, but in reduced opposition. The structures of the old station are still falling apart and increasingly choked by overgrown plants, but the enthusiasm for selling or leasing the island is gradually decreasing. It seems those with the power to decide these issues subconsciously prefer to hold back.

Liberty

Andree Maria Polturak, daughter of a Polish officer killed at the start of the Second World War, sailed after the war from Sweden to join her family in America. She was 17 at the time. She was detained at Ellis Island because she had a passport issued by the communist Polish consulate. While awaiting a ruling, she was so offended that the Statue of Liberty was standing with its back to her window that later, after graduating college, she wrote a short story titled "The Rear End of the

Statue of Liberty" and got an A for it.[214] The ambiguous title of this story concerns physicality and morality. It is about the real bronze-cast back (backside?) of the Statue of Liberty and the feelings of those, like Andree, imprisoned at Ellis Island in the rear end of their imagined freedom. In the mid-sixties — by which time Andree has set herself up in America, taken her husband's name Marks, and become a social worker — the Statue of Liberty takes on a dual caretaker role for Ellis Island. First, it opens its massive pedestal to store collections of documents and mementos left over from the immigrants' odyssey, with a view to making them available to visitors in 1972. Second, it takes Ellis under its legal authority. In May 1965 President Lyndon B. Johnson places Ellis Island, alongside the Statue of Liberty, under the joint administration of a National Park:

> ... WHEREAS the millions of people who passed through the Ellis Island Depot were important to America for their contribution in making the United States of America the world leader it is today; and
>
> WHEREAS the Statue of Liberty is a symbol to the world of the dreams and aspirations which have drawn so many millions of immigrants to America ...
>
> I, LYNDON B. JOHNSON, President of the United States of America ... do proclaim that the property known as Ellis Island ... is hereby added to and made a part of the Statue of Liberty National Monument ...
>
> Warning is hereby expressly given to all unauthorized persons not to appropriate, injure, destroy, or remove any feature of the National Monument.[215]

Soon after this proclamation is made, the outstanding architect Philip Johnson[216] receives a commission for a design for the island to honor its history.

Edward Corsi, who in 1907 couldn't make out the Statue of Liberty through the mist, hears of this decision with joy. He is 69, has a great deal of energy, and wants to use it for Ellis Island. He knows the island like few others, he is well prepared to discuss what needs to be done there. On 13 December 1965 he is killed in a car accident — never managing to serve the new Ellis.

The Tower of 16 Million

Wright's Key Island had many towers enwrapped in golden cables. On Philip Johnson's island there is to be one wide tower, round as a doughnut or alternatively — according to some critics — a fuel tank; ramps spiral up around it and it's hard to resist the sense Wright's Guggenheim Museum has left its footprints here. This hollow tower is the island's most important point. It's 130 feet high and a monument to all the immigrants who passed through Ellis; its designers taking their number as 16 million. As they climb the ramps, visitors will be able to read the names of arrivals listed on the ships' manifests and carved on the wall.

The tower will stand on an empty lawn at the southern part of Ellis Island. From the tower's spiral and top visitors will be able to admire the Manhattan skyline and practically touch the Statue of Liberty. To those

who fear the giant cylinder will encroach on the statue's splendid solitude, the designer replies the statue's pedestal alone will be 20 feet higher
than the Tower of 16 Million, while the tower's shape feels at home in
New York Harbor — because it alludes to circular Castle Garden.

Johnson intends to strip the island of nearly all its former structures.
He will leave the main station building standing with the baggage room
and dormitory, the infectious diseases division, and the morgue. Yet he
proposes not a fundamental renovation, but merely a procedure known
as *stabilization*. The buildings are to be protected from further decay,
but maintained as a permanent ruin. The press cites Johnson's view
that existing turn-of-the-century architecture is rarely worth a Mass,
but nostalgia naturally is. Therefore the ferryboat *Ellis Island* will be
stabilized as well, but only for display.

The glass and wood are to be removed from all the buildings, and
the walls and roofs preserved. Grapevines, sycamores, and poplars will
be planted around the walls. The trees and vines will be able to grow
unhindered and work their way inside, as they do now without the
sanction of design.

This cluster of historic buildings, separated from the rest of the
island by a moat, will be open to viewing from raised footpaths.

The press suggests a site visit was the deciding factor in Johnson's
radical approach to the island's older structures. When the architect
came to Ellis Island, the entire grounds already looked so pathetic he
was discouraged from restoring them.

Separately, apart from the open-air museum of the ruins, Johnson
foresees the island having all that tourists require beyond nostalgia — a
modern restaurant plus a space for picnics and dances. (This would
have been a wonderful site for the 75th birthday of Cecilia Greenstone,
the former little angel of Ellis. Cecilia invited 260 guests and when they
raised a toast, she told them the story of the impoverished men and
women sailing in from all over the world. People are now starting to

forget what poverty was, but she remembers, though she has long been kept busy with family life.)

The government of New York and one of its senators endorse the project. Secretary of the Interior Stewart L. Udall, who commissioned the design, says it shows what can be achieved when art, architecture, and history combine. The press, however, is in no mood for praise. They call the transformation of functional buildings into permanent ruins a romantic folly, and view the memorial tower as ugly and more reminiscent of gates slamming shut than opening, which is unjust to Ellis Island.

Regardless of all this — there isn't enough money. Completing the project would cost much more than the $6 million designated by the United States Congress. In 1964, the Vietnam War is building up steam. It turns out that even the promised $6 million will never materialize, and the project is shelved.

Red Power, Black Power

We don't know if there are any Lenni Lenape among the eight people who suddenly declare themselves ready to take possession of the island, but as the original inhabitants of America's eastern regions, there ought to be. The group presents itself as Indians of All Tribes, and it's led by John White Fox of the Shoshone, who in November 1969 took over Alcatraz Island in San Francisco Bay so that, as the student LaNada Boyer, one of the occupiers, put it, *[We would be] recognized as a people, as human beings ... to raise not only the consciousness of other American people, but our own people as well, to reestablish our identity.*[217]

Now, in the dark March dawn, the Native Americans get in a small boat on the New Jersey coast. They've loaded it with essentials to set up a camp on the island. Once out on the water, their motor refuses to obey, they start to drift, and the Coast Guard must come to their rescue. Humiliated, they declare they'll return. White Fox declares at a press conference that they have a moral right to the island, that they want to create a Native American cultural center there, where young Indians can learn how to combat the tragedies that whites have brought into the world — pollution of the air, earth, and water. And that's not all. At Ellis they intend to create a museum about the harm done to Native Americans. It will have spaces for disease, alcoholism, and the desecration of ancient culture.

They don't invoke their ancestors buried on the island. Perhaps they don't know.

Red Power is just being born. There's no talk yet in the US of repaying debts to the Native Americans, or of political correctness. The one visible result of the failed landing is shoring up the Coast Guard. They are to guard Ellis carefully. They establish a secure zone around the island based on the Espionage Act of 1917 — the same one that sent "enemy aliens" to Ellis during the First World War. Patrol boats now circle Ellis. They're meant to enter the ferry channel between the first and second islands, but they have to be careful there, because as of recently the ferryboat *Ellis Island* is resting at the bottom of the channel.

The ferryboat held out for a million miles but was riddled with leaks; in one January storm it sank peacefully beneath the waves and did not rise again.

The boats ward off the Native Americans, but the African-American squatters who arrive a few months later — at a strength of 63 men, women, and children — stay out of the way of the Coast Guard, which also clearly prefers not to trouble them. Black Power has already made itself known and is prompting anxiety. The arrivals introduce themselves as NEGRO — the National Economic Growth and Reconstruction Organization, Inc. Their leader is Thomas W. Matthew, a 46-year-old neurosurgeon, an opponent of welfare — which in his opinion renders people helpless — and a supporter of resocialization through work, especially in black-founded companies. The group spends 13 days on the island and over that whole period negotiates intensively with the National Park. Matthew announces a fundraiser to purchase the island, build a resocialization center, found a range of workshops — from shoemaking to electronics — and restore the Great Hall as a monument to immigration and a meeting place for different ethnic groups. As a result NEGRO secures the right to use the island for five years, but the Nayional Park restricts them to the south end of Ellis Island (right where the Tower of 16 Million was to stand), forbids any interference with the Great Hall, and retains the right to inspect.

Dr Matthew's fundraiser doesn't succeed. The approaching winter leaves barely four of his supporters on the island. NEGRO slowly abandons its project. The island once again is empty.

Peter Sammartino Looks at his Mother

The bicentennial of American independence is approaching.

Ellis Island has never been in more desperate condition.

The government is completely sick of the island. In 1973 the Secretary of the Interior announces that he intends to ask the president to hand Ellis back over to the General Service Administration. But his words set off such a furore that the secretary resigns and once again nothing happens.

Or not until January of the following year, when an angel appears over the island. He flies in concentric circles overhead and calls out: America, aren't you ashamed to forget your stepping stone?

This angel, by the name of Peter Sammartino, later wrote about what he saw. First, he saw his mother. She sailed to Ellis Island to join his father, who arrived from Italy in 1901. She was slim, stylish, and wore a gold watch on a chain in her left breast pocket — which surprised her relatives, who expected a chubby woman in peasant clothes, but filled his father with pride. Peter Sammartino watched from above as his parents stood in the enormous throng of newcomers, and then saw them again at the photographer's they visited together and realizes he remembers the name of the studio — Pigafotta — and its address: 199 Bleecker Street. But that was only a moment, then his mother and father vanished from sight, the overgrown ruins of the island emerged, and when the helicopter landed and Sammartino entered the Great Hall, some bats took flight.

Peter Sammartino takes his ride over the island at the age of exactly 70, barely 128 years younger than the US (the bicentennial won't fall until two years later, in 1976).

Sammartino is a writer and educator, founder and first president of Fairleigh Dickinson University in New Jersey.[218] He and his wife Sally, who took part in creating the school, are two well-known local citizens and they chair the committee on celebrating the United States bicentennial.

Sally, a year older than her husband, is not in the helicopter, but he surely tells her the whole story that evening. She hears how the untended island moved Peter: *What an ugly sight next to the greatest symbol in the world — the Statue of Liberty! For shame, America ...*[219]

The two of them decide to get down to business; for as long as they've known one another, they've done everything together. So, they meet with influential people, organize pressure groups, write letters to the authorities, including President Gerald Ford, and work out how much money is initially needed to get things off the ground. The amount needed to truly save the island is better kept quiet for now — it comes to $20 million. But they can start with small steps — for instance purchasing thousands of large bags for trash and debris. The debris is needed for the construction of a large park in New Jersey — the park is happy to take it, since it keeps things cheap, so it's a win-win. Volunteers can handle the clean-up, and it turns out there's no shortage of them — Ellis Island takes up more and more space in Americans' hearts and minds, and the bicentennial surely contributes to that.

Peter and Sally go on a lobbying tour around the United States — they fly to Washington to seek support in Congress, then to Chicago, to Texas, to the west coast. It would appear no one can say no to this elderly, good-natured couple. But that's too good a story. More likely America now really is ashamed, has long been awaiting the stubborn Sammartinos' business-like proposals, is relieved to welcome the charitable organization the Restore Ellis Island Committee under Peter's chairmanship, and is glad to accept his views:

> Yes, we have problems, we have inequities, and who hasn't?
>
> But ... we must rejoice in the fact that we are the most favored of any land in the history of civilization. ... And if we have now become too soft, too demanding, too wasteful, perhaps this island can be a reminder that we must be thankful for what we have.[220]

President Ford pledges a million dollars.

This allows them to repair the roof of the main building, put in windows, clear the overgrown plants, install toilets, light the building and some of the grounds, hire 24-hour security, and fix up the island enough for boats holding 100 passengers to moor there, for the Sammartinos' committee wants Americans to see the island.

The provisional opening ceremony of the Great Hall is held in May 1976; the great soprano Lucia Albanese had probably never performed in such a run-down venue. Albanese sings the American national anthem and then a university orchestra plays a symphonic poem composed in honor of Peter and Sally.

That very month, sightseeing trips begin. A ferry takes tourists to

Liberty Island and then to Ellis. Six times a day, seven days a week, until the autumn. Park ranger guides make sure groups stick together and don't stray from the safe path where nothing will fall on their heads.

The Great Hall is as empty and raw as a factory floor. Yet that summer 45,000 people go inside. They don't complain about not being shown enough. Testifying to their emotion is a poem printed in June 1978 in the magazine *Island Images*, recalling the underground publications in Poland — ink smeared on poor-quality paper:

> There once was a ranger named Cort
> Tour guide of the dramatic sort
> His audience was so thick
> That they loved his rhetoric
> And cried all the way home to Batter's Port.

On Sadness, Meredith Monk

> When your heart is very tender, every moment has a kind
> of existential sadness to it ... It's not sadness like having
> to cry all the time but it's really the sadness of existence.
> It's like seeing everything with that tenderness has a kind
> of a sadness to it ...

So thinks Meredith Monk. She's talking about Poland,[221] but because she means *seeing everything*, she also therefore means Ellis Island.

Meredith finds herself at the island just as it's coming to life.

Meredith was born in New York City. Her mother was an American professional singer; she performed hundreds of advertising jingles and theme songs for soap operas. Meredith's maternal grandfather was a popular baritone and violinist in Russia (he emigrated to the United States at the end of the 19th century), and

her great-grandfather a well-known cantor in Moscow. She was born to sing, but had flawed eyesight that hindered her spatial perception. But she discovered that if she sang with her whole body, her whole self, she could locate her place in space.

Meredith's singing is astonishing because it seems not like the voice of a singer, but of the wind, of birds, cicadas, reeds, branches, water; sometimes it's a sickly moan, an elderly huff, a mad shriek, a baby's cry. Meredith needs no lyrics or accompaniment. This singing, with its enormous range, is combined with movement, and even when Meredith is standing still, she seems to dance.

> I work in between the cracks, where the voice starts
> dancing, where the body starts singing.[222]

She is petite, slim, with a long face and dozens of tiny braids tumbling over her shoulders and back. Offstage she dresses in a way that makes you suspect she has no idea what she's wearing, that if you handed her some cheap secondhand rags she'd put them on in good faith. It's hard to say whether she's beautiful, but it's difficult to take your eyes off her.

She composes, sings, acts, makes films, collaborates with famous American artists, and wins prestigious prizes.

Meredith is curious about the island, like Shirley C. Burden was before her, and like him she finds her way there. She directs the film *Ellis Island* according to her own concept, with her own music and her own singing. The movie has two sets of main characters. One is a modern tourist visit, filmed realistically, like a newsreel. The second is the immigrants and staff of Ellis Island — ghosts who are ever-present there, but invisible to the

tourists, as they were to Shirley Burden. Yet the film's main character is an object — a black-and-white measuring stick. Sometimes the role of the measuring stick is taken over by a hand drawing symbols.

First we see black.

Then the outline of the island. The sky brightens.

Water flows, the island flows, the sky flows, everything is in motion.

Dilapidated pillars, peeling walls, the metallic clang of bells, or of pots, or ships' sirens.

A motionless black-and-white crowd of turn-of-the-century immigrants amid the modern debris of the island. One of the women comes to life, brushes some invisible dust from the lapel of the man next to her, and freezes again.

A man in a white lab coat and a woman in a long dress and hat take a few ceremonial steps, as though inviting one another to dance. When they stand facing one another, he moves his hands toward her face. In one hand he holds a small object. We see the immigrant woman's handsome face, her eye is large, bulging, cow-like, we're almost sure the buttonhook will cut through the glassy white sclera like the razor in Buñuel's *Un Chien Andalou*. But it doesn't come to that, because the woman swoons and sinks down in slow motion, while the doctor stands motionless with his arm raised.

A handsome young couple: they have their eyes open but don't see anything. Someone unseen holds the measuring stick to their chests, as though slicing through them crosswise.

A man in black clothing, a Mediterranean type in black stockings and flat shoes, like something out of *commedia dell'arte*, seizes the measuring stick and places himself beside it.

Now a surprise, because color appears on the screen. The firm but friendly face of a tour guide. Behind her, tourists climb stairs and vanish into the murky depths of a corridor.

Back to black-and-white. A group of women and children in white dresses, or rather robes, lie arranged fairly haphazardly, but beautifully, on the floor. They're sleeping. A few men in black frock coats, black shoes, and hats are stretched out symmetrically alongside one another, as if removed from coffins. They're sleeping.

Women with long, lovely hair, bent over, hair covering their faces. Motions of washing their hair and searching it for lice. A group of men with focused gazes like in an old genre painting. They're counting money.

Colorful tourists walk through empty rooms.

A portrait of a woman, attractive, gentle, in black. Someone's hand draws a horizontal line over her eyebrows and writes on her temple *125 mm*. A bird-like sound, intermittent, like a plaintive whine.

Men's faces. A hand draws a semicircle on one's cheek and a zigzag on another's. And always at that moment, the bird sound.

On another man's face someone writes SERB.

An inspector asks a man his name.

A name appears on the screen:

Ellessen Rahmsauer,

and then its subsequent, increasingly reduced versions:

Elias Ramseur,

Elias Ramser,

Eli Ram.

A teacher in a black hat, white blouse, tie, with a pointer in her hand (it's also the measuring stick) points at English words on a blackboard and pronounces them loudly, emphatically. Immigrants, staring at her mouth, silently repeat the syllables, their muteness suggesting labor beyond their power.

The last shot, color again: a young man, a guard, sits in a chair, turns on a transistor radio and opens up a newspaper. The radio gives a detailed weather report.[223]

How They Came, Ludmila Foxlee

This film would surely make a strong impression on Ludmila Foxlee, sensitive as she was to sound, dance, costumes, and props, and conscious of the experiences that go along with them. Yet Ludmila did not live to see Meredith's work; she died in 1971, nine years after her husband. After he passed away she stopped running the antiques store. Reliable and organized as always, before her own passing she managed to write down her recollections, which she titled *How They Came: The Drama of Ellis Island.*

Liberty

She's almost a hundred years old and suffering from degenerating bone structure. This is particularly evident wherever her iron ribs touch her noble metal skin, causing unpleasant erosion. When she was young, her iron skeleton didn't directly touch her bronze plating, they were separated by the cartilage of insulation, which time has caused to dry up and fall out. Her hand holding the torch is in the worst condition, because water collects in the handle. There's a fear that one day her diseased arm may drop America's lamp.

Luckily magic exists, or perhaps only the pressure of round-numbered anniversaries. For her centennial, the symbol of the free world must exhibit health, strength, and beauty. Not only do the Statue of Liberty's owners insist on it, but so do its donors. Just as she did nearly a century ago, the statue unleashes the generosity of both governments and nations. France and America recall their fraternal gift and once again feel a pleasant thrill.

The anniversaries of the Statue of Liberty and of Ellis Island, which by order of President Johnson are a combined monument to

America's history, are barely six years apart. The statue's centennial falls in 1986, the immigration station's in 1992. It's becoming obvious a fundamental renovation of the Statue of Liberty must go along with truly returning Ellis to health; at the moment it's just being kept on a weak drip.

In May 1982, President Reagan announces the creation of the 21-person Statue of Liberty–Ellis Island Restoration Commission. Chairing it is Lee Iacocca, the energetic head of the Chrysler automotive corporation. In its first year of existence the commission already raises $40 million.

This is almost as much of a miracle as pulling Chrysler out of bankruptcy.[224]

Iacocca describes his management techniques in his autobiography, which so fascinates Americans that between November 1984 and May 1985 it goes through 31 editions. Its last paragraph reads:

> Since most of my life has been selling — selling products, or ideas, or values — I guess it would be out of character to close this book without asking for the order. So here goes:
>
> Please help me in the restoration of Ellis Island and the Statue of Liberty. Please send your tax-deductible contribution to [the following address]. Don't let the flame in the Statue go out! And remember, if nothing else, Christopher Columbus, my father, and I will be forever grateful.[225]

In 2001 it's calculated that the committee has raised a total of $500 million.

Lee Iacocca Looks at His Mother

Peter Sammartino, as he flew circles around the island, saw his mother and the watch in her breast pocket. As Lee Iacocca enters the main building of the immigration station, he sees his future mother Antoinette, wobbling as she heads for the stairs for the six-second inspection, weak and uncertain — and silver-tongued Nicola saving her from exclusion.

Lee is convinced he inherited his ambition in life and his managerial ingenuity from his father. Nicola Iacocca was, to his mind, a promotional genius. For instance, when he founded a chain of small movie theaters, he announced: today the ten kids with the dirtiest faces get in free.

Antoinette Iacocca came through Ellis in 1921. Three years later the stairs were dismantled and traffic was redirected. Now Lee Iacocca is shocked to hear the National Park has no intention of rebuilding them. It would go against the conservational concept of rebuilding the station from the final period of its activity.

Antoinette's son categorically demands the steps. He defines his work for the island as a labor of love. If he allows them to rebuild the building without the steps, he'll let down his emotions and his parents' memory.

Part VII

Pearl Divers

Travel Chests

The steps Lee Iacocca was so stubborn about were, of course, rebuilt.

In 1907, at the immigration peak, about a million newcomers landed at Ellis Island. The Ellis Island National Museum of Immigration opens on the island in 1990 and doubles that record. Every year it receives two million people from the United States and around the world. They pour out at the ferry dock (the sunken ferryboat *Ellis Island* still reposes at the bottom of the canal, a wave occasionally revealing the roof of its superstructure) and walk through the large doors of the main building, which look like new, and encounter a city of travel trunks.

Right near Antoinette's steps, a glassed-in tunnel stretches away. It's packed with travel trunks, made many years ago in housewright's fashion, on a frame. They are stacked up like buildings in a densely populated district that has no better or worse streets, but packs in tenements, granaries, barns, corncribs, and houses of worship side by side. The most beautiful chest has a barrel-vaulted roof with thick ribs resting on the frame and fastened to it with iron clasps, each with an elaborate rosette stamped or engraved on it. Its sides are clad in beautifully glistening polka-dot pink and lilac tin, not only for decoration, but protection, like armor. In the city behind glass, this chest could play the role of a synagogue.

The trunk-building touching the corner of the synagogue-chest is even bigger, but primitive, made of reddish planks pretending to be brick. Its ambitious owner was also thinking about decoration and protection — he's painted on its walls three black flowers, regular as Gothic tracery, and has fortified the construction with a wooden crosspiece around the middle. Next to it stands a shack woven from bast, and pressed around this are even poorer shelters, tent-swellings made of rags. On some trunk-buildings we see traces of repeated renovations: here part of the wall has been tarred, here a hole has been covered over with plywood; yurts made of old kilims, carpets, and blankets are patched up, roped together, fortified with braids, and fastened with leather straps.

Here and there a little apartment-house stands, tall but narrow, with colorful patterned walls. Yet they're not painted like the apartment-houses in the old towns of Lublin, Warsaw, or Gdansk, but upholstered in thick, strong fabric, probably pounded in a fulling mill.

The barns squeezed in between the burgher houses are poorly planed but their corners are well aligned. Some are made of lumber not from the saw, but from the axe; we can see how the blade slid through the tree trunk.

If the baggage handler Peter McDonald were to walk along this wall, we can be sure he'd be able to name the origins of these boxes, trunks, sacks, and bundles. He'd marvel that they'd found their way back to Ellis Island. Some were stored for years by their former owners' descendants before being handed over to the museum. They are displayed anonymously. Yet we can be sure that if the trunk belonging to Annie Moore and her two brothers, Philip and Anthony, found itself among them, it would be marked as the first historic piece of luggage on the island.

Annie Moore's Ten Dollars

It emerges that the Annie Moore who died in the car accident in Texas in 1924 was not the Annie Moore who sailed to Ellis Island in 1892.

This was established recently by Megan Smolenyak Smolenyak (her maiden name is coincidentally the same as her husband's last name, though they're entirely unrelated). While performing genealogical research on immigration, she discovered that the Annie Moore killed in the collision was not an immigrant, and was probably born in Illinois. What's more, this Annie's family settled in Texas in 1880, in other words more than a decade before the Irish Moores sailed from Cork to America.

What then happened to the real Annie in America?

For a few years Smolenyak didn't devote much attention to this question. Then at a genealogical exhibition in Philadelphia, she saw the 1910 photograph of the Texan Annie that was probably the artist's model for the statue of the Irish girl at the Ellis Island museum. At that moment Megan with the two identical last names decided to track down the one and only Annie Moore from Cork.

This involved a certain moral dilemma. Tracking down the real Annie meant disinheriting the Texan family from a tradition they now partially believed in, having been invited not only to Ellis Island but to Ireland as well for various anniversaries. But the truth was more important and in its name Megan Smolenyak resorted to a simple, even rather blunt method. She announced online that whoever put her on track to uncover the American life of Annie Moore from Cork would receive a $1,000 reward.

The response was practically instantaneous. New York City's commissioner of records, Brian G. Andersson, located the naturalization certificate of Philip Moore, Annie's youngest brother, and offered Megan Smolenyak further help with her search. They found information from the 1930 census, in which Philip appears alongside his daughter, Anna. This Anna they found in the Social Security death index, which led them to her son. Annie Moore was his great-aunt. Megan Smolenyak was gradually getting closer to the family life of Annie Moore from Cork.

As it happens, Annie never left New York. First she and her family stayed in a *tenement house*, a rental apartment building for poor immigrants who, packed into cramped rooms with no amenities, earned a living shoemaking, weaving, tailoring. She married the German immigrant Joseph Schayer, a bakery worker. They settled on the Lower East Side of Manhattan and changed address numerous times, probably in search of cheaper accommodation, though they never moved more than a couple blocks away. They had 11 children, but only five survived childhood. Annie's heart gave out in 1924 (the same year Annie Moore from Texas died), at the age (like her) of 47. She was buried in Calvary Cemetery in Queens, a few miles from Ellis Island. In the same grave, overgrown with grass, six of her children were laid to rest.

Her other little brother, Anthony, whom Annie had also taken care of on their journey to America, died young, in 1902. He was buried in a pauper's grave, but when their father died five years later, the son was exhumed and the two were buried together.

Of the five children Annie Moore raised, two had none of their own.

Megan Smolenyak Smolenyak told journalists that Annie's life was a struggle that she dedicated to future generations.

Her search led her to meet some of Annie's descendants. They live in America and bear ten last names, including Irish, Jewish, Italian, and Scandinavian ones. According to Megan Smolenyak, they're poster children for America.[226] This would make Annie's descendants a picture-perfect synthesis of American heritage. But the words *poster children* also calls to mind *foster children*, adoptees who must cope with a difficult start.

The archivist Brian Andersson didn't help Megan for the money. Half of her prize money he donated to charity, the second half he gave to fix up Annie and her children's untended grave. Edward Wood, a plumber from New Jersey who came from the Texan Annie's family, declared publicly: *I'm disappointed but I'm not heartbroken.*

Knowing what Annie Moore from Cork's life was like, it's hard to be certain if she stuck to her resolution of 1 January 1892: that day she told Commissioner Weber she'd never part with the gold Liberty coin.

Before Megan Smolenyak Smolenyak announced her discovery, Margaret O'Connell Middleton of Tucson, Arizona, went to Ellis

Island. She introduced herself as a granddaughter of Annie Moore. She took part in a press conference setting out plans for a computerized genealogical center on Ellis and she said she wanted to pay back the gift her grandmother had received.[227]

From scattered information, we can conclude that Middleton was descended from the Annie from Texas, not from Cork. But at that time the problem of Annie's dual nature didn't yet exist. The good-faith proposal of a refund was accepted. Annie Moore's ten dollars returned to Ellis.

Sammartino, Peter and Sally

In close proximity to the six-second stairs and the city of traveling trunks, a plaque hangs on the wall:

> Dr Peter Sammartino, who, as founder-president of the
> Restore Ellis Island Committee, persuaded Congress to
> begin the restoration of this national shrine.

Having influence over the highest authorities of the United States does not mean having authority over one's own fate.

On 30 March 1992 the *New York Times* prints a note under the headline *Peter Sammartino, 87, Is Dead; Was Fairleigh Dickinson Founder*. It reports that Peter Sammartino and his wife were found shot in their home in Rutherford, New Jersey. The police determined the incident was a murder-suicide. Mrs Sammartino was 88. The prosecutor told the press they were both in poor health: Mrs Sammartino with Alzheimer's and Dr Sammartino with kidney problems.

In his final months Peter Sammartino couldn't come to grips with his or his wife's life, but this was a decision he could manage.

In a film on the Fairleigh Dickinson University website, they sit on a bench among flowers, their house in Rutherford in the background, and talk about founding the school. First he speaks, then she, then he again — they help one another along with looks and hand gestures, and, though they ought to look at the camera, their eyes are really fixed on one another.

Sherman's Walls, Weber's Wall

Augustus Sherman never sought publicity and would certainly be moved to see his subjects blown up larger than life on the walls of the museum. Their solemn gazes, oftentimes full of trepidation, follow the visitors and it's sometimes hard to hold their gaze.

The majority of Sherman's estate was left to his niece, Mary Sherman Peters. In 1969 she donated more than 150 of her uncle's photos to the Statue of Liberty National Monument, which includes Ellis Island. A second corpus of his photos found their way to the New York Public Library along with the papers of Commissioner William Williams, who admired Sherman's talent and frequently asked him for prints.

These photographs continually prompt investigations and keep saying something new. The museum at Ellis Island asks ethnographers and dress historians for commentary on the immigrants' clothing; psychologists research the models' faces and gestures; sociologists, their domestic and social lives. Someone took on the Russo-German Mittelstadts, who, as we know, arrived with eight children in May 1905, and managed to establish the following:

Their only daughter, Matilda, married, but had no children.

Their eldest son, Adolf, fathered 12 children.

The next-eldest, Jake — six children.

Reinhold died at the age of 16 (he's maybe 12 in the photo).

John had 12 children — like Adolf.

Fred — seven.

Benjamin — four.

Alfred — three.

The mother of the eight siblings, Rosana, didn't live to enjoy any of her grandchildren, for she died the same year she arrived at Ellis Island while giving birth to yet another child — her tenth (one was stillborn). In the picture she stands straight, her hands folded on her stomach; judging from the date, she must already know about her next pregnancy. Rosana's calm expression tells us she is not afraid. She is 39.

Augustus Sherman is one of the main figures behind the Ellis Island National Museum of Immigration, though he didn't live to see it founded. He couldn't have anyway — the museum's opening year would have been his 125th birthday.

Colonel Weber, who hired Sherman to work at Ellis, has his own museum too. It was set up in the city of Lackawanna, where he

enjoyed his grandchildren, where he sat down to lunch in a raincoat when his daughter put on a rainy melody, and where he died just before Christmas in 1926.

The John B. Weber Museum is small, taking up the ground floor of Lackawanna's elegant colonial-style public library. Enthusiasts of one of the Civil War's youngest colonels did not stop at collecting small mementos. They've introduced John Weber's life story into the curriculum of the local schools (they've named one after him), and his home into the city's sightseeing program. They tend the commissioner's grave, and will soon erect a monument to him, after raising money for it at events such as Valentine's Day picnics. The soul of these endeavors is Bill Tojek, who in his early youth saw the colonel's war photos and realized in amazement that the boy was the same age as he was. A place for the monument has already been designated. It will have two levels: a vertical one — a statue of John Weber in his field uniform — and a horizontal one — a granite wall showing Weber leading the African-American troops and giving Annie Moore her gold $10 coin. The panel also shows a locomotive, the dependable steam-engine of history, giving off clouds of white smoke.

Guastavino

While the Great Hall was being renovated, the ceiling panels were examined. They were filthy. It was decided to check how they were holding up, and they were struck, one by one, with a rubber mallet. The strong panels let out a tone, the weak ones a dull thunk. There were 17 weak ones and 29,000 good ones. And so a quiet, lengthy percussion piece was played on the ceiling of the hall in honor of Guastavino.

Liberty

Twenty years before the foundation of the Ellis Island museum, the World Trade Center opened in Manhattan. Eleven years after the inauguration of the museum, the Manhattan skyline — visible clear as day from the island — is missing two towers.

On 11 September 2001, Ranger Vincent DiPietro was putting out hangers for children's coats in the educational part of the museum. He heard a distant explosion. When he ran out to the water's edge, a group of his colleagues was already standing there, watching the tip of Manhattan. DiPietro later says everyone was wondering: are we seeing the same thing?

The horticulturalist Alfred Farrugio stood at the flagpole. He later said the seagulls that usually circled the patio around the cafeteria keeping an eye out for food had landed on the ground, their heads pressed into their torsos.

The stillness didn't last long. People started running back and forth and dialing cell-phone numbers. They were afraid. The symbols of America — the Statue of Liberty and Ellis Island itself — could be the targets of yet another attack. Liberty Island was immediately ordered to be evacuated and, surrounded with a cordon of police boats, meant at least to prevent an attack by sea. Around 200 Ellis employees congregated on the lawn, surrounded by the Wall of Honor as if behind a barricade, waiting for the boats that would take them to New York or New Jersey. The narrow freight bridge connecting Ellis Island and Jersey City was immediately closed; it would have been easy to blow up.

It was early enough that no tourists had yet arrived at either island. The first evacuation boat, the *Liberty IV*, with employees picked up from the Statue of Liberty and Ellis Island, landed at the Battery in Manhattan just as the first tower collapsed. The evacuees found themselves in a cloud of dust and ash. Police directed them to the Staten Island Ferry. They landed there safely. The captain of the *Liberty IV* therefore returned to Ellis Island and collected the next group of employees. Yet before he managed to repeat his mistake and let his passengers off at the Battery, the second tower collapsed and *Liberty IV* returned to Ellis.

Now no one doubts the evacuation ought to run in the opposite direction — from Manhattan to Ellis Island. Ellis has to take on the role of a rescue station. It's fairly well prepared for this — it has a large open space with fresh air and a roof over people's heads, sanitary facilities, a kitchen, and some of its personnel are familiar with managing crowds and know how to administer first aid. Above all, Ellis has what's always been its advantage — isolation from the metropolis, which on this day more than ever is threatened with chaos.

The Ellis Island staff therefore gear themselves up for the first victims. They bring chairs, tables, and portable toilets out into the open air. They prepare medical equipment on the front lawn. The first boatloads of wounded arrive shortly. Most are not badly injured, but they look gravely ill. They come off the boats gasping for air, choking and coughing, covered in grease, smeared in soot. Their faces are expressionless, their eyes empty, as if unseeing. They wave their arms in front of them. Their clothes have turned to rags. Many are barefoot.

Three teams are organized. The first — emergency doctors who've come from a hospital in New Jersey, administering first aid; the second — caregivers doing their best to calm the arrivals; the third — suppliers, providing food, water, tissues, towels, blankets, makeshift baby bottles and whatever else they can.

Boat after boat arrives, each bringing 50–70 passengers. Every passenger has to have the dust cleaned off; often staff have to use a hose. Then they record the passenger's name, address, time of arrival, and personal and contact telephone numbers, immediately entering them into a computer to create a database. Someone else makes a list of boats, a precise schedule of their movements, and cross-references the passenger list with the appropriate boat. All this information goes straight to the police, so families can locate their loved ones. Just in case, each arrival gets a bracelet, like a newborn, with their name and Social Security number if they're able to give it.

Someone, surely a supplier for the gift shop, offers new T-shirts to serve as replacement clothes, and diapers.

Burn victims and the more gravely injured continue on to nearby hospitals.

There are few with severe injuries. The crisis center at Ellis Island keeps waiting for more people from the towers and after a while everyone begins to realize — over there, it's mostly the dead. Then simultaneously the island receives an order to prepare to receive corpses. That night it is to be a morgue for New York City.

So the staff quickly clear out one of the large store rooms and install lights. They bring in freezers from New Jersey. The island once more has a house of the dead, yet the dead do not arrive. They've been crushed under heaps of concrete. The makeshift morgue will never be used. The freezers go back.

A few months after these events, Vincent DiPietro noticed one of the stamps used by the education program was still set for 11 September. Apparently no one had used it since. DiPietro didn't let anyone change the date.

The employees from Ellis and Liberty Islands were sent home for a few days. Then they were invited to meet with an anti-stress team, to talk through what was troubling them. They didn't complain about the worst things, but rather of the hole in the familiar Manhattan skyline, the stench of burning and smoke, the dust still hanging in the air. Then they returned to work. It was a return to remember, because all their bosses came out to the dock and lined up in a row, as if, as happened long ago, stepping out of the official boat would come President Theodore Roosevelt or William Howard Taft.[228]

The museum at Ellis Island was reopened to visitors on 19 December 2001.

The Statue of Liberty did not resume receiving tourists until 3 August 2004. They were only allowed to visit the pedestal at the statue's feet, however. On that day, anyone going up to the top floor of that base

will find themselves under a glass ceiling and, upon tilting their head back, can peer into a gigantic tunnel — the interior of Liberty.

It is filled with a thicket of trusses riveted together according to the design of the great engineer Gustave Eiffel, and only here and there can one see, glistening through the steel skeleton, that golden-green body, now out of reach.

The Wall of Honor, the Jagielskis, the Mormons

Inscribing a name on the Wall of Honor is very simple. There's no need to prove anything. In any case it's hard to imagine someone wanting themselves illegitimately inscribed there. Why would they? So many families in America today are entitled to it. Nearly everyone has come from somewhere. If not through Ellis Island, then through another seaport or airport, through a legal land crossing, or smuggled

across the border.

The Wall of Honor at Ellis Island, despite its name, cannot exalt anyone. For those wishing to write their family's name there, it's clearly a necessary point of departure, their American place of birth. We might say the Wall of Honor, which surrounds a lawn and forms a perfectly round bowl, is America's secular baptismal font.

But what happened to Franciszka Jagielska from Dulsk in Golub-Dobrzyń county, and her husband Józef, who waited so many years for her in the city of Pittsburgh, Pennsylvania? They are not among the nearly 775,000 names etched on the wall.

This time, no censor had a hand in their absence. It may be only the circumstances of their lives that are to blame. Perhaps their reunion came too late, the family didn't fully connect, and Franciszka and Józef Jagielski left no descendants in America. Or subsequent generations' lives didn't give them the desire to remember their ancestors' first footsteps in the United States. Or maybe they didn't want to spend the money?

A name must be paid for. Józef and Franciszka Jagielski have a few options to choose from:

An inscription for one person, costing $150:

Józef Jagielski

or

The Józef Jagielski Family.

An inscription for two people for $225:

Józef and Franciszka Jagielski

or

The Józef and Franciszka Jagielski Family.

In both cases you can also, for the same price, add a wife's maiden name (we don't know Franciszka's). But it probably wouldn't fit, because the whole line, including spaces, cannot exceed 40 characters. For this reason — and out of concern for the equality of this assembly — additional descriptions are not accepted, such as *Mr* or *Mrs*, *Rev*, *Gen*, *MD*, *Esq*, and so on.

However, this equality has limits. Anyone spending $1,000, $5,000, or $10,000 can have two lines and receive the title of Leader, Benefactor, or Patron of Ellis Island, respectively.

Anyone who pays the basic $150 receives a matching certificate as well. They are now known as a Friend of Ellis.

You can arrange all this online or in person — at the place that was once known as the Kissing Gate and which made such a strong impression on matron Maud Mosher. At the bottom of the stairs, a bronze plaque hangs on the wall bearing a quote from Maud's notebook.

You have to stand in a line made up mainly of descendants of former arrivals who, as well as a space on the Wall of Honor, want a copy of the ship's manifest bearing their ancestors' names, a precise description of the information on it (because the manifests aren't always legible), a photograph of the ship they arrived on, and whatever else the database knows about them.

The line is patient and a familiar, friendly mood prevails, as though all these customers were descended from the same great-grandmother and were meeting at a family holiday celebration.

The office at the Kissing Gate provides information about the 22 million passengers (American citizens and foreigners) received at the Port of New York between 1892 and 1924.

Working to create this database were 12,000 volunteers belonging to the

Church of Jesus Christ of Latter-day Saints, popularly known as Mormons. They have the largest supply of genealogical information in the world, collected in the belief that their Church can accept into its bosom even those baptized after death. But first they have to be found in the registers.

A Horse-Drawn Cart in Stawiski, Meredith Monk

Meredith Monk doesn't search for her relatives in the computers on the island. She goes to Poland. We see her kneeling on the grass in Stawiski, about a hundred miles northeast of Warsaw. She kisses and strokes the grass. Her long, thin braids crisscross on the ground. At this moment Meredith looks so unostentatious, even ugly, that her gestures seem in no way theatrical. It's hard to imagine her onstage, where she electrifies not only with her singing but her whole person. She's wearing an odd newsboy-type cap, a baggy jacket, and large clunky boots. These are clothes for a journey, or a pilgrimage even. They express an intention to come nearer to a place Meredith has long been thinking of.

Meredith rises, having suddenly spotted a horse pulling a cart. The horse is large, powerful, and the cart is solidly built, with tilted wooden sides. The young man sitting on it loosens the reins in curiosity. Meredith goes up to the horse, touches its face, says something to it. This would look funny and childish if we weren't aware Meredith knows the language of nature, meaning surely the language of horses as well, and beyond that, in the opera she composed, *Atlas*, a horse-guide appears, playing a metaphysical role. Meredith speaks for a moment with this horse from Stawiski as though he were something more than a heavy draft animal, and then sits in the driver's seat and takes the reins. The boy lets her take his seat, then walks around the cart and probably finds the situation entertaining, while Meredith keeps choking back tears. Her grandma Zdrojewska had a horse-drawn cart in Stawiski before she emigrated to America, and drove it herself. It was probably no worse a cart than the one Meredith is riding now, because grandpa Zdrojewski had a bicycle shop in neighboring Łomża, and the family was not as poor as the majority of the area's Jews.

Meredith Monk knows a thing or two about one line of her ancestors, the one descended from the famous cantor, but almost nothing about the other, the branch that came from here. Meredith's parents were born in America and didn't like her asking about the homeland of her grandparents from Stawiski and Łomża.

The locals observe from behind wicket gates as Meredith goes door to door in her newsboy cap and asks at each: did the Zdrojewskis live here? She asks in English and someone interprets. An old man thinks hard and replies: *Zdrojewscy? Pamiętam…*

Then Meredith bursts into tears, because she knows that sound. *Pamiętam, pamiętam*, she repeats through her tears: *I remember, I remember*. But she doesn't remember how she knows that word, *pamiętam*. At any rate, the old man doesn't remember anything except the name Zdrojewski and offers his age as an excuse; he's 95. Maybe those Zdrojewskis lived here, maybe there… It's easy to tell the old Jewish houses if you run your hand over the door. One side of the doorframe is smooth, because they kissed the wood. They used to hang the Ten Commandments there.

We don't know what the Zdrojewskis' first names were, we only know they were very lucky, because they left.

Maybe they were called Chaim or Chane, or Frana, or Kleloime, or Lajzer, or Lalmen, or Mordche, or Feivel, or Stanisław; all of these have the same last name — Zdrojewski — and are named in the ships' manifests at Ellis Island as arrivals from Łomża and the surrounding area in the first quarter of the 20th century. There were an awful lot of these Zdrojewskis.

They might have looked like the motionless characters in Meredith's film about immigrants, the ones who come to life for a moment when a man in a white coat brings his hand to their eye, brandishing a buttonhook.[229]

Buttonhook, Trachoma

The 1930s saw the twilight of the buttonhook as a practical fastening tool. It still held out as a diagnostic aid for some time at Ellis Island, but infrequently; as medical inspections improved at European ports it was required less and less.

Yet few small objects for trivial uses have such an eventful afterlife. The Buttonhook Society, founded in 1979 in Maidstone, England, publishes the color magazine *The Boutonneur*, organizes annual exhibits of the most interesting specimens; maintains print, illustration, and photography archives (with over 50,000 entries); publishes compendiums

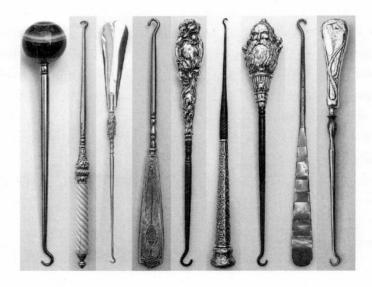

for collectors; and organizes social weekends for them, for instance at the White Hart Hotel in Salisbury.

Unfortunately trachoma also has an eventful life. Yet by the 21st century it circulates in entirely different regions from the buttonhook and its fans.

Jeff Dosik, the museum librarian at Ellis Island, receives a letter from Jonathan Struthers of the International Trachoma Initiative, fighting trachoma in the countries of the developing world. Struthers wants to familiarize himself with long-ago research on trachoma from Ellis. The affliction of yesterday's immigrants likely had the same source as the trachoma in Burkina Faso, Ethiopia, Guinea-Bissau, Kenya, Mali, Nepal, and seven other countries where ITI oversees care. The organization calculates over 40 million people around the world suffer from trachoma, while 10 million are completely or partially blind as a result of the disease. However, Struthers is thinking positively. He declares Morocco has almost completely dealt with trachoma, while the Gambia, Ghana, Vietnam, and Mauritania are on the right path. Thanks to the organization, 352,000 sufferers have been operated on and 77 million doses of the medication Zithromax have been given. According to the organization's optimistic predictions, the world should be able to completely regain its sight around 2020, though we don't know if that optimism takes into account the desperate lack of water for washing and drinking in trachoma-affected regions. One-sixth of the world's population has no access to clean water, even though water covers over 70 per cent of the surface of the globe.

Jacob Auerbach's Buttons

Jacob Auerbach, who came to Ellis Island like Jonah in the belly of the whale and in time became an inspector on the island, really did keep the most important elements of his first uniform: 15 buttons, six epaulettes, the eagle from his shirt, and the emblem from his cap. He offered all this to the museum along with a manuscript of his memoirs.

The museum has received many objects as gifts. Most have left no doubt as to their nature — things like shawls, formal dresses, silverware, Bibles, menorahs, Hanukkah candles, images of Our Lady of Częstochowa, felt boots, tablecloths, a Polish passport featuring a proud spread-winged and crowned eagle, issued to Perla Rajter from Grójec in 1922, a peasant accordion with keys as round as coat buttons, an elegant zither from Norway painted with flowers and fruits like an Old Master's still life, the aforementioned travel chests, and so on. But some objects take a moment's thought to work out what they actually are. Something black, hard, and threadbare turns out to be a coconut, brought across the ocean from its country of origin and kept for decades. A pile of gray cardboard is an empty box of chocolates. It is identified by a worn-out overprint in Polish: *Suchard Czekolada Gorzka*. This treasure was kept for many years by Nathan Solomon, who received it from his mother in 1923, probably to ease his journey.

Today, the museum struggles rather with too many items than too few, but it wasn't so from the start.

Historic furnishings from the immigration station fell apart and were destroyed during the years of still waters. The team creating the museum eagerly waited for them to be cleaned, renovated, reconstructed. The publication *Stewed Prunes* (probably so named because in a certain period prunes dominated the immigrants' menu at Ellis), made by friendly hands on photocopiers at the island, carried this lament:

> I think I shall never find
> Artifacts of any kind
> Used by immigrants at their peak
> Before these roofs did start to leak.
> No desk, no books, no buttonhooks,

No beds that like the photo looks.
Bring back the artifacts oh ye crooks
To place in Ellis' empty nooks.
Artifacts are searched by big fools like me
But only God knows where they be.

The poem was written by a concerned Diana P., meaning Diana Pardue. That was in 1980. The author stayed for long enough to see the objects she needed. Today she runs the museum.

Janet Levine and Assadourian

Janet Levine, PhD, was working at a university. She was researching the relationship between psychology and art. That is, up until the moment she read about the Oral History Project at Ellis Island. She always wanted to interview people, find out how they built their destiny, get to know *those who had to recreate their entire lives*. In 1991 she called Diana Pardue at the Ellis Island museum, took a ferry to the island, and was hired.

She conducted her first interview with a German woman named Annabel, who came to America after the First World War. She was poor, alone, and terrified, but she had spirit. She created a large, happy family and provided her children with the safety and comfort she could only have dreamed about. She showed Janet photos of this huge family. Both Janet and Annabel were nervous because neither had experience recording conversations, but a few years later Annabel's great-grandson visited Janet at the island, listened to the tape, and asked for a copy to give to his loved ones.

One of Levine's last interviews was with a Hungarian named Steven. In the mid-thirties his family discovered their grandfather had

Jewish blood, *and they were beginning to feel the — the pressures of being Jewish in Europe*. Steven and his three brothers left for America. Steven told Jane that when he first saw Manhattan in 1937, he looked up at the skyscraper windows and wondered which would belong to him. He got some windows, but he remained lonely. Annabel and Steven were both successful, but each in a different way. The variety of these successes, the variety of human achievements, fascinated Levine.

She recorded hundreds of interviews before her retirement. You can hear them using headphones and read them; they've been transcribed with exceptional fidelity. Every *uh-huh, mm-hm, yeah, oh yeah, uh-hm, well,* and *so* has been retained, because these mutterings and exclamations have historical significance.

We listen to these stories and hear a cat meowing, a clock ticking, a lawnmower rumbling in the distance, a wheelchair creaking, because most of these sessions take place in the houses or apartments of those being recorded. From time to time Janet Levine flew all the way to Florida with her tape recorder, because that's where people from the great metropolises of the east and north move in their old age. She spoke to all her Danish interviewees in Florida, in the city of St Petersburg.

One of these people in Florida spoke too fast, incomprehensibly. But he couldn't hold himself back. He was in a great hurry; he was very old. Though not so old as the man of 97 who still went dancing, or the woman of 106 who looked like a little angel and gave Janet home-made cookies.

A certain younger interviewee remembered America as a country all in the dark. That was his impression from the abyss of the subway. Levine says such visions of reality are *child-like*. In moments of great emotion, great stress, adults are sometimes subject to such strong impressions, like children. They remain under their influence for a long time and talk about them the way they actually perceived them as a child.

Janet recorded immigration stories in various cities and states of America, in various apartments, in various circumstances. She drew a conclusion: it's good to talk to people in their gardens, it's not so good in their retirement homes.[230]

The transcribed accounts, oftentimes dozens of pages long, stand clipped into three-ring binders on the shelves of the Oral History division of the Bob Hope Memorial Library, on the top floor of the museum.

Each account is accompanied by a summary, noting the most important elements of its contents, as well as sentences that might be worth quoting — for instance, in museum educational programs. So after Levine's recording of an interview with the Armenian woman Ervanthouhi Garabidian Assadourian, born in 1906, who came to America on the ship *Gul Gjemel* at the age of 14, one of her colleagues, Paul E. Sigrist Jr, made the following summary:

> Details about the relationship between the Turks and
> the Christians in her town: 3– 4, interesting quote about
> animals having feelings like humans in times of great
> adversity: 4, information about being kept safe by an
> American woman: 5, description of atrocities committed
> by the Turks: 5–6, quotable description of being left alone
> and praying to her dead grandmother: 6, mention of the
> great loss of life in her family: 7, details about attending
> Turkish school: 7–8, mention of learning Armenian when
> she eventually went to Constantinople to live with her
> uncle: 8, mention of being robbed of all worldly goods
> by the Turks: 9, extended story about recently meeting
> up with a long-lost cousin: 9–11, details about her family:
> 11–12, details about writing on a slate in kindergarten:
> 12, mention of table etiquette: 13, description of clothing:
> 13, details about her grandfather's business raising and

slaughtering lambs: 13–14, more family details: 14–16,
description of her mother and her mother's ability to
write: 16, story about the excavation of an old Russian
Bible that was later sold to Oxford University: 17–18,
description of a secret cave where Christians would
sometimes hide: 18, various atrocities committed by
the Turks: 19–20, information about the American
woman who saved her the translation of an Armenian
book into English: 20–21, information about well-
known Armenian Catholics whom Mrs. Assadourian
knew: 21–22, information about the American woman's
efforts to save Armenian children: 23–24 ... details
about when her father and husband-to-be came to the
U.S.: 25 ... description of her excitement and eventual
disappointment in America: 31, information about being
at Ellis Island: 32 ... quotable description of being forced
by her father into an arranged marriage upon arrival
in New York: 35, details about her inability to attend
school because she had to help in her husband's grocery
business: 36 ... description of her good relationship
with her husband's family: 37 ... her sentiment that the
U.S. had become "a jungle": 39, her desire to travel to
Armenia but her decision to stay in the U.S. because of
her advanced age: 39 ...

Beneath this abstract from the life of Ervanthouhi Garabidian
Assadourian, Sigrist added: *Interview date 5/26/1993, age at time of
interview: 87, running time: 57:57, interviewer: Janet Levine.*
The rules require that an interview last no longer than an hour.
Someone has to take this all in, and there have already been more than
2,000 interviews.

Divisions, Corridors

Sometimes a conversation goes along with a site visit. This time it's
Paul Sigrist doing the interviewing himself, and the guest of the Oral
History Project is John C., a former American merchant marine sailor
detained at Ellis Island in 1947 on suspicion of psychological problems.
Forty-three years later, in November 1990, the museum employees
walk with John C. and his wife through the empty hospital buildings
on Island 2. John C. is looking for something.

We hear the rustle of wind and the shuffling of feet, the voices cut
in and out. John C.'s voice emerges:

> Well, I remember ... that you can look out the window
> and see the Statue of Liberty ... Then I had to be on this
> side. Because that's where we went to, when you woke up
> in the morning.

He addresses Sigrist:

> One place I would like to see now... Are you going to
> edit this?

Sigrist doesn't completely understand the question. John C. is
asking if the recording will be corrected. He adds: *Because I don't want
to say nothing wrong in here.*

Sigrist reassures him: *Oh, don't worry. You say whatever you want to
say. It doesn't matter.*

John C.: Because I come out with very frank things.

Sigrist: That's quite all right ... What would you like to
see?

John C.: The main room upstairs is where we used to get
our shock treatments.

Sigrist: I see. Well, we're going to try and find it, which room.

John C.: Fascinating though, really.

Sigrist asks about the nurses. John C. doesn't remember any women there.

Mrs C.: No, I think they were the big guys because they had to handle them after they had shock treatments and everything ...

John C.: But what it was after [the treatment], you were out. You were completely out. Then one of the attendants would grab your hands, arms, the other one would grab your legs, pick you off, and that's why I wanted to see this main, it looked like an auditorium to me, or a gymnasium, and just dump you on some old dirty mattress on the floor. And when you went in there, if you were one of the last ones, you had maybe fifteen or twenty guys laying around on that floor. And when you got up[,] you got up and said, "Okay." And you say, "Well, where do I go from here?" They said, "You go back to your room."

We hear shuffling and wind.

John C.: I'd do it all over again. I'd do my whole life over again.

Mrs C.: Get out of here!

John C.: Really, I would ... That part of my life was very interesting. It was a good part of my life ...

Sigrist: And surely the shock treatment would have had some effect, you know?

330

Mrs C.: Well I don't think he really needed any at the time.

John C.: Not really. I wasn't that, knowing now, there was no need for shock treatments.

Sigrist remarks his feet are getting cold. Mrs C. is glad she put on old shoes. The voices fade.

Someone says in the distance:

This certainly is the longest hallway in the entire complex.

Mrs C.: In the entire world.

Antek with Zoska, Eric Byron

Eric Byron misses his weekends in Washington Square Park, but he had to give them up. He hasn't got the energy to drag all the machinery there with him anymore.

He built it himself. It's made out of an ancient gramophone with a crank, a five-foot horn Eric constructed out of heating or ventilation ducts and a small platform on rubber wheels. Eric, as befits an artistic soul, lives in the East Village, not far from the park, and even a few years ago would throw the horn on his back, fasten a harness across his chest, and haul his musical equipment to his concert venue. He did this for at least ten years, solely for pleasure.

First he'd make a careful selection of records, which he'd also load on to the cart, and put a box of needles in his pocket, because he never used the same one twice. Some of the records were very old, from the start of the 20th century, and required very delicate treatment. He bought the needles in bulk, so they cost two cents apiece.

As Eric parked his music by a bench, the square would be full of people. He didn't mind, just the opposite. He played "Willie the Weeper" featuring Louis Armstrong, or "Hallelujah, I'm a Bum" by Jack Kaufmann. He most enjoyed putting on Eric Carus, because once when he did this, something remarkable happened. A blind woman was walking slowly down the path, supported by two people holding her arms. She stopped, raised a finger as if to test the wind direction, and headed toward the melody. She stopped next to Eric Byron and listened. She knew what was on the record because she'd been to see that opera, she remembered the singer and the auditorium of the old Metropolitan Opera perfectly, she could see it again.

Eric is tender-hearted, so he had to react quickly. Luckily he had on hand two foolproof American ditties from 1919: the Prohibition song "How Are You Goin' to Wet Your Whistle When The Whole Darn World Goes Dry?", sung by Billy Murray, and a song posing no less dramatic a question: "How You Gonna Keep 'Em Down On the Farm After They've Seen Paree?" in a version by Arthur Fields.

But as he listened to Fields, Eric fell into a sentimental reverie, because he remembered the singer's last days — a stroke, then dying in a fire at his retirement home in Florida.

Eric Byron is coordinator of the Ellis Island museum's Discography Project. He collects recordings produced for immigrants from the start to the middle of the 20th century. It turns out that over those fifty years, a range of American labels released no fewer than 30,000 records for foreigners to familiarize themselves with American life. They included skits, songs, short theatrical scenes; many of them taught basic English expressions.

The museum has managed to acquire over 1,200 records. Making out foreign words, particularly sung, from scratchy records demands great patience. One album Eric Byron acquired is from 1927, with a little music, a little chat, and a little singing in Polish. Its title: *Antek with Zośka on the Ship.*

Zośka: Antoś, my goodness! What's that dance they're doing?

Antek: See, they're dancing the foxtrot to a waltz.

Zośka: Heavens! They're jiggling like aspic ... What is she doing, why, her legs are flying in the air.

Antek: Don't be scared, they're normal legs, she can spin one around three times and it doesn't hurt.

Zośka: Well, I'd get my legs all twisted up. Oh, Antoś, I think looking at them is making me feel sick.

Antek: Oh no, Zosia, that's not from looking at them. Come here, Zosia, take a look down where the water's flowing around the ship, that'll make you feel better for sure.

The next bit of the album brings Antek on land more or less permanently and is titled *Antek the American in the Tavern*.

Eric doesn't know Polish, but he has volunteers who know various languages. They sit by a creaky record player, listen closely, transcribe the text in the original language and translate it into English. They help with cataloguing, tracking down bibliographic details, and other jobs. One of these volunteers, Charles Lemonick, has racked up approximately 9,000 hours of this work.

According to Eric, *Antek and Zośka* and similar recordings create an opportunity to understand other cultures.[231] He's convinced they are valuable research material, though he fears they favor ethnic and racial stereotypes. He never plays them in the park; they could offend someone.

Levine, Byron, Dosik, Moreno

The collection of books at Ellis Island, the Oral History Project, and the Discography Project are located side by side on the top floor of the museum. Eric Byron sits on the opposite side of the wall from where Janet Levine used to work, and a little further along is a small foyer and the library, where Jeffrey Dosik and Barry Moreno work.

The museum employees say one-third of the island's current staff come from families who came through here to the United States. Park Ranger Dennis Mulligan can even show the tourists his family's manifest. A copy of the document is displayed in the Great Hall on one of the high podiums where the inspectors used to sit. The manifest declares that on 19 July 1901, Elisabeth Mulligan sailed to New York with her four children. One of them, Thomas, is Dennis's grandfather.

Levine's grandparents on her father's side were Abraham Levine and Celie Eig from Minsk. Janet couldn't find them in the passenger lists, though. She gave up, because the name Levine appeared so often in the manifests that she'd have had to waste an enormous amount of time searching, and she had her interviews with the living to do.

Without searching far, Eric Byron found that his grandmother was named Rose Levine (no relation to Janet's grandfather) and also arrived

from today's Belarus. Eric also knows that his maternal grandfather, Isaac Fleischman, emigrated from Lithuania. This is all the knowledge he needs. He has no desire to dig around in the past. He says to him the future is more important, and the present most important of all. He didn't drag his machinery to Washington Square Park for the sake of the past, but for a lovely present moment.

Jeffrey Dosik, for his part, loaded the appropriate software and entered a whole series of queries, but was driven more by professional duty than personal curiosity. The people at the museum were simply testing out the search engines linked to the database so wonderfully prepared by the Mormons on themselves and their ancestors. Jeff typed his grandfathers Mozes and Alexander, and grandmothers Yetta and Anna into the search boxes. He established that Mozes Dosik, who sewed caps in a Russian shtetl, came to America in steerage in 1906; his wife Yetta a year later; Alexander Rogersin in 1913; and his wife Anna Sadleck from Slovakia not until 1924. The search engines performed well. Dosik fulfilled his professional duty and obtained something else valuable. He's always liked the island, but now he feels more at home here.

The librarian and historian Barry Moreno's grandfather sailed to America after 1930, on a different wave of immigration — for education. Presbyterian missionaries founded American universities in Cairo and Beirut and offered scholarships in the US to young Arab Christians. Barry's mother is an Egyptian Copt; his father is a refugee from Fidel Castro's Cuba.

Barry sits at his computer beneath a glass ceiling; over his head he has one of the station building's four copper-domed towers, as well as jet streams and bird formations. He's written over a dozen books on immigration. One of them, the *Encyclopedia of Ellis Island*, is the basic source of knowledge about the island. The book is dedicated to his nephews — Victor and Sergio Moreno. That's an unusual dedication, because most authors of books about Ellis Island dedicate them not to their descendants, but to their ancestors — parents, grandparents, great-grandparents who came through here. It seems as though every book about Ellis Island has been written by people driven by such a familial impulse.

One dedication is simultaneously an appeal. Peter Morton Coan, who collected interviews with immigrants (*Ellis Island Interviews: in their own words*), confides in his readers:

> I am looking for my biological parents. I have never met
> them. It is ironic that I would feel the need, the spiritual
> pull, to write a book about Ellis Island genealogy, and
> roots when I, myself, lack knowledge of my own past.
> Perhaps that is the reason.[232]

He gives some meager information about his mother, attaches his address and asks for a response if anyone knows of some path to her, or more likely to a memory of her.

The Train Station in Jersey City

A flimsy bridge runs between Ellis Island and the New Jersey waterfront, built in the mid-1980s, during the period of the greatest renovation work on the island. Once massive trucks would cross it bearing materials, now it's closed to the public. The official version is it requires fundamental reconstruction; the unofficial one is that pedestrian traffic from Jersey City to Ellis Island would threaten the profits of the private ferry company.

If we want to view the bridge from the Ellis Island side, we have to exit the main building into a long annex, where the former kitchen and laundry used to operate, and emerge into an area of empty, untended wharf to which tourists have no access. We now have our backs to the old electric plant with its yellowed smokestack, the water tower — a

white cistern on steel legs, and, behind it, the large dormitory and the luggage building, which is still waiting to be renovated. We can see how much still remains to be reclaimed, but after all we're standing on the original part of Ellis, Island 1. The wealth of Islands 2 and 3, mostly closed off to visitors, is even greater — they hold dozens of former hospital buildings which have been re-roofed, their windows re-glazed or covered in shutters, yet whose interiors are thus far untouched and still look as they did when Shirley Burden visited. Rusting equipment still stands inside, leftovers of the station's former possessions; plaster still rains down on them and the floors of endless corridors still creak. But now we know that assigning these buildings new, suitable functions and getting them into as good shape as the main museum building will happen sooner or later, that no one will lay a hand on the island's historic grounds, because Ellis Island is approaching closer to Plymouth Rock.

If the bridge were open, it would lead us to Liberty State Park in New Jersey, right near Black Tom wharf, which in 1916 was rocked by the explosion Dr Frederick A. Theis described so vividly. Today, the epicenter of that explosion is a green lawn surrounded by American flags on tall poles.

The paths of Liberty State Park lead to the old rail station that served immigrants who'd secured the right to enter the US at Ellis Island. This station is also a museum. On weekdays it's mostly empty. No one asks for anything or stops anyone.

The train station closed in 1967. The tracks were torn out from under the twenty platforms, lying beneath an enormous concrete roof held up with cast-iron columns. The symmetrical openings in this roof surely once held panes of glass. Now sunlight and rain fall through them, so the trackbed is overgrown with wild greenery, ivy has wrapped around the columns and their capitals, and in sunlight the whole space looks like a boundless orangery, and in the rain like an aquarium. Nature has been allowed to overwhelm the platforms, yet it hasn't been permitted into the main hall, which is in such beautiful condition it seems ready at any moment to receive passengers heading for the express to Philadelphia from Platform 3 (at 5.42 pm) or for the Crusader from Platform 7 (4.32 pm), or for the Blue Comet to Atlantic City from Platform 10 (10.13 am), and so on.

From Liberty State Park we can see more easily than from Ellis Island how close the two buildings stand across the water: the immigration station on the island, where life could begin — or also end — and the train station on the mainland, which meant a new birth.

Lenni Lenape

Not far from the Wall of Honor, on the grass in the shade of a few paradisiacal apple trees, lies a small gray-red stone from the Lenape Indians.

In the middle of the stone is carved a bird's-eye view of a turtle. It looks like an inkblot. Its head, feet, and tail protrude from its shell. On its left lies the seal of the Delaware-Lenape tribe, on its right, that of the

Mohican people. Both are full of symbols: a wolf, a bear, a predator's footprints, a cross, a shield, a bow, a leaf.

Beneath these is written:

Delaware Indian Burials — Uncovered on Ellis and Liberty Islands. Re-Interred May 1, 2003.

On the morning of that day, a group of men and women walked out of the museum building on Ellis in ordinary clothing: sweaters, jeans, jackets. It must have been cold, though according to Lenape tradition on 1 May the tribe welcomes spring. That is why this date was chosen to celebrate their ancestors' return home.

The group includes National Park employees and Lenape tribal elders. Three of them bear small cedar boxes containing remains discovered on the island in the mid-eighties. Archeologists had no doubt these bones, intermixed with oyster shells, dating to the 17th century at the latest, belonged to the Lenape. They communicated with tribal representatives and determined that, as long as ren-ovations were underway on the island, the park would tend to the remains.

Afterwards they would be buried in a jointly chosen place on Ellis Island.

Seventeen years have passed since that agreement. On the last day of April 2003, the graves were dug. This was done by the Delaware

Chief Joe Brooks, tribal member John Sumpter (both American Army veterans), and Bruce Gonzales, president of the Delaware Nation, of Andarko, Oklahoma.

Now, on this May morning, the Native Americans slowly lower and release the boxes into the hole in the ground. Jimmy Jackson from the Lenape elders sings a traditional song in the Lenape language. First the cawing of gulls drowns him out, then the roar of a jet plane.

The mourners waft pleasant-smelling smoke from burning sweetgrass over the grave. In this way they drive away evil spirits. Earlier, Lenape women prayed for the peace of their ancestors. Linda Poolaw led the prayer meeting. Usually men take care of burying the Lenape dead, but Linda said women should participate in the funeral, share in the general emotion, and feel the relief. And so this happened too.

Linda Poolaw, like Bruce Gonzales, came from Andarko. She's the daughter of Horace Poolaw, a Native American who all his life photographed other Native Americans, and in 1942 joined the US Air Force and taught the crew how to take photographs from the air, because anyone who could interpret such photos could better spot bombing targets.

Linda worked with the New York branch of the National Museum of the American Indian, housed in the beautiful rotunda of the former Customs House at the southern tip of Manhattan, which itself is a work by Rafael Guastavino Sr and holds an important place on every tour of New York architecture. She wrote a book about her father and his photographs. She noted her father didn't want them to commemorate his person. He wished to commemorate *his people*, the Indians of Oklahoma.[233]

Oysters

Strict penalties for polluters have been brought in and the water in New York Bay is getting cleaner. The bluefish have returned, and sturgeons, shad, and yellow perch are multiplying. One year near the coast of New Jersey, a perch was caught measuring nearly four-and-a-half feet long and weighing almost eighty pounds. Sometimes a seal is spotted here. Scuba divers have discovered oyster beds still lying beneath the water. Their shells are large, empty, corroded by acidity.

Twenty years ago environmental defenders decided to encourage the oysters back to life in their former lost paradise. They prepared an artificial reef near Liberty and Ellis Islands and after some time noticed juvenile mollusks growing on it. They established they weren't suitable for consumption, but they could be workers, expanding the reef and cleansing the water. Apparently nothing purifies water like living shellfish.

So there's a hope the Bay will keep getting cleaner thanks to penalties, pangs of conscience, and fear for the future — among humans anyway — as well as the patient work of the mollusks whom fate has at least granted a reprieve from being eaten alive along with their small three-chambered hearts (as the author and gourmand Jonathan Swift put it, *he was a bold man that first ate an oyster*). So, one day, fat, delicious oysters will grow around Ellis Island, as in days gone by.

We must patiently await a healthy harvest, because an oyster sickened by the humans who poisoned its water will in turn poison the human who eats it. In the first quarter of the 20th century they poisoned humans not only with typhus, but with suspicion — that the poor countries of Europe were to blame for all kinds of infection.

No one can be sure when the oysters in the beds around Ellis Island, and the water of the Bay along with them, will return to their condition in the days of the Lenape Indians — whether in ten, twenty, fifty, or a hundred years, or whether it's possible at all.

From the Author

I sailed to Ellis Island over ten years ago to see the museum. In the very first moments, by the city of traveling chests, I felt a curiosity that grew with each following step. What happened here? Who were the people of the island — the keepers of the gates? What was their interaction like with those pressing in on those gates? How did they reconcile the virtues they learned in their homes and democratic institutions with the cruelty their service often demanded?

After returning to Poland, I started to look for books about the island. I was sure there would be many, including by Polish authors. I found nothing. In the catalogues of the largest Polish libraries the island's name didn't appear at all, while in the large book collections of Britain and America titles about Ellis Island are very easy to find and too numerous to count. These works are documentary, academic, memoirs, photo books, films, poems, novels. But they have not reached Poland, either in the original editions or in translation. As if we, occupied with the course of events at home, had no attention left for Ellis Island.

So I decided to do something about this within the measure of my abilities — to write a book about Ellis Island. I asked the Ellis Island National Museum of Immigration for help tracking down information and I received a generous, encouraging response. I went to America, and as I worked at Ellis Island I found it just as easy to obtain testimony of the United States' generosity as of its selfishness. I could forget the ambivalent word *key* to describe the island's former role; throughout the period of my work, the island lay open before me.

Thank you to the museum's director Diana Pardue and to Dr Janet Levine, Barry Moreno, Jeffrey Dosik, and Eric Byron for sharing books, manuscripts, films, recordings, and photographs. I am particularly grateful to Barry Moreno, librarian, historian and writer, author of that important source of information about the island, the *Encyclopedia of Ellis Island*, for his wise assistance and great patience. I am grateful for an invaluable piece of practical assistance — a daily spot on the official National Park boat running between the tip of Manhattan and Ellis Island.

H.G. Wells, on whom Ellis Island made a tremendous impression, confessed in his book *The Future in America*:

> And always I have been saying to myself, "Remember the immigrants; don't leave them out of your reckoning."[234]

As I gathered this information, I became convinced that the attention paid to immigrants should be accompanied by attention to those who accepted them (or rejected them). *Ellis Island* is an expression of that conviction.

List of Illustrations

Nebraska, p. 37. From Barry Moreno, *Children of Ellis Island*, Charleston, SC: Arcadia, 2005.

The second station on Ellis Island, pp. 46–47. US National Archives.

The Temple of Music at the Pan-American Exposition in Buffalo, p. 48.

The pavilion over Plymouth Rock, p. 50. www.visit-plymouth.com/ images/rockportico1.jpg.

President Theodore Roosevelt (with arm extended) on Ellis Island, William Williams on the right, p. 51. William Williams Papers, Manuscripts and Archives Division, The New York Public Library, Astor, Lenox and Tilden Foundations.

A crowd of immigrants in front of Ellis Island station, p. 54. Burt G. Phillips/Museum of the City of New York/Print Archives.

Perumall Sammy, p. 57. Photo by Augustus F. Sherman, from the book Augustus F. Sherman, *Ellis Island Portraits 1905–1920*, New York: Aperture Foundation, 2005.

The University Club building in Manhattan, p. 68.

Zbyszko Cyganiewicz, p. 71. Photo by Augustus F. Sherman, from the book Augustus F. Sherman, *Ellis Island Portraits 1905–1920*, New York: Aperture Foundation, 2005.

Jewish orphans who sailed from Russia after the pogrom of 1905, p. 72. Photo by Augustus F. Sherman, from the book Augustus F. Sherman, *Ellis Island Portraits 1905–1920*, New York: Aperture Foundation, 2005.

After 1904, the shape of the island resembles a radiator, p. 73. US National Park Service, Ellis Island.

Eye examinations, p. 76. US National Park Service, Ellis Island.

The medical service at Ellis Island, p. 79. US National Archives.

Immigrants with chalk symbols on their clothes, p. 81. Culver Picture.

Henry James, p. 82. Time Life Pictures/Getty Images.

The children's playground on the roof of the station building, p. 85. Photo by Augustus F. Sherman, from the book Augustus F.

Black Tom wharf after the explosion in 1916, p. 158.

Fiorello La Guardia as a pilot during the First World War, p. 168.
Wide World Photos.

Dutch siblings, p. 170. Photo by Augustus F. Sherman, from the book
Augustus F. Sherman, *Ellis Island Portraits 1905–1920*, New York:
Aperture Foundation, 2005.

Young Italian soldier, p. 172. Photo by Augustus F. Sherman, from the
book Augustus F. Sherman, *Ellis Island Portraits 1905–1920*, New
York: Aperture Foundation, 2005.

Emma Goldman, p. 176. Photo by Augustus F. Sherman, from the
book Augustus F. Sherman, *Ellis Island Portraits 1905–1920*, New
York: Aperture Foundation, 2005.

New York cemetery, paupers' area, p. 184. Museum of the City of
New York/Jacob A. Riis Collection/90.13.1.87.

Robert Watchorn with his wife and son, Emory, p. 193. As appears in
The Autobiography of Robert Watchorn, ed. Hebert Faulkner West,
Oklahoma City: The Robert Watchorn Charities Ltd., 1959.

Women in the detention room, p. 196. US National Archives.

Ludmila Foxlee in Slavic folk dress, c. 1920, p. 208. US National Park
Service, Ellis Island.

Caricature of Henry H. Curran, p. 218. *New Yorker*, June 14, 1930.

Cartoon by Hendrik Willem van Loon from 1924, p. 222.

Ku Klux Klan demonstration in New Jersey in 1924, p. 223.
Bettmann/Getty Images.

Italian woman, p. 228. Photo by Augustus F. Sherman, from the book
Augustus F. Sherman, *Ellis Island Portraits 1905–1920*, New York:
Aperture Foundation, 2005.

Cossacks, p. 229. Photo by Augustus F. Sherman, from the book
Augustus F. Sherman, *Ellis Island Portraits 1905–1920*, New York:
Aperture Foundation, 2005.

Dr Thomas W. Salmon memorial plaque at the New York Psychiatric
Institute, p. 234.

The Mittelstadt family, p. 311. Photo by Augustus F. Sherman, from the book Augustus F. Sherman, *Ellis Island Portraits 1905–1920*, New York: Aperture Foundation, 2005.

Main Hall of the Station, Guastavino's ceiling, p. 313. CC Image courtesy of Paul Beavers on Flickr.

Interior view of the Statue of Liberty, p. 316. Courtesy of Daniel Schwen [CC BY-SA (https://creativecommons.org/licenses/by-sa/4.0)].

The Wall of Honor, p. 317. US National Park Service, Ellis Island.

Buttonhooks, p. 322.

The librarian and author Barry Moreno, p. 334. US National Park Service, Ellis Island.

Liberty State Park in New Jersey, the former Black Tom wharf, site of the devastating explosion in 1916, p. 337. Michael S. Yamashita/Corbis.

Horace Poolaw photographed by Jerry Poolaw, Lenni Lenape, p. 339. US National Park Service, Ellis Island.

End Notes

The Ellis Island National Museum of Immigration is referred to as Ellis Island Immigration Museum in the following notes.

1 Rising Tide

1 Barry Moreno, *Encyclopedia of Ellis Island* (Westport, Connecticut, Greenwood Press, 2004), p. 53.

2 Samuel Ellis' ad appeared on 20 January 1785 in Loudon's New-York Packet, a local newspaper published by Samuel Loudon. Moreno quotes it in his *Encyclopedia of Ellis Island*, p. xii.

3 Information about this initiative of the tsarist authorities, and quotes from the letters, come from an extraordinarily interesting and moving book edited by Witold Kula, Nina Assorodobrai-Kula, and Marcin Kula, *Listy emigrantów z Brazylii i Stanów Zjednoczonych [Letters of Emigrants from Brazil and the United States 1890–1891]* (Warsaw, Ludowa Spółdzielnia Wydawnicza, 1973), pp. 5–13, 273–4. The history of this book is itself interesting. In 1941, during the German occupation, Witold Kula was a volunteer teaching assistant at the underground Free Polish University. He had prepared his exercises on the auxiliary sciences of modern history, using, among other things, a textbook by the archivist Kazimierz Konarski. In the section on sorting files, Konarski stated that the Polish Historical Records Archive had inherited from the tsarist authorities an enormous collection of letters sent by emigrants but never delivered to their families. He went on to say something even more tantalizing: that the archive had considered destroying the collection, since it had no direct connection with the files they were collecting. Yet thanks to some influence or suggestion, they decided to keep them. The day after he read this revelation, Witold Kula raced to the archive on Jezuicka Street. The German occupiers had closed the academic workroom, but were still employing Polish archivists. One was an acquaintance of Witold Kula's, who escorted him down to the basement. Among the stacks of files marked for sorting stood some boxes with embossed lids. From then on, Witold Kula and his students systematically read, copied (by hand, since there were no other possibilities at the time), and edited the material. Every now and then they would pick up about a hundred letters from the archive. Then in 1944, the Warsaw Uprising broke out.

The archive collection burned. What remained were notes from around 700 letters that had been brought back to the archive before the uprising, and 300 originals, which luckily the researchers had not yet returned.

These letters are a rich, utterly priceless source of a wide range of information. They talk about the economic life of towns and villages, family relationships, customs, national and linguistic consciousness, seeking a better life, unfulfilled longing, and anxiety for loved ones, because at the will of the police chiefs and censors, silence fell between the senders and their addressees. If these letters had been destroyed, we would be ignorant of one of the most dramatic episodes in the history of emigration.

Apart from the Kulas' book, this episode has not received its due place in the literature and research on Polish and global emigration. Nor is it known by the present-day inhabitants of the Golub-Dobrzyń region, so terribly injured by the tsarist correspondence blockade. According to information from Professor Marcin Kula, in the mid-seventies his students went to Golub-Dobrzyń to look for traces of this long-ago tragedy, but no one could remember it any longer. It had been erased by two world wars, political and systemic changes, and the 20th-century displacement of people, due, among other things, to the socialist transformations.

4 Ibid., pp. 239–42, 255, 281, 327–8, 393, 397–8.

5 This quote comes from an account by Treasury Secretary William Windom, cited by the historian Thomas M. Pitkin in his book *Keepers of the Gate: a history of Ellis Island* (New York, New York University Press, 1975), p. 13.

6 For Ellis Island's entire existence, from 1892 to 1954, it was the largest immigration station in the United States. The Commissioner of Immigration at the Port of New York was responsible for overseeing it and the work of all the services on the island, and had the final say on settling difficult and delicate issues concerning, for instance, the deportation of persons with a high public profile or who found themselves in a particularly tragic situation.

The station was run successively by 12 commissioners (five of whom were born outside the United States):

John B. Weber (1890–1893), Joseph H. Senner (1893–1897), Thomas Fitchie (1897–1902), William C. Williams (1902–1905), Robert Watchorn (1905–1909), William C. Williams once again (1909–1913), Frederic C. Howe (1914–1919), Frederic A. Wallis (1920–1921), Robert E. Tod (1921–1923), Henry H. Curran (1923–1926), Benjamin M. Day (1926–1931), Edward Corsi (1931–1934), and Rudolph Reimer (1934–1940).

No more commissioners were appointed after 1940. The function was handed over to interim officials, including Byron H. Uhl (1940–1942).

7 All quotes by Astolphe Louis Léonor, Marquis de Custine, come from his book

La Russie en 1839, vol. 1 (Paris, Librarie d'Amyot, 1843), pp. 230–31, 271, 313–14. Quotes translated from the French by Sean Gasper Bye.

8　This and the following quotes concerning Weber's journey around Russia as well as all the information about the trip come from the chapters "Russia" and "Ordered to Appear Before the Pristav" in *The Autobiography of John B. Weber* (Buffalo, J.W. Clement Company, 1924), pp. 112, 120, 123–5, 127, 130. I also drew some information from this book about the various stages of the commissioner's life.

9　The information about the death of Colonel Weber's first wife comes from a story by his 88-year-old grandson Dyas Carden, recorded in 1994 by Paul E. Sigrist Jr as part of the Oral History Project for the Ellis Island Immigration Museum.

10　Peter McDonald spoke about his observations to a journalist of the *New York Evening Telegraph*, who reported them on 29 December 1912 in "Baggage in Fifty Languages Fails to Rattle 'Peter Mac'." Information about the baggage handler's personal life comes from the recollections of one of his grandchildren, located in the manuscript division of the Bob Hope Memorial Library, Ellis Island. Bob Hope, a popular American comedian and actor in vaudeville and on film, was chosen as the patron of this library because he himself passed through Ellis Island in 1908 (he was five years old at the time; he remembers rebelling in the vaccination line). He worked hard for his success in the United States and later, as a star, performed at Ellis Island for the Coast Guard during the Second World War.

11　I have quoted Victor M. Safford's observations about baggage from his book *Immigration Problems: personal experiences of an official* (New York, Dodd, Mead and Company, 1925), p. 2.

12　I take this from Pitkin, *Keepers of the Gate*, op. cit., p. 19. The author does not mention the name of the reporter or the date of publication.

13　"Button Hook Kills Child — Pierces Nostril and Penetrates Brain of Four-Year-Old," *Toronto Star*, 14 February 1921.

14　Since we are talking about Shavinovitz's original profession, it's worth mentioning the occupations of most arrivals from the Polish lands at the start of the 20th century.

Edward Pinkowski, author of numerous works on immigration, gives a list of these professions in 1900. The Polish immigrants included 58,084 unskilled laborers; 26,834 agricultural workers; 15,364 miners and quarrymen; 13,270 iron and steelworkers; 12,388 tailors (9,097 of them men's); 8,815 servants and waitresses; 4,210 steam railway employees; 4,128 salesmen and women; 3,425 hucksters and peddlers; 2,947 carpenters and joiners; 2,090 clerks; 1,945 painters, glaziers, and varnishers; 1,701 laundry workers; 1,540 restaurant owners; 972

masons; 841 teachers of various kinds; 666 hat and cap makers; 614 barbers and hairdressers; 496 housekeepers; 487 bartenders; 469 watchmen, policemen, and firemen; 468 clergymen; 246 janitors and sextons; 243 watchmakers; 184 plasterers; 125 fishermen and oystermen; 74 paper hangers; and 4 bootblacks.

Edward Pinkowski provided this information in "The Great Influx of Polish Immigrants and the Industries They Entered" from Frank Mocha, ed., *Poles in America: bicentennial essays* (Stevens Point, Wisconsin, Worzalla Publishing Company, 1978), pp. 330, 334, 339, 347–8, 360.

We don't know if Shavinovitz was included in these statistics, for instance under "shopkeepers," since manufacturing buttonhooks is too narrow a specialty to single out. (There are very few bootblacks, but they hold a special place in the American popular imagination.) It would probably depend on what language he spoke — Polish or Yiddish — and what ethnic background he declared for himself. The large number of tailors, specifically men's tailors, in this list suggests it could also include Jews, among whom this was a common profession.

15 Both posters can be seen in the exhibition at the Ellis Island Immigration Museum.

16 Quote from the chapter "Immigration Service" in *The Autobiography of John B. Weber*, op. cit., p. 89.

17 The Chinese Exclusion Act of 6 May 1882 halted the immigration of Chinese workers to the United States for ten years. Chinese workers previously resident in the United States who went temporarily to China were required, on returning to the United States, to present permission to cross the border once again. Chinese men and women were refused the right to United States citizenship. Congress renewed these discriminatory practices in subsequent legislation up until 17 December 1943. Abolishing the law was a gesture to America's wartime ally. The Chinese Exclusion Act was rigorously enforced, even in exceptional situations — like the sinking of the *Titanic* in 1912. Survivors of that catastrophe were sent to Ellis Island and received permission to enter the United States (Commissioner William Williams did his best to ease the rules of inspection) — with the exception of six sailors of Chinese descent, who were deported.

18 Quote from John B. Weber's article "Our National Dumping-Ground: A Study of Immigration," *North American Review*, vol. 154, April 1892.

19 Weber, *The Autobiography of John B. Weber*, p. 92.

20 *New York Times*, 21 February 1892. Citation from Howard Markel, *Quarantine!: East European Jewish immigrants and the New York City epidemics of 1892* (Baltimore, Johns Hopkins University Press), 1997.

Lorie Conway, in her book *Forgotten Ellis Island: the extraordinary story of America's immigrant hospital* (New York, HarperCollins Publishers, 2007), includes a statement from Senator William Chandler of New Hampshire, a supporter of strict limits on immigration, of a similar tone: *No one has suggested a race distinction. We are confronted with the fact, however, that the poorest immigrants do come from certain races* (p. 4).

We already know from Pitkin's *Keepers of the Gate* (op. cit. p. 20) that Chandler took advantage of the cholera incident to propose in Congress a year-long suspension of immigration from Europe to the United States. It did not receive sufficient support. However, the 1893 Immigration Act empowered the president to forbid entry to the United States to all persons from countries where cholera or other epidemic illnesses were confirmed. This also applied to transportation of baggage.

21 This manifest can be found online in the "Passenger Search" section of www.libertyellisfoundation.org.

22 Leon Czolgosz testified in court that he owed his radicalism to a speech by the anarchist Emma Goldman. He resolved to assassinate the president after Congress added anarchists to the categories of persons subject to deportation in the 1903 Immigration Act.

23 Years later, William Williams composed a lengthy commentary on this dispute: "Reminiscences of the Bering Sea Arbitration," *American Journal of International Law*, vol. 37, no. 37, October 1943.

24 According to information cited by Pitkin in *Keepers of the Gate*, op. cit., p. 38.

25 The Contract Labor Act, enacted in 1885, forbade contract laborers entry to the United States. Its goal was to protect American workers from foreign competition. The only exceptions to the ban were actors, artists, lecturers, skilled workmen in new branches of industry not yet established in the United States, private secretaries, and domestic or personal servants. The Immigration Act of 1888 provided that foreign contract laborers were to be deported within one year of their entry into the Unites States, and provided for financial awards for informers who put the authorities on their trail. Special inspectors enforcing this law had a separate office on Ellis Island and detention rooms for their use. From 1892 to 1954, around 40,000 contract laborers were detained at immigration stations and deported to their home countries. The largest number, over 28,400, were deported in the two decades from 1901 to 1920.

Based on information in Moreno, *Encyclopedia of Ellis Island*, op. cit., p. 42.

26 Safford, *Immigration Problems*, op. cit., p. 201.

27 Ibid., p. 10.

28 Barry Moreno, in his *Encyclopedia of Ellis Island*, lists under the entry "Races and Peoples" (op. cit. pp. 200–201) how many representatives of various races came to the United States from 1899 to 1931 according to Federal Bureau of Immigration statistics. They include:

South Italian: 3,310,015

German: 1,644,107

Polish: 1,508,653

English: 1,313,716

Scandinavian: 1,065,624

Irish: 1,053,500

Mexican: 700,134

North Italian: 621,279

One reason for such a dramatic influx of Southern Italians, particularly from Sicily, was the massive earthquake that on 28 December 1908 destroyed 90 per cent of the houses, public buildings, churches, and palaces in Messina. The deaths — according to various sources — totaled 60,000, 70,000, or 80,000 people. Those left behind were unable to rebuild their lives there.

29 The regulations and information about the number of staff are based on Harlan D. Unrau's *Ellis Island, Statue of Liberty National Monument: historic resource study* (Denver, Colorado, US Department of the Interior, National Park Service, 1984), pp. 359–72, in the collection of the Bob Hope Memorial Library, Ellis Island Immigration Museum.

30 Here are the seventeen organizational divisions of Ellis Island station:

Executive — focused around the office of the commissioner and overseeing all work; Boarding — in charge of disembarking cabin passengers, among other things; Medical — responsible for medical inspection of immigrants and the hospitals' work on the island; Registry — handling initial immigrant inspection; Special Inquiry — handling immigrants interned temporarily; Information — gathering documents concerning immigrants; Discharging — for releasing temporarily detained immigrants; Deporting — handling immigrants set for exclusion; Statistical — gathering information about immigrants and their movements; Treasurer's — handling the station's and immigrants' financial transactions; Watchmen's and Gatesmen's; Matrons'; Engineers' — servicing the complex equipment at the station; Laborers' — providing unskilled labor; Night — which oversaw all activities outside business hours; Marine — serving tugboats, ships, and ferries; Miscellaneous — such as gardening, carpentry, and painting.

31 These quotes come from the memoirs of Maud Mosher, *Ellis Island as the Matron Sees It*, Maud Mosher Papers, Manuscript Department of Bob Hope Memorial Library, Ellis Island Immigration Museum, pp. 2–6, 20.

32 Victor Safford's remarks on the smell of ships and vessels are based on his descriptions in "Chapter 2 Impressions of Old Ellis Island," of his book *Immigration Problems*, op. cit.

Moses A. Safford's diary is stored in the USS *Constellation* Archive Collection in

Baltimore, Maryland, edited by Victor Safford and titled "A Man-of-War Man's Diary: a cruise in an old frigate prefaced by an autobiography of the diarist". It appeared in print newly edited by Lawrence J. Bopp and Stephen R. Bockmiller under the title *Showing the Flag: the Civil War naval diary of Moses Safford, USS Constellation* (Charleston, South Carolina, History Press, 2004). Both editors are volunteers at the museum ship. In the year the book was published, Bopp was a retired history teacher in Baltimore, while Bockmiller worked in the municipal administration of Hagerstown, Maryland, in the Baltimore–Washington greater metropolitan area.

33 In the United States, statistical reports always cover not the calendar year, but the fiscal year. Until 1976 this began on 1 July, currently it begins on 1 October. For simplicity's sake, I do not make the distinction.

34 Based on Alexandra W. James, *A History of the University Club of New York 1865–1915* (New York, Charles Scribner's Sons, 1915).

35 This description comes from a letter quoted in Daile Kaplan, ed., *Photo Story: selected letters and photographs of Lewis W. Hine* (Washington, DC, Smithsonian Institution Press, 1992), cited in Peter Mesenhöller's essay in Augustus F. Sherman, *Ellis Island Portraits 1905–1920* (New York, Aperture Foundation, 2000), pp. 8–9.

36 The professional wrestler Stanisław Jan Cyganiewicz, aka Zbyszko I (his brother, also a wrestler, performed as Zbyszko II), was born in 1881 in Jodłowa near Jasło in today's Podkarpackie province of Poland. He died in 1967 in St Joseph, Missouri. He won the professional world championship three times, in 1906 (Paris), 1921, and 1922 (New York). In 1924 he emigrated to the United States and lived there for the rest of his life. He won over a thousand matches. His opponents struggled not only with his strength and dexterity, but also his distinctive "turtle-like" physical build.

37 Tomasz Kuczkowski (1786–1843), *O epidemicznem zapaleniu oczów, a w szczególności o téy epidemii, która w garnizonie warszawskim panowała* [*On Ophthalmia and Specifically the Epidemic that Raged in the Warsaw Garrison*] (Warsaw, Drukarnia Woyskowéy, 1822).

38 Medical Council of the Kingdom of Poland, *Krótka wiadomość o tak zwanym egipskiém zapaleniu oczu podana przez Radę Lekarską Królestwa Polskiego* [*A Short Notice on the So-Called Egyptian Ophthalmia from the Medical Council of the Kingdom of Poland*] (Warsaw, Drukarnia J. Glücksberga, 1850).

39 Dr Grover A. Kempf, a doctor on Ellis Island from 1912 to 1916, spoke about his experiences in 1977. A part of his account is available in the Ellis Island Immigration Museum in the room dedicated to medical inspection.

The United States Public Health Service divided diseases brought by immigrants into three classes: A, B, and C. Class A included the most dangerous infectious diseases, requiring deportation. The classification was updated every few years. On every list — from 1903 to 1930 — trachoma was in Class A. According to Barry Moreno, *Encyclopedia of Ellis Island*, op. cit., p. 42.

40 Photo and recollection in Georges Pérec and Robert Bober, *Ellis Island*, tr. Harry Mathews and Jessica Blatt (New York, The New Press, 1995), pp. 63, 156.

41 According to Lorie Conway, *Forgotten Ellis Island*, op. cit., pp. 75–6.

42 Safford, *Immigration Problems*, op. cit., pp. 244–5.

43 Interview conducted 12 August 1998 by Paul E. Sigrist Jr for the Oral History Project, Ellis Island Immigration Museum.

44 Henry James, *The American Scene* (London, Chapman & Hall, 1907), p. 85.

45 Pitkin, *Keepers of the Gate*, op. cit., p. 66.

46 Ibid., p. 44.

47 William Williams was the first commissioner of Ellis Island to resign before the end of his term. Another six out of 12 commissioners followed in his footsteps: Frederic C. Howe, Frederick A. Wallis, Robert E. Tod, Henry H. Curran, Benjamin M. Day, and Edward Corsi. A majority of these resignations were influenced by conflict between official duties on the one hand and personal and moral convictions on the other, as well as criticism from various wings of public opinion.

48 Quotation from Pitkin, *Keepers of the Gate*, op. cit., p. 65.

II   Flood

49 This and the following quote are from *The Autobiography of Robert Watchorn*, ed. Herbert Faulkner West (Oklahoma City, The Robert Watchorn Charities Ltd, 1959), pp. 37–8.

50 The words "wire filter" accurately describe the appearance and character of this room in those years. To deal with moving huge numbers of people, in 1900 it was divided up with tall metal barriers, between which inspection subjects waited or moved along. There were no seats. In a picture from 1909 we see benches between the barriers for the immigrants. In a picture from 1912 the barriers are gone and we can see tightly packed benches full of people. Pictures from 1918 and 1919 show white rows of hospital beds, and from 1924 onwards, almost empty space.

51 H.G. Wells, *The Future in America* (New York, Harper & Brothers, 1906), p. 140.

52 Both quotes come from Edward A. Steiner, *On the Trail of the Immigrant* (New York, Chicago, Toronto, Fleming H. Revell Company, 1906) pp. 87–8, 111, and both allude to the Bible. The first, to the Gospel of Luke (17:34–36): *I tell you, in that night there shall be two men in one bed; the one shall be taken, and the other shall be left.* (...) *Two men shall be in the field; the one shall be taken, and the other left.*

The second, to the Book of Revelation (14:6): *And I saw another angel fly in the midst of heaven, having the everlasting gospel to preach unto them that dwell on the earth, and to every nation, and kindred, and tongue, and people.* (These quotes from the King James Version.)

53 Cartoon from the *New York Evening World*, in the collections of Watchorn Methodist Church, Alfreton, England, displayed in Room 204 of the Ellis Island Immigration Museum.

54 Steiner, *On the Trail of the Immigrant*, op. cit., p. 37.

55 Excerpt of a letter from Stanisław Kazmirkiewicz of Pennsylvania to his family in Golub-Dobrzyń county, quoted in Witold Kula, Nina Assorodobrai-Kula, and Marcin Kula, eds, *Listy emigrantów z Brazylii i Stanów Zjednoczonych* [*Letters of Emigrants from Brazil and the United States 1890–1891*] (Warsaw, Ludowa Spółdzielnia Wydawnicza, 1973) p. 299. This letter was withheld by the tsarist censor, but similar information reached families by other routes and at other times.

56 "For the Improvement of Steerage Conditions," Speech of the Hon. Adolph J. Sabath of Illinois in the House of Representatives, Wednesday, 27 May 1908 (Immigration Collection of Prescott Farnsworth Hall, Widener Library, Harvard University). On the title page of this publication appears an epigraph from the author: "I am not willing to sacrifice the health and the lives of poor and oppressed people on behalf of greedy steamship companies. It is time that steerage conditions, such as I have described, come to an end."

57 Conditions were still this way in 1920. An immigrant from Slovakia sailing to New York from Rotterdam described them to Ludmila K. Foxlee, an employee of the Young Women's Christian Association on Ellis Island, who recorded it in her memoir, *How They Came*, finished in 1968, located in the manuscript division of the Bob Hope Memorial Library. I will write more about the extraordinary character of Foxlee and her work on the island later.

58 Years later, Francesco Martoccia recounted this to Commissioner Edward Corsi, who included the story in his book, *In the Shadow of Liberty: the chronicle of Ellis Island* (New York, The Macmillan Company, 1935), p. 77.

59 Information about Dr Salmon's life and the quote about the poor hospital in Greyson County come from Earl D. Bond, *Thomas W. Salmon, Psychiatrist* (New York, Norton, 1950), pp. 61–2.

60 The Boards of Special Inquiry were convened on the station based on the Immigration Act of 1893. They were made up of three or four inspectors and looked into immigrants' cases, deciding to deport them if they didn't meet the conditions demanded. They most often assessed whether a newcomer would be a burden on American society, if they intended to take on contract work, and if they were morally or politically suspicious. During the peak immigration period

(1900–1924) between four and eight such boards operated on the island. They benefited from the help of interpreters. In 1912, 47 station employees at Ellis Island had authorization to sit on the boards. The public could not listen in on the boards' work and journalists sometimes called them secret courts. Immigrants had the right to appeal to a superior board in Washington.

61 Bertha M. Boody, PhD, *A Psychological Study of Immigrant Children at Ellis Island* (Baltimore, The Williams & Wilkins Company, 1926), p. 2.

62 Quote from Lorie Conway, *Forgotten Ellis Island: the extraordinary story of America's immigrant hospital* (New York, HarperCollins Publishers, 2007), p. 121.

63 According to Barry Moreno, *Encyclopedia of Ellis Island* (Westport, Connecticut, Greenwood Press, 2004), p. 124.

64 Ibid.

65 Quote from Corsi, *In the Shadow of Liberty*, op. cit., p. 76.

66 Both quotes from Fiorello La Guardia, *The Making of an Insurgent: an autobiography, 1882–1919* (Philadelphia, J.B. Lippincott & Co., 1948).

67 Based on an account by Francesco Martoccia in Corsi's *In the Shadow of Liberty*, op. cit., p. 80.

68 La Guardia, *The Making of an Insurgent*, op. cit., p. 66.

69 Both quotes by Watchorn from Thomas M. Pitkin, *Keepers of the Gate: a history of Ellis Island* (New York, New York University Press, 1975), pp. 65, 48.

70 According to William Williams' report, "Ellis Island: its organization and some of its work," 1912 (William Williams Papers, New York Public Library). At that time around 650 people were working on the island, including 130 doctors and medical personnel.

71 Interview conducted 23 September 1978 by Harvey Dixon for the Oral History Project, Ellis Island Immigration Museum.

72 This and the following quote from Watchorn, *Autobiography*, op. cit., pp. 155, 157.

73 Based on the interview with Colonel Weber's grandson, Dyas Carden, recorded in 1994 by Paul E. Sigrist Jr for the Oral History Project, Ellis Island Immigration Museum.

74 According to an account from Jeske Paterson, Cecilia Greenstone's great-grandson, from 1997, Manuscript Division of Bob Hope Memorial Library.

75 This and the previous quotes come from the document "Importing Women for Immoral Purposes: presented by Mr Dillingham" (Washington, Government Printing Office, 1909), pp. 4, 22–3, 33, 9.

76   Quote from La Guardia, *The Making of an Insurgent*, op. cit., p. 71.

77   Edith Abbott, *Immigration: select documents and case records* (Chicago, Illinois, The University of Chicago Press, 1924), p. 609.

78   Based on La Guardia's book, *The Making of an Insurgent*, op. cit., and Alyn Brodsky's *The Great Mayor: Fiorello La Guardia and the making of the city of New York* (New York, St Martin's Press, 2003). The quote comes from Brodsky's book (p. 40). The note in it that the guests mocking immigrants spared the Irish is explained by the fact that this particular minority wielded great influence in Tammany Hall. In time, Italians took it over, which must have been very unpleasant for La Guardia, who always emphasized his Italian heritage and who fought Tammany for years.

79   According to an interview with Teresa Duffy-Gavin, born in 1892, conducted in 1991 by Paul E. Sigrist Jr for the Oral History Project, Ellis Island Immigration Museum.

80   Inspection of first- and second-class passengers took place not on Ellis Island, but on the ships at the Port of New York. It was superficial and random, especially for first class, whose passengers protested against "indiscreet" questioning. Second-class inspections centered on searching for infectious diseases. Suspected cases were taken to Ellis Island for further testing, though this happened very rarely. While the steerage passengers were sent straight to Ellis Island on ferries, first- and second-class travelers disembarked on American soil at the New York wharf, directly from the ships.

81   The cartoon is from 1929. An enlarged copy can be found as an exhibit in the Ellis Island Immigration Museum, which says it comes from the collections of the YIVO Institute for Jewish Research and the New York Public Library.

82   The quotes of William Williams' opinion I take from Conway, *Forgotten Ellis Island*, op. cit., p. 119. She drew them from the article "The Invasion of the Unfit," *Medical Record: a weekly journal of medicine and surgery*, 14 December 1912.

83   Taken from Hans Pols' *Thomas W. Salmon, Ellis Island, and the Origins of Mental Hygiene in the United States*, 2004, Manuscript Division, Bob Hope Memorial Library, Ellis Island Immigration Museum.

84   *New York Times*, 27 November 1912.

85   Based on John T.E. Richardson, *Howard Andrew Knox: pioneer of intelligence testing at Ellis Island* (New York, Columbia University Press, 2011), p. 154.

86   The presents were practical and came from charitable organizations. The women received sewing and toiletry kits, scissors, gloves, aprons, handkerchiefs, and stockings. The men: socks, toiletries, and shaving gear. For the girls, a doll, a miniature set of tableware, a notebook, and a pencil case. For the boys, something

similar, only instead of a doll and dishes, a game of some kind. Also included in the women's packages was some inexpensive jewelry. In 1985 the daughter of an immigrant woman from Germany offered the Ellis Island museum collection a glass necklace her mother had received for Christmas and considered a treasure. It is exhibited in a display case in room 227 of the Ellis Island Immigration Museum.

87   Father Gaspare Moretti, director of the St Raphael Society for the Protection of Italian Immigrants, was a talented photographer and preserved many scenes from the lives of Italian immigrants. He delivered this speech in 1910. At the time he was 30 years old. Quotation from Moreno, *Encyclopedia of Ellis Island*, op. cit. pp. 35–36

88   Ludmila Foxlee, *How They Came*, op. cit. p. 130.

89   La Guardia, *The Making of an Insurgent*, op. cit., p. 65. The author of the memoir's foreword, La Guardia's secretary M.R. Werner, writes that La Guardia dictated and edited his memoir over the last six months of his life. La Guardia's opinions about unjustified deportations comes from the same book.

90   Based on information from "Kills His Children, Wife and Himself," *New York Times*, 22 January 1914.

91   From John T.E. Richardson, *Howard Andrew Knox*, op. cit., p. 182.

92   The Smithsonian Institution, one of the first institutions in the world for the support of science, was founded in 1846 by the US Congress based on a bequest from the chemist and mineralogist James Smithson. The Smithsonian complex is made up of dozens of museums and research institutions in Washington DC and other US cities, including the Smithsonian American Art Museum, the National Museum of American History, the National Museum of Natural History, and the National Air and Space Museum.

93   From Boody, *A Psychological Study of Immigrant Children*, op. cit., p. 63.

94   La Guardia, *The Making of an Insurgent*, op. cit., p. 77.

95   From Harlan D. Unrau, *Ellis Island, Statue of Liberty National Monument: historic resource study* (Denver, Colorado, US Department of the Interior, National Park Service, 1984), p. 546.

96   From Peter Morton Coan, *Ellis Island Interviews in Their Own Words* (New York, Checkmark Books, 1997), pp. 221, 278. Theodore Spako gave his interview at the age of 102.

97   From an interview with Anna Wittman Wilhelm conducted in 1991 by Janet Levine for the Oral History Project, Ellis Island Immigration Museum.

98   Corsi, *In the Shadow of Liberty*, op. cit., p. 4

99   From an interview with Betty Dornbaum Schubert, conducted in 1990 by Paul E.

Sigrist Jr for the Oral History Project, Ellis Island Immigration Museum.

100 From an interview with Paul H. Laric conducted in 1991 by Paul E. Sigrist Jr for the Oral History Project, Ellis Island Immigration Museum.

III   Becalmed

101 Woodrow Thomas Wilson, a Democrat, was President of the United States from 1913 to 1921. In his re-election campaign he promised to keep the country out of the war, but on 2 April 1917, in light of the developing situation, particularly German aggression on the seas, he asked Congress for a declaration of war on Germany. Wilson's peace program, announced on 8 January 1918 in an address to Congress (Wilson's famous "Fourteen Points") called for, in its 13th point, the creation of an independent Polish state with free access to the sea.

102 Quotes from Frederic C. Howe, *The Confessions of a Reformer* (Kent, Ohio, Kent State University Press, 1988), pp. 252–3.

103 Quote from Thomas M. Pitkin, *Keepers of the Gate: a history of Ellis Island* (New York, New York University Press, 1975), p. 113.

104 Howe, *Confessions of a Reformer*, op. cit., p. 254.

105 The Hebrew Immigrant Aid Society (HIAS) was among the most active aid organizations on Ellis Island and had its own office on the island. Thanks to its financial support and interventions, many Jewish immigrants avoided deportation. The organization went to great lengths to ensure Jews detained on the island could observe Jewish holidays and benefit from a kosher kitchen, which was introduced to Ellis Island by 1911, because many Orthodox Jews preferred to go hungry rather than eat non-kosher food. In 1940, this kitchen produced around 86,000 meals. It operated until the closing of the station on Ellis Island.

106 The story of this journey is according to Jeske Paterson, Cecilia Greenstone's great-grandson, from 1997, Manuscript Division of Bob Hope Memorial Library, Ellis Island Immigration Museum.

107 Howe, *Confessions of a Reformer*, op. cit., p. 256.

108 Francesco Martoccia's story about Cohen appears in Edward Corsi, *In the Shadow of Liberty: the chronicle of Ellis Island* (New York, The Macmillan Company, 1935), pp. 83–4.

109 The Knights of Pythias present themselves in their informational materials as an international, non-sectarian, fraternal organization, founded in 1864 in Washington, operating in many cities and towns in the US and Canada and engaging in a wide range of charitable and social activities. More information can be found at www.pythias.org, which also features, among other things, a

long film describing their work for young people and those with health problems. Pythias, a literary hero of antiquity, is a model of friendly loyalty.

110 Information about Paula Pitum comes from Corsi, *In the Shadow of Liberty*, op. cit., pp. 106–112.

111 Quotations from Dr Frederick Theis' story come from Corsi, *In the Shadow of Liberty*, op. cit., pp. 118–19.

112 Investigations and disagreements about this case lasted all the way to 1939, when an international commission declared Germany's responsibility and required payment to the United States of $50 million in compensation.

113 Quote from Howe, *Confessions of a Reformer*, op. cit., pp. 256–8.

114 The renowned architect Rafael Guastavino Sr, a Spaniard born in Valencia, used anti-fire methods and materials in his designs. The United States developed an interest in his achievements after the Great Chicago Fire of 1871. Guastavino and his family moved to the United States, settled in New York, and founded an architectural and construction firm, which built cupolas and vaults for many historic buildings, including the enormous Cathedral of St John the Divine, Pennsylvania Station, and the Custom House in lower Manhattan, which today houses a branch of the National Museum of the American Indian. Rafael Guastavino Jr inherited his father's talents. After building a vault over the Great Hall at Ellis Island, he co-designed the extraordinary Cloisters museum (now The Met Cloisters) in upper Manhattan, housing medieval works of art. There, he created an intriguing and atmospheric combination of medieval cloisters and architectural fragments transported over from Europe. A popular work by Guastavino *fils* is the Oyster Bar at Grand Central Station on 42nd Street, and the nearby arches, where a whisper gathers strength like in a Greek theater; New Yorkers call this place the Whispering Gallery.

115 This test was introduced by the Immigration Act of 1917. The immigrant had to read at least 40 words in his or her own language. Political refugees, people experiencing religious persecution, children under 16, wives, and older relatives of immigrants already accepted into the United States were exempt. Supporters of staunching the flow of "worse" immigration had long sought to exclude the illiterate. As early as the second Grover Cleveland administration (1893–1897), the Immigration Restriction League successfully lobbied for a restriction bill, which received the support of Congress. President Cleveland vetoed it and in a sharp speech described it as a radical move away from the national policies of the United States. He noted that what the bill's authors said now about the level of new immigrants was said years before about newcomers whose numerous descendants were now among the finest citizens in the country. For the next several years the issue kept being raised in political speeches and journalistic articles, and the bill was vetoed a total of four times. In 1903 Commissioner William Williams in his first term at Ellis Island was in favor of excluding the

illiterate to winnow down the growing mass of newcomers.

The 1917 Act closed off access to the United States for 33 categories of aliens. One of the most important were illiterates. Congress passed the bill, overriding a veto by President Woodrow Wilson. It was in force until 1952.

Based on material in Barry Moreno, *Encyclopedia of Ellis Island* (Westport, Connecticut, Greenwood Press, 2004) and Pitkin, *Keepers of the Gate*, op. cit.

116 Quotes from the King James Version of the Bible, Joshua 9:12–13, Job 1:18–19, Hebrews 13:1–2.

117 Quotes from Howe, *Confessions of a Reformer*, op. cit., pp. 266–7.

118 Quotes regarding war neuroses are from Earl D. Bond, *Thomas W. Salmon, Psychiatrist* (New York, Norton, 1950), p. 108.

119 Ibid., p. 85.

120 According to an article by Joseph Mitchell, "Mr. Hunter's Grave," *The New Yorker*, 22 September 1956.

121 The International Workers of the World (IWW) was founded in Chicago in 1905 by 200 socialists, anarchists, and radical labor union activists from various cities in the US. They declared that the working class and the employers' class had nothing in common and that struggle against the employers could not cease until workers gained control of the means of production and overthrew the existing wage system. In 1912, the IWW numbered 50,000 members. It now has 2,000 in the United States, Australia, Canada, Ireland, and the United Kingdom.

122 Quote from Pitkin, *Keepers of the Gate*, op. cit., p. 123.

123 The information in this paragraph is based on Alyn Brodsky's *The Great Mayor: Fiorello La Guardia and the making of the city of New York* (New York, St Martin's Press, 2003), pp. 100–103.

124 Quoted from Pitkin, *Keepers of the Gate*, op. cit. p. 124. Pitkin also quotes the accusations against Howe from the House Committee on Immigration and Naturalization, as well as his counter-arguments. According to the Commission: out of over 600 immigrants sent to Ellis Island since 1917 for deportation, only 60 were repatriated; Howe had received friendly letters from the anarchist Emma Goldman and other notorious agitators; left-wing literature had circulated at Ellis Island; women detained on accusation of immorality had enjoyed too much freedom on the island; etc.

Howe intended to defend himself to the Commission, but they did not wish to hear him out. He presented his explanations in the *New York World*, which was absolutely in favor of deporting the Bolsheviks, though it usually took the side of immigrants. He said he never released any foreigner unless he had approval from Washington. He only insisted that every person sent to the island for deportation was able to receive the legal attention guaranteed them by the United States' Constitution. He knew such an attitude would meet with criticism, but his conscience did not allow him to become merely a rubber stamp. The *New York World* still came out against the Bolsheviks, but respected Howe's response and did not attack him.

125 All these posters are hanging in the permanent exhibition of the Ellis Island Immigration Museum.

126 The story of Miji Cogic is according to August C. Bolino, *The Ellis Island Source Book* (Washington DC, Kensington Historical Press, 1990), pp. 84–5.

127 Information about Paula and the quote come from Corsi, *In the Shadow of Liberty*, op. cit., pp. 108–109.

128 Edward Corsi's opinion of Emma Goldman I draw from his memoir (ibid., p. 190), along with her recollections (p. 200) and information about her speech before her deportation (pp. 195–8).

129 Information about Uhl's report based on material in Moreno, *Encyclopedia of Ellis Island*, op. cit., p. 205.

IV   Pitch and Toss

130 These excerpts from an interview with Josephine Lutomski, née Friedman, a hospital assistant at Ellis Island in 1922–1923, conducted in 1986 by Edward Applebome for the Oral History Project, Ellis Island Immigration Museum.

131 Excerpt from the poem "The Mercy" by Philip Levine in Philip Levine, *The Mercy* (New York, Alfred A. Knopf, 1999), p. 73.

132 Information about burials and births based on Barry Moreno, *Encyclopedia of Ellis Island* (Westport, Connecticut, Greenwood Press, 2004), pp. 14, 51–2, and Harlan D. Unrau, *Ellis Island, Statue of Liberty National Monument: historic resource study* (Denver, Colorado, US Department of the Interior, National Park Service, 1984), pp. 603–4.

133 Quote from Thomas M. Pitkin, *Keepers of the Gate: a history of Ellis Island* (New York, New York University Press, 1975), p. 134.

134 Ibid., pp. 134–35.

135 Ibid., p. 134.

136 In 1915–17 the Armenian population of the Ottoman Empire was exterminated. An estimated 1.5 million people were murdered in this period. Around the world, public opinion was indifferent to this atrocity. Hitler is said to have invoked this apathy in a speech to Wehrmacht commanders at his residence in Obersalzberg on 22 August 1939. He ordered that during the attack on Poland they mercilessly kill men, women, and children, because only in this way could Germany obtain

its *Lebensraum*, then added: Who, after all, speaks today of the annihilation of the Armenians? However, some researchers question whether Hitler actually spoke those words in his address.

137 Lee Iacocca and William Novak, *Iacocca: An Autobiography* (New York, Bantam, 1986), p. 5.

138 Pierce-Arrow Motorcar Company — founded in 1901 in Buffalo, Colonel Weber's home city — specialized in luxury cars, but also produced trucks and fire engines. The model the colonel was haggling over was most likely a 1903 Motorette, an elegant convertible with a coachman's box for the driver, a wide leather seat for the passengers, shining headlights and narrow spoked wheels. The Motorette had one cylinder and two gears. It had no reverse.

The old advertising pamphlets are masterpieces of design — the Motorette stands in the background, framed by tall antique columns, awaiting a lady in an athletic costume with a floor-length skirt and a dog on a leash. The columns conceal part of the automobile, mysterious and charming like its owner. No technical specifications are given, as if that were beneath the dignity of the product.

In 1909, President Taft ordered two automobiles from Pierce-Arrow. They were the White House's first official cars. Other drivers of Pierce-Arrows included Emperor Hirohito of Japan and the Shah of Persia (his model had metal detailing and was upholstered in silk and Siberian wolf fur).

A restored 1919 Pierce-Arrow stands in the Woodrow Wilson Library.

139 Based on the interview with Dyas Carden recorded in 1994 by Paul E. Sigrist Jr for the Oral History Project, Ellis Island Immigration Museum.

140 The University Club long defended itself against women. In 1987, 53 per cent of its members voted against admitting them. Yet they were forced to submit to anti-discrimination laws, especially since the case caught the interest of the city's Human Rights Commission. Therefore in 2007 I could write to Mr Andrew Berner, the club librarian, asking if it would be possible to visit this marvelous building, and I received a prompt and polite response. Mr Berner checked if the club archive contained information on William Williams and promised to show me the interior, where the commissioner stayed. The promise was not uncon- ditional. He warned me the club had a dress code (nothing casual such as jeans or tennis shoes), and that I would not be allowed to take any pictures. I arrived appropriately attired, but right at the entrance I encountered some middle-aged women, clearly regulars, in wrinkled trousers and worn-out sneakers. In the main hall, people were shouting into mobile phones, even though a bronze plaque forbade their use. In the three-story-high dining room, I heard Polish being spoken. Some doctors attending a conference on slowing the aging process had just sat down to lunch; a couple of them had come from Kraków. Mr Berner himself (in a very discreet gray suit) proved to be approachable, hospitable, and helpful. The club library was quiet and empty. The computer stations were

hidden away in side nooks, so as not to detract from the space's dignity.

141 All quotes in this section and information about Watchorn's donations comes from *The Autobiography of Robert Watchorn*, ed. Herbert Faulkner West (Oklahoma City, The Robert Watchorn Charities Ltd, 1959) pp. 127, 129–30, 4, 174–5.

142 Information in this chapter is based on Ludmila Foxlee's memoir, *How They Came: the drama of Ellis Island 1920–1935*, written in Montvale, New Jersey, in 1968, as well as *The Papers of Ludmila Kuchar Foxlee* (1885–1971), arranged and described by Stacy F. Roth, *Historical Notes: Lise Hirschberg, 1985*. Both are found in the Manuscript Division of Bob Hope Memorial Library, Ellis Island Immigration Museum. The quotes come from the former title (pp. 36–7).

143 According to Pitkin, *Keepers of the Gate*, op. cit., p. 136

144 Based on the memoirs of Henry Curran, quoted in Susan Jonas, ed., *Ellis Island: Echoes from a Nation's Past* (New York, Aperture Foundation, 2005), p. 76.

145 According to Pitkin, *Keepers of the Gate*, op. cit., p. 137.

146 Ibid.

147 Elizabeth Gardiner, "Red Cross Narrative Report," Ellis Island Hospital, 1920, Bob Hope Memorial Library.

148 According to Alyn Brodsky, *The Great Mayor: Fiorello La Guardia and the making of the city of New York* (New York, St Martin's Press, 2003), p. 152.

149 Based on Jacob Auerbach's brief memoir, *Ellis Island and I*, Manuscript Division of Bob Hope Memorial Library (pp. 9, 11), and an interview with Jacob Auerbach conducted by Janet Levine in 1992 for the Oral History Project, Ellis Island Immigration Museum.

The words *Mene, Tekel, Upharsin*, written by the hand of God on the wall of Belshazzar's Babylonian palace, are interpreted as: measured, weighed, divided, meant to herald the destruction of Babylon (Daniel 5:25).

150 Ludmila Foxlee, *How They Came*, op. cit., p. 116.

151 Ibid., p. 22.

152 Ibid., p. 131.

153 Based on Edward Corsi's book *In the Shadow of Liberty: the chronicle of Ellis Island* (New York, The Macmillan Company, 1935), p. 111.

154 Based on Ludmila Foxlee's memoir *How They Came*, op. cit., pp. 144, 107, 202.

155 Opinions and quotes from *Despatch from H.M. Ambassador at Washington Reporting on Conditions at Ellis Island Immigration Station: Presented to Parliament by Command of His Majesty*, London, Parliamentary Paper, 1923, pp. 2–7.

156 According to Pitkin, *Keepers of the Gate*, op. cit., p. 147.

157 Quote from Louis Adamic's memoir, *Laughing in the Jungle* (New York and London, Harper & Brothers, 1932), quoted in Barbara Benton, *Ellis Island: A Pictorial History* (New York, Facts on File Publications, 1987), p. 130.

158 From Pitkin, *Keepers of the Gate*, op. cit., p. 150.

159 Henry H. Curran, *Pillar to Post* (New York, Charles Scribner's Sons, 1941), p. 294.

160 Based on Henry F. Pringle, "Wet Hope," *The New Yorker*, 14 June 1930, p. 24.

161 Based on the chapter "A Digression: Britain and America," written after the First World War in *The Autobiography of Robert Watchorn*, op. cit., pp. 118–120. The verse Watchorn quotes is from George Pope Morris's poem, "Woodman, Spare That Tree" (1830).

162 Quote from Ronald H. Bayor, *Fiorello La Guardia: Ethnicity and Reform* (Wheeling, Illinois, Harlan Davidson, Inc., 1993), p. 70.

163 Quote from Duff Gilford, "Americans We Like: Congressman La Guardia," *The Nation*, 21 March 1928. Quoted in Brodsky, *The Great Mayor*, op. cit., p. 178.

164 Illustration in the collections of the Bob Hope Memorial Library. The artist, Hendrik Willem van Loon, born in Rotterdam, came to the United States in 1903 and became a reporter for the American press, a writer, and an illustrator. He was a correspondent in Russia during the 1905 revolution and in Belgium at the start of the First World War. His most popular book, *The Story of Mankind*, has been reissued many times.

165 Pictures of these pogroms are featured in the permanent exhibition at the Ellis Island Immigration Museum. In them, we see the murdered and wounded, destroyed equipment, and a woman despairing. They're displayed in a place less accessible to young school groups, on the other side of a large panel of photographs showing a market in Stryj, in Austrian-ruled Galicia (today's Stryi, Ukraine), in 1905: the masonry structures of the market square; some handsome multi-story buildings, with the handsomest labeled Main Tavern; church towers in the background; in the foreground, carts of hay and some modest cargo; women in headscarves, men in white shirts and waistcoats, all in hats or caps. An empty dirt road leads to the market, a gutter runs between the road and the market street, covered in one place with planks. Near this picture, whose background shows a view further into town, we find information stating that from 1880 to 1924, 800,000 people emigrated to the United States from Galicia, which straddles the current border of Poland and Ukraine.

166 The first Ku Klux Klan was founded after the Civil War in 1866 as a club of Confederate veterans with racist convictions. It quickly transformed itself into a terrorist organization that set out to reimpose white domination over the

liberated black citizens of the southern states. In the election year of 1868, around 2,000 blacks and whites supporting them were murdered. The Klan's terrorism delayed the liberation of African-Americans, but it also provoked a reaction from Congress, which opposed the Klan's methods and passed laws restricting them. In the 1870s the organization started to melt away and its activities gradually ceased.

The second Ku Klux Klan was founded in Georgia and Alabama in 1915, hearkening back to the views and methods of the first. Initially frail, it quickly grew in strength. It was fortified by fear of communism, of population changes in the United States, and of the strengthening labor union movement. In the 1920s the Klan numbered over 4 million members spread across a number of states, including Illinois, New Jersey, Ohio, Pennsylvania, Indiana, and the Midwest. It had a hierarchical structure, publishing houses, propaganda specialists, and door-to-door recruiters, who received a commission of 25 per cent of each $10 joining fee. It also included women in a separate organization. Members were elected as sheriffs, aldermen, and mayors, and joined school boards and parish councils. The Klan weakened during the Great Depression; in 1930 its membership had fallen to barely 30,000. It bounced back in the 1960s to oppose the fight for civil rights for the black population, once again resorting to acts of violence and killings.

In 1990 the Georgia Supreme Court published an interesting ruling on the case of a Ku Klux Klan member convicted for using the traditional Klan costume. His conviction was based on the "Anti-Mask Act" promulgated by the state of Georgia. The defendant evoked the First Amendment to the United States Constitution, guaranteeing freedom of expression, and accused the state law of being unconstitutional. The court rejected this argument and presented its own: the ban on wearing a Ku Klux Klan mask did not infringe freedom of speech, but wearing the mask in public infringed citizens' right to freedom from violence and intimidation.

By that time, the Ku Klux Klan numbered a few thousand people and played a very small role in the life of the United States. Today it is a fragmented organization, with many groups claiming to be the "true heirs" of the Klan.

V   Ebb Tide

167 The information about Sherman's photographs being used without attribution comes from Peter Mesenhöller's essay in Augustus F. Sherman, *Ellis Island Portraits 1905–1920* (New York, Aperture Foundation, 2000), pp. 12–13.

168 *Manual of the Mental Examination of Aliens*, Treasury Department, United States Public Health Service, Miscellaneous Publication No. 18, Prepared Under Direction of the Surgeon General (Washington, DC, Government Printing Office, 1918).

169 Ibid., p. 5.

170 Bertha M. Boody, PhD, *A Psychological Study of Immigrant Children at Ellis Island* (Baltimore, The Williams & Wilkins Company, 1926), p. 54.

171 Information and quotes from Earl D. Bond, *Thomas W. Salmon, Psychiatrist* (New York, Norton, 1950), pp. 162–3, 227.

172 Amtorg Trading Corporation, the first representative of the USSR in the United States, was founded in New York in 1924. It was the only official Soviet mission in the United States until 1933, when the United States recognized the USSR and a Soviet embassy was opened in Washington. Amtorg oversaw trade projects as well as espionage disguised as trade.

173 Emma Goldman's book was published in the United States in 1923, titled *My Disillusionment in Russia* (Garden City, New York, Doubleday, Page & Co.). Her publisher removed some of the chapters without the author's approval. They were reinstated in the next edition in 1924, under the title *My Further Disillusionment in Russia*. The excerpt quoted comes from the latter, p. 139.

174 Foreigners leaving the US for a time had to apply for a reentry permit. A *New York Times* journalist wrote in a report on Ellis Island from 8 October 1933: "Each year more than 50,000 re-entry permits are issued. The clerks likewise make 20,000 verifications of landings and arrivals each month for naturalizations and other purposes. (…) In the Great Halls where once aliens waited for the ferries to the mainland now stands case after case of immigrants' records. There are records of more than 20,000,000 individuals." From Barry Moreno, *Encyclopedia of Ellis Island* (Westport, Connecticut, Greenwood Press, 2004), p. 207.

175 Ludmila Foxlee, *How They Came: the drama of Ellis Island 1920–1935*, written in Montvale, New Jersey, in 1968, and located in the Manuscript Division of Bob Hope Memorial Library, pp. 190–1.

176 Ellenor Cook and Ludmila Foxlee, *The Shepherds' Christmas Eve: A Musical Play* (New York, G. Schirmer, 1929), with color cover by Sergei Soudeikine, still available from online secondhand book sellers.

177 Information about Ludmila Foxlee's tasks is based on her memoir, *How They Came*, op. cit.

178 St John of Capestrano, born in 1386, a Franciscan and papal legate canonized in 1690, traveled throughout Europe as a preacher and confessor. In 1454 he spent a few months in Poland, where he called for Christian forces to unite against the Muslim invasion of the Balkans. He contributed to the victory over the Turks at the Battle of Belgrade in 1456. Quote from Edward Corsi, *In the Shadow of Liberty: the chronicle of Ellis Island* (New York, The Macmillan Company, 1935), p. 28.

179 Giuseppe Mazzini, born in Genoa in 1805, journalist, republican, conspirator, Freemason, ideological comrade of Garibaldi, prisoner, and émigré to Switzerland and the United Kingdom.

180 Quotes from Corsi, *In the Shadow of Liberty*, op. cit., p. 24.

181 Ibid., p. 26.

182 Ibid., pp. 30–31.

183 Ibid., p. 281.

184 Based on the interview with Jacob Auerbach conducted by Janet Levine in 1992 for the Oral History Project, Ellis Island Immigration Museum.

185 "Mrs. Roosevelt Takes Students to Ellis Island," *New York Herald Tribune*, 14 December 1932, p. 20.

186 The New Deal was a program of economic and social reform introduced by President Franklin D. Roosevelt in 1933, aiming to ease the effects of the Great Depression. It consisted of introducing benefits for the unemployed; public works; federal financial support for businesses; legal regulations on industry, agriculture, and banking, and in support for the creation of new workplaces; and the end of Prohibition. The New Deal reforms earned Roosevelt the respect of voters. He led his administration into four consecutive terms, though this record violated the old democratic convention that the president would step down after two terms.

187 From the Foreword to Corsi, *In the Shadow of Liberty*, op. cit., p. v.

188 Thomas M. Pitkin, *Keepers of the Gate: a history of Ellis Island* (New York, New York University Press, 1975), p. 167.

189 Based on a wide-ranging interview with Sumi Shimatsu Utsushigawa conducted in 1998 by Janet Levine for the Oral History Project, Ellis Island Immigration Museum.

The cuts and light adaptations I have made do not affect the essential content of her statement.

190 According to the *New York Herald Tribune*, 18 August 1942, p. 6.

191 Irving Johnson, "Byron H. Uhl Tells a La Guardia Story," *New York Herald Tribune*, 18 August 1942.

192 Guy St Clair, *A Venerable and Cherished Institution: the University Club of New York 1865–1990* (New York, University Club of New York, 1991), pp. 190–1.

The modern Dreadnought-class battleship, launched in 1906, was the most famous ship in the British Navy at the time. Its name dated from 16th-century tradition and meant "fearless." Before the First World War, Winston Churchill forced through the construction of Superdreadnoughts, which strengthened

Britain's position on the seas. *Dreadnought* was also the name of the first British nuclear ship, built in the 1950s.

193 Information in this chapter based on the club's chronicles and the book by Guy St Clair, *A Venerable and Cherished Institution*, op. cit.

194 Frances W. Kerr, *Ellis Island: Immigration and Naturalization Service Monthly Review*, May 1949. Quoted in Moreno, *Encyclopedia of Ellis Island*, op. cit., pp. 62–3.

195 The Displaced Persons Act, passed under the Harry Truman administration, permitted entry to the United States for holders of so-called "Nansen passports" (issued to stateless persons since 1922 on the initiative of Fridtjof Nansen, the first League of Nations High Commissioner for Refugees) and established special quotas for refugees in the American, British, and French occupation zones in Germany, Italy, and Austria.

196 Quote about the waters of Jordan from Pitkin, *Keepers of the Gate*, op. cit., p. 172.

197 The Internal Security Act was passed by Congress in 1950, overriding a veto by President Truman, amid the atmosphere of the Cold War and the tension of the Korean conflict. It denied right of entry to the US to all members of totalitarian, fascist, and communist organizations, regardless of the circumstances under which they joined. This led to numerous detentions and deportations. Under pressure of protests, in 1951 Congress passed a slight amendment to the law regarding people who had joined totalitarian parties when they were under 16 years old, as well as those whose party membership was compelled by political pressure or living conditions (e.g. acquiring food or work).

198 The presence of Chinese people on the island was due to the repeal on 17 December 1943 of the Chinese Exclusion Act.

199 Based on an interview with Joseph Gallo, conducted in 1993 by Paul E. Sigrist Jr for the Oral History Project, Ellis Island Immigration Museum.

200 The case of Voskovec, who was finally cleared of all accusations, was described in detail by Andy Logan in her article "It Doesn't Cost Them a Cent," *The New Yorker*, 12 May 1951, p. 68. I drew information and quotes from her piece.

201 Based on the memories of Eugenia Korfanty (née Noakowska), Zbigniew Korfanty's widow, who died in 2006 in Dallas, Texas; shared with me by the journalist Barbara Szmatloch, author of numerous articles on the famous Silesian activist Wojciech Korfanty and his family.

202 C.L.R. James, *Mariners, Renegades & Castaways: the story of Herman Melville and the world we live in* (Dartmouth College, Hanover and London: University Press of New England, 2001). The quotes by James come from this book, pp. 125–7, and the epigraph appears on p. 4.

203 Based on an interview with Dr James Louis Baker, conducted by Janet Levine in

1993 for the Oral History Project, Ellis Island Immigration Museum.

204 The airport was not called LaGuardia at first. Initially it was named after Glenn Hammond Curtiss (1878–1930), an American aviation pioneer, construction engineer, and inventor who broke many speed records in his vehicles. For instance, he achieved a speed of 180 mph on a motorcycle of his own construction, which apparently had no brakes at all. As evidence of his inventiveness, in one of his motorbikes he used an empty tomato can as a carburetor.

On 2 November 1939 the airport, which meanwhile had been renamed North Beach Airport, officially received the name New York Municipal Airport — LaGuardia.

205 Based on an interview with Eleanor Irwin Park conducted in 1987 by Andrew Phillips for the Oral History Project, Ellis Island Immigration Museum.

206 Barry Moreno provides this information in all seriousness in his *Encyclopedia of Ellis Island*, op.cit., p. 83.

207 Ibid., pp. 78–9.

208 Ibid., pp. 37–8.

VI Still Waters

209 Excerpts from Joseph Brodsky's long poem "Elegy for John Donne," in Joseph Brodsky: *Selected Poems*, tr. George L. Kline (Baltimore, Penguin Books, 1973), pp. 39, 41–4.

210 Shirley C. Burden's confession of his encounter with the island is found in the permanent exhibition of the Ellis Island Immigration Museum alongside his photographs of the abandoned buildings. Burden was the long-serving chairman of the photography publishing house Aperture. He sat on the board of the Museum of Modern Art and donated valuable items to it. He died in 1989 on a medical flight from Los Angeles to New York. He was killed by an attack of an untreatable neurological disease. One of his last photo essays was the book *Chairs* (New York, Aperture, 1985). He photographed chairs in Parisian parks, revealing their individuality through his shots and commentary.

Almost forty years after Shirley Burden started photographing the abandoned buildings of Ellis, the well-known American photographer Stephen Wilkes joined in with equal passion. The oldest part of Ellis Island had already been renovated, but in the hospital complex on Islands 2 and 3, little had changed since Burden's visit. Wilkes therefore got a similar impression. He describes the disintegration of material substances and adds: *But mostly I saw life*. I quote from Stephen Wilkes' foreword to his book of 75 color photographs, *Ellis Island: ghosts of freedom* (New York, London, W.W. Norton & Co., 2006).

211 Quotes from Thea von Harbou's novel, *Metropolis*, anonymous translation (Norfolk, Virginia, The Donning Company, 1988), pp. 9, 8, 24.

212 Thea von Harbou, *Metropolis* (Cabin John, Maryland, Wildside Press, 2003), p. 5.

213 Taliesin, the name of Frank Lloyd Wright's house in Wisconsin, was also bestowed at the start of the 1930s on the architectural school he founded there — an international fraternity of enthusiasts who learned through a shared practice and way of life. The house and school's name comes from Taliesin — a Welsh sixth-century poet (Wright was of Welsh descent). Wright demanded his students understand and practice painting, sculpture, music, drama, and dance. The fraternity also ran a cooperative farm which we would now call organic. Alexander Woollcott wrote in *The New Yorker* on 19 July 1930 (p. 25): *I knew ... that in Taliesin I would find nothing alien, nothing automatic, nothing unreasonable. Perhaps that's the essence of it — reasonableness. With the sweetness of warm milk, of new-mown hay, and of water, fresh-cupped from a bubbling spring.*

Wright and his students founded the firm Taliesin Associated Architects. After Wright's death, William Wesley Peters, a faithful student of the great architect and husband to his daughter Svetlana, became its chairman. He'd worked with Wright on many projects, including the Guggenheim Museum in New York. Known in the United States as an outstanding construction engineer, he was also famous for a short second marriage to another Svetlana — Alliluyeva, Stalin's daughter. He died in 1991.

214 Based on an interview with Andree Maria Marks, née Polturak, conducted in 1993 by Paul E. Sigrist Jr for the Oral History Project, Ellis Island Immigration Museum.

215 President Lyndon B. Johnson, Proclamation 3656 Adding Ellis Island to the Statue of Liberty, The American Presidency Project, www.presidency.ucsb.edu.

216 Philip Johnson (1906–2005), one of America's most outstanding architects, co-designer of famous Manhattan buildings such as the Seagram Building (with Ludwig Mies van der Rohe) and the New York State Theater (now the David H. Koch Theater) at Lincoln Center (with Richard Foster), as well as designer of the AT&T Building (later Sony Tower) and an expansion of the Museum of Modern Art, also in Manhattan. He was the first architect to win the Pritzker Prize (1979), the highest honor in the field.

217 *Alcatraz is not an Island*, documentary, 60 minutes, directed by James M. Fortier, 2002.

218 The university's name is an expression of gratitude to its benefactor, Colonel Fairleigh S. Dickinson (1858–1942). Founded in 1942 as a two-year junior college, it slowly transformed into a senior college and in 1954 obtained university status. In 2009, more than 9,000 people from 32 American states and 72 other countries studied there. It has two campuses in New Jersey, one in Canada,

and one in the UK. The latter is situated in a modernized 17th-century Jacobean manor house built on the foundations of a 13th-century priory, made available by Trinity College, Oxford. The university states it is dedicated to the preparation of world citizens through global education (https://view2.fdu.edu/about-fdu/history-and-mission/, accessed 30 July 2019).

219 Based on the autobiography of Peter Sammartino, *Of Colleges and Kings* (New York, Cornwall Books, 1985), p. 112, and Margherita Marchione, *Peter and Sally Sammartino: biographical notes* (New York, Cornwall Books, 1994).

220 Quote from Peter Sammartino, *Of Colleges and Kings*, op. cit., pp. 115–6.

221 In 1995 Meredith Monk came to Poland for a retrospective of her work, performed for Polish audiences, and searched for her family's place of origin. The director Mariusz Grzegorzek made a film about this titled *Meredith* for the Łód branch of Telewizja Polska. The singer's words about sadness come from that film. Meredith Monk visited Poland again in 2005 and performed at a concert in the town of Cieszyn in Silesia.

222 Jan Greenwald, "An Interview with Meredith Monk," 28 February 1981, *EAR Magazine*, April–May 1981, quoted in Deborah Jowitt, ed., *Meredith Monk* (Baltimore and London, Johns Hopkins University Press, 1997), p. 2.

223 *Ellis Island*, black-and-white film, 28 minutes, conceived, directed, and with music by Meredith Monk, 1981.

224 In 1979 Lee Iacocca became chairman of the car company Chrysler. At that time it was threatened with bankruptcy due to unsuccessful investments in producing compact cars. He secured a federal loan to the tune of $1.5 billion. Thanks to his skillful leadership, the company stayed competitive in the automotive industry and paid off its debts seven years ahead of schedule.

225 Quote from Lee Iacocca and William Novak, *Iacocca: An Autobiography* (New York, Bantam, 1986), p. 341.

VII Pearl Divers

226 Based on articles by Sam Roberts, "Story of the First Through Ellis Island is Rewritten," *New York Times*, 14 September 2006, and Ray O'Hanlon "Putting Things Right: If Only Annie Could Have Seen This," *Irish Echo Online*, 14–20 February 2007.

227 According to August C. Bolino, *The Ellis Island Source Book* (Washington dc, Kensington Historical Press, 1990).

228 Description of these events based on Janet A. McDonnell's work, *Responding to the September 11 Terrorist Attacks*, National Park Service, US Department of the Interior, Washington dc, 2004.

229 The description of Meredith Monk's encounter with the town of Stawiski is based on *Meredith*, the 1995 film made by Mariusz Grzegorzek for the Łód branch of Telewizja Polska.

230 I made use of a recorded account by Janet Levine about her work. It begins with the words: *This is Janet Levine* ... It's August 21st, 1994, and I'm here in the Ellis Island Oral History Studio. She opens all the recordings of this project with a similar formula. Oral History Project, Ellis Island Immigration Museum.

231 Information about the Discography Project from Eric Byron's article "English Acquisition by Immigrants (1880–1940): the confrontation as reflected in early sound recordings" on the Columbia Journal of American Studies website, http://www.columbia.edu/cu/cjas/byron1.html (accessed 9 August 2019).

232 Peter Morton Coan, *Ellis Island Interviews in Their Own Words* (New York, Checkmark Books, 1997), p. 419.

233 The account of the Lenape funeral is based on an article by Fawn Wilson Poacha, "Ancestral Delaware Remains Finally Laid to Rest," National Association of Tribal Historic Preservation Officers, 2003, http://nathpo.org/News/NAGPRA/News-NAGPRA31.htm, (accessed 30 July 2019).

From the Author

234 H.G. Wells, *The Future in America* (New York: St Martin's Press, 1987), p. 100.

Index